FOUR CENTURIES OF SILVER

PERSONAL ADORNMENT IN THE QING DYNASTY AND AFTER

FOUR CENTURIES OF SILVER

PERSONAL ADORNMENT IN THE QING DYNASTY AND AFTER

by Margaret Duda

photographs by Paul Duda

drawings by Chunming Gao

Illustrations: page 2 (*A talisman*, from Ch 6);
  page 8 (*Symbolic locks*, from Ch 2)
Text & Photographs © 2002 Margaret Duda
Photographs by Paul Duda
Antique photographs on pages 11, 93, 121, 137 & 149
  courtesy of Peabody Essex Museum
Drawings by Chunming Gao

Project designer: Geoslyn Lim

Copublished and distributed in the USA by
Art Media Resources, Ltd.
1507 South Michigan Avenue
Chicago, IL 60605 USA
Tel: 312-663-5351
Fax: 312-663-5177
Email: info@artmediaresources.com
www.artmediaresources.com

Published by Times Editions
An imprint of Times Media Private Limited
A member of the Times Publishing Group
Times Centre, 1 New Industrial Road, Singapore 536196
Tel: (65) 62139288 Fax: (65) 62854871
Email: te@tpl.com.sg

Times Subang
Lot 46, Subang Hi-Tech Industrial Park
Batu Tiga, 40000 Shah Alam
Selangor Darul Ehsan, Malaysia
Tel & Fax: (603) 56363517
Email: cchong@tpg.com.my

Printed in Singapore.

ISBN 1-58886-031-0

Dedicated to:
SYDNEY and SKYE,
ALI, BROOKE, and TY,
and all those who follow.

Acknowledgements

In any project of this sort, there are so many people to thank.

I can never express enough gratitude to my son Paul, a professional photographer, for capturing the beauty of the hundreds of artifacts in this book. He not only created masterpieces of design, but also tolerated my changes as I kept learning and rearranging.

In addition to his invaluable knowledge in this area and his time, Chunming Gao deserves my appreciation for his original drawings at the beginning of each chapter showing the way in which the artifacts were worn.

Good friends Jim and Kathy Morrow offered their priceless editing expertise and I will always be in their debt. Violet Phoon, my editor at Times Publishing, added encouragement, fast e-mail responses, and friendship, to her great editing, and has earned my gratitude. My deepest appreciation is also extended to Geoslyn Lim who performed miracles fitting all of the illustrations into the book.

Special thanks also go to good friend Brooke Jaron for her expertise, her encouragement, her patience, and her daily replies to my constant queries.

With so little in the literature, I had to request information from experts all over the world. Since I do not read or speak Chinese, others interpreted for me, and still others offered their constant encouragement. For reasons best known to them, I'd like to thank:

Joan Ahrens, Adele Anderson, Ida Balashova, Andrea Barbalich, Terese Tse Bartholomew, Nancy Berliner, Baolin Duan, Melinda Brown, Barbara Bush, Ian Chalmers, Philip Chang, Heding Chen, Dominic Cheung, Dennis Crow, Rommy Dai, Meli Diamanti, David and Aurelie Edwards, Trudi Engel, Kathy Flynn, Mary Gage, Chunming Gao, Deming Gao, Valery Garrett, Rolf Gilberg, Diane Greenfield, Sue Hacker, Beverley Jackson, Dov Jaron, Julia Jaw, Eleanor Johnson, Annie Lee, Feng Li, Jikai Li, Michelle Liao, Robert Liu, Shusen Liu, Kaiyin Lo, Ruth Malloy, Steve Miska, Lonnie Morelli, Susan Murphy, Peter Rasmussen, Eliska Repaskey, Valrae Reynolds, Nancy Row, Jun Shao, Zhiqiang Shan, Susan Shyn, Nancy Stites, Kenny Sun, Kemei Tang, Linda Thiel, Glenn and

Lucille Vessa, Xiaoyin Wang, Mary Ellen Ward, Erica Wellman, Corinne West, Julia White, Emily Harris Wing, Chungsun Yuan, Jieying Yuan, Wei Zhang, and Yujun Zhong.

As I composed the text, Terese Tse Bartholomew, Jin Cao, Shur Er Lee, and Mary Liu translated the Chinese characters on the silver for me, as Barbara Abbott, Erik Connors, and Norbert Leutzow provided technical support.

For having the courage to publish chapters of this book as articles, I'd like to thank Robert Liu of *Ornament* magazine, and Robin Markbreiter, Stephen Markbreiter, and Tuyet Nguyet of *Arts of Asia* magazine.

Special gratitude also goes to The Bead Society of Greater Washington for awarding me a research grant to help support my work.

Within my family, I will always be grateful to my parents who encouraged my every scholarly and creative effort. I also owe a huge debt to my husband, Larry. If he hadn't told me that I probably couldn't sell a book on this subject, I would never have tried so hard to prove him wrong. Once I embarked upon the project, of course, he offered his full moral support, which was a constant reminder of the reason that I married him.

I have my children to thank for their understanding when I had to be in China instead of at family reunion football games. On an individual level, I want to thank my son Paul again for taking the photographs, my son David for supporting my writing as he supplied me with valuable references, my son John for his interest in my work and instructions on how to meet my deadline ("just cram, mom"), and my daughter Laura for listening to my writing problems as she tried to keep track of her three toddlers. I want to thank all of their spouses for supporting me as well, and for tolerating my intrusions. Finally, I'd like to thank my five grandchildren, whose very presence in this world encourages me to keep writing.

Margaret Duda
November, 2002

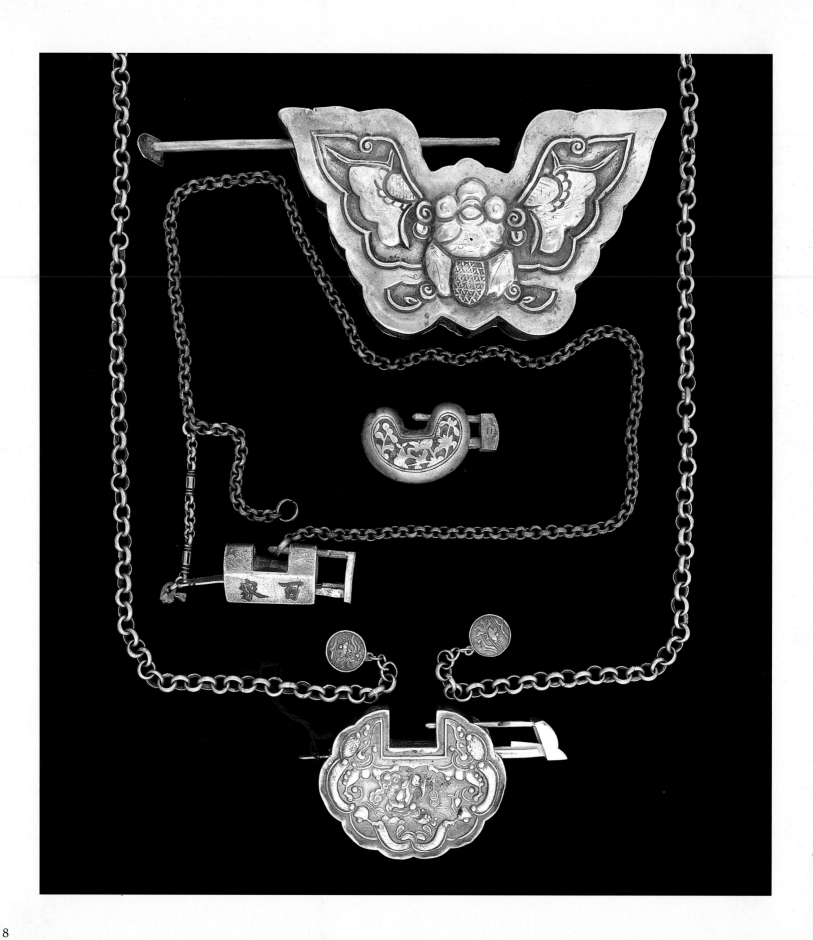

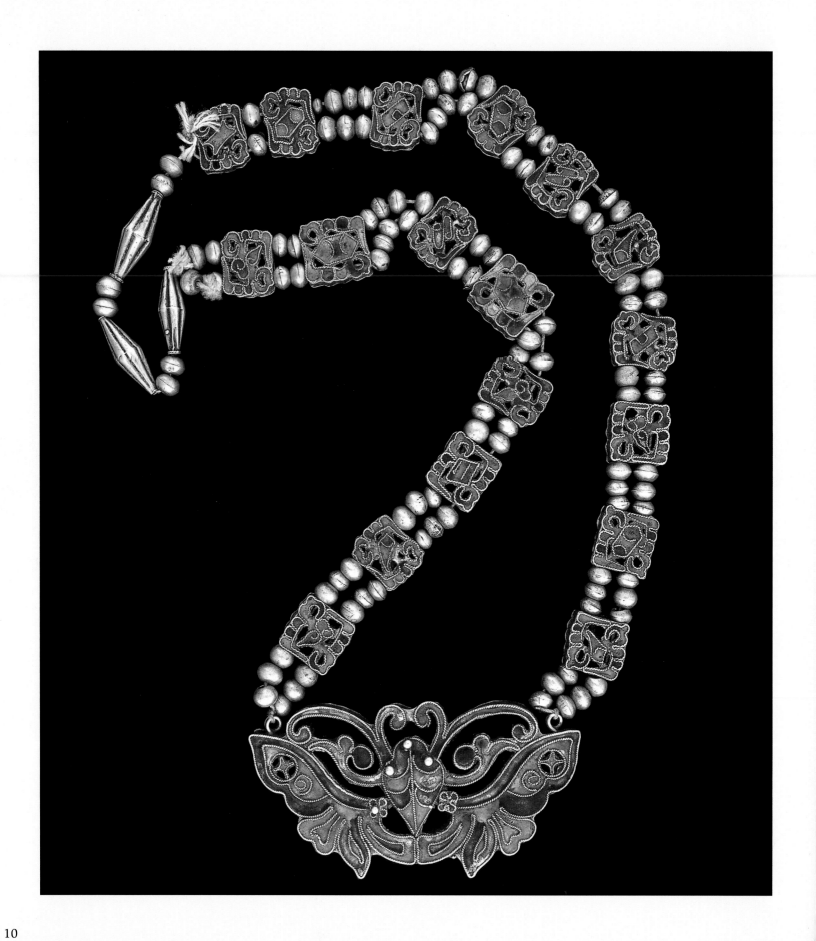

Introduction

The artistry that formed China during the Qing dynasty, an era that lasted from 1644 to 1911, testifies to the power of cultural interaction. The Manchus maintained political control, but their domain included the Han Chinese, the Inner Mongolians, the Tibetans, and fifty-five ethnic minority groups, all of whom wove their customs and creativity into the intricate fabric that constituted this astonishing society. This process is especially evident in the silver adornments produced during this period.

The Qing silversmiths fashioned pieces for aristocrats and peasants alike, leaving behind an enormous body of work that includes both fine art and folk art. Some artisans labored in the cities, filling orders for noblemen and businessmen, while others followed the nomads or tramped through the countryside, crafting adornments for daily use and special celebrations.

These silversmiths followed traditions that we can trace back more than a millennium to artifacts found in ancient China. Gilded-silver filigree ornaments appear in the Zhou dynasty (second century B.C.), but silversmithing did not develop fully until the Tang dynasty (A.D. 618–907). Extending all the way from Korea to Kashgar, the Chinese empire of the Tang dynasty drew artistic inspiration from sources both inside and outside its borders. The busy flow of trade along the Silk Road meant that the craftsmen of Persia, India, Arabia, and Turkey all eventually influenced Chinese artisans, who began to produce the finest silverwork in the Far East. Minute granulation, filigree with jewels, and elaborate repoussé-decorated hairpins and personal toilet articles appear as early as the ninth and tenth centuries. Recognizing the value of new techniques, an emperor in the Yuan dynasty (1279–1368) spared the lives of prisoners-of-war who were goldsmiths and silversmiths if they agreed to labor in the Imperial workshops.

By the Qing dynasty, Chinese silversmiths had developed sophisticated techniques for creating miniature masterpieces. Scenes from folk stories encircled needle cases, depictions of the Eight Immortals garnished baby locks, Buddhist symbols embellished grooming kits, flowers bobbed from springs on hairpins, and qilins displayed scaly backs and flowing manes. These craftsmen created some of the world's most compelling metal artifacts, but today, Chinese silver still does not receive the same attention accorded gold, jade, and ivory items. Little exists in the literature about either the high artistic achievement or the functions of these pieces.

Qing dynasty silver adornments, prohibitively expensive for a peasant, were fundamentally crafted for the wealthy commoners and members of the aristocracy. The royal concubines also valued these works, especially when they were gilded. During the Qing dynasty, the Imperial Palace employed both goldsmiths and silversmiths to produce their jewelry.

In addition, silver artifacts had their place in Qing tradition. During mourning, the only jewelry pieces permitted a Manchu woman were tiny silver earrings and a small silver bar in her hair. A wealthy Han matron followed even stricter rules, using no ornamentation for the first hundred days of bereavement, then only silver for the remainder of the mourning period.

Certain artifacts, such as the needle cases, appeared only in silver or gilded silver: they had no jade or gold equivalent. Although the aristocratic women employed seamstresses, they themselves loved to embroider. They probably valued their elaborate silver or gilded-silver needle cases not only as useful containers, but also as beautiful bodily adornments. Commoners who could afford them bought less expensive models, as every mother dreamed of giving her daughter a silver needle case for her dowry. Other types of silver accessories were equally treasured.

Although the Chinese had always placed a substantial price on their silver adornment, these pieces became especially valuable after the Opium War (1839–1842). Following their defeat by the British, the Chinese had to pay reparations, causing a scarcity of the metal. The government nationalized silver mining, and the cost of the ore skyrocketed. Hand-crafted artifacts became increasingly more expensive and difficult to obtain, and the silver content of the newer items dropped drastically. Many modern Chinese antique dealers can date a given Qing piece not only by its style, but also by the amount of silver it contains.

Subsequent historical events served to further degrade, mutilate, and bury this great heritage. After the downfall of the Qing dynasty in 1911, entrepreneurs sold thousands of silver, gold, and gilded-silver Imperial artifacts—court necklaces, hairpins, coronets—to international markets. During World War II, the Japanese plundered the country and carted the best adornments

they could find back to their homeland. Still other silver pieces disappeared during the subsequent Civil War, which ravaged China before the expulsion of the Kuomintang.

With peace came Communism and, later, the Cultural Revolution, which banned bodily adornments and made the surrender of such pieces a matter of patriotic duty. The government collected countless specimens from the people and warehoused them in and near Beijing. The owners must have hated parting with their treasures (some people evidently buried them), but an individual faced imprisonment for possessing such objects. The confiscated items remained in storage for many years, although I was told that a large quantity was melted down for coinage.

In the early 1970's, the government allowed a few overseas antique dealers of Chinese heritage to view and buy silver pieces. If he had government connections (and a Chinese lineage), such

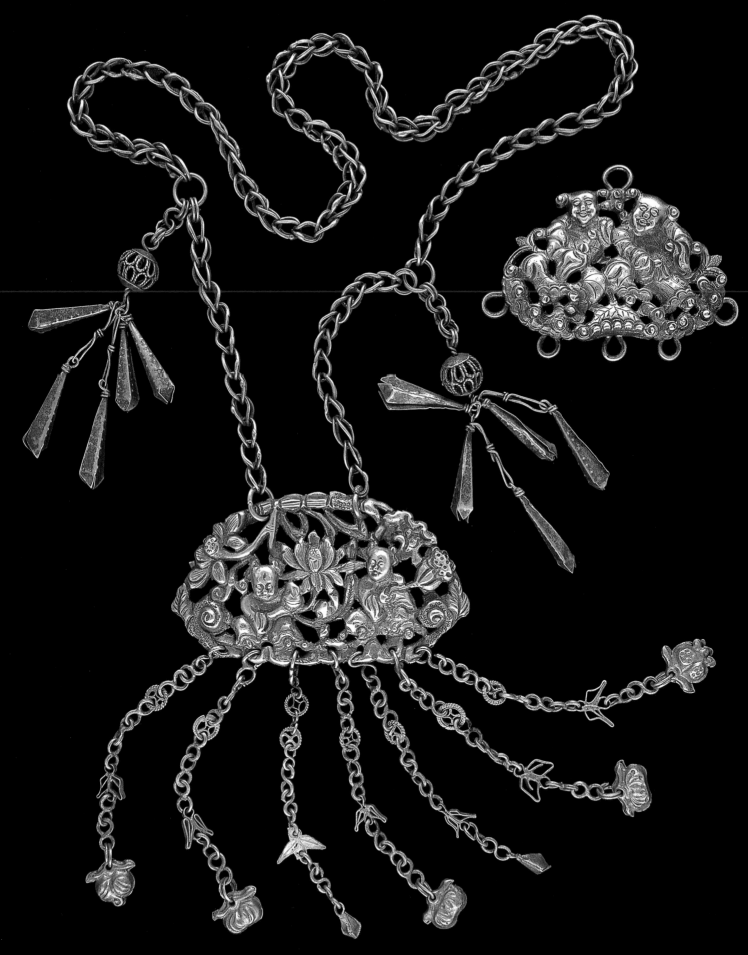

an entrepreneur could acquire silver artifacts by the kilo. Normally, he would have to decide whether or not to purchase a box of pieces after viewing only the top layer. With luck, he would receive permission to pick and choose from the entire inventory. The Chinese bureaucrats called the items Mongolian, but in fact they represented every culture in the country. After Richard Nixon's celebrated mission to China, a limited number of American dealers were allowed to enter the Qing silver trade.

From the 1970's to the mid-1980's, a government-owned company hired workers to add old beads to Qing artifacts, thus transforming them into jewelry for Western women. Most of these items went to dealers in America and Europe. This brought much-needed revenue to China, but by the mid-1980's, the government realized that the country was losing valuable cultural artifacts. Wholesale operations ceased in 1985, and it became illegal to remove any piece over one hundred years old without the government's red wax seal of approval.

Until this ban, however, a staggering number of Qing dynasty silver articles reached the United States—selling very cheaply, because most were only 65-75 percent silver. Many went for as little as five or ten dollars each. Throughout this boom, Chinese and American entrepreneurs routinely violated the artistic integrity and damaged the cultural significance of the adornments. Small pieces found themselves randomly attached to large ones. Intricate old chains yielded to newer, simpler ones. The addition of semi-precious stones and longer chains transformed locks and qilins, originally worn by children, into necklaces for Western women. Grooming kits, usually hung from a man's belt or the button of a woman's dress, became Westernized necklaces with mismatched dangles—an offense to the symmetry created by the original silversmiths. Hairpins and earrings were twisted into pendants. Hat adornments became earrings. Few entrepreneurs realized how these radical alterations all but nullified the social meaning of the artifacts.

In 1992, I found my first pieces. I spotted five ornate silver needle cases in a booth in a southern Pennsylvania antiques mall and asked the manager what they were. He didn't know, but arranged for me to telephone the owner on the spot. This dealer told me she'd bought them many years before from an elderly couple who'd been missionaries in China during the early 1900's.

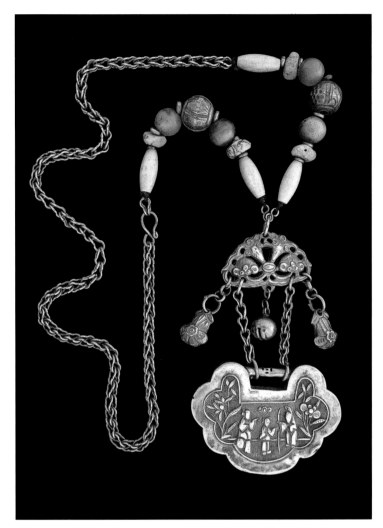

She also told me that the cases were used to hold needles for opium smoking. Fascinated, I purchased them all.

Although I know now that these cases once contained simple sewing and embroidery needles—they aren't connected to anything as exotic as the opium trade—I still love them. Searching for other needle cases in antique shops and flea markets, I came upon a wide variety of Qing dynasty silver adornments, as well as similar pieces from the Republic era. I stumbled upon pieces fashioned in many grades of silver, as well as in paktong, a combination of copper, zinc and nickel that has a silvery finish. Because they never tarnish, paktong pieces became popular with the wealthy of the Qing dynasty. My search continued and continued...

By the mid-1990's, the bonanza had ended and Chinese silversmiths had begun crafting reproductions to fill the void. While the first such replicas were easy to identify, the forgers eventually became so adept that even museum curators told me they had trouble distinguishing some copies from the originals. Whenever I did find an authentic piece, it cost five to ten times as much as I was used to paying and American dealers complained that they could not easily replenish their supply of Chinese silver pieces.

Authentic Qing dynasty silver in the United States is still available, but you must seek it in private collections, antiques malls, and Oriental antique shops, or through Internet auctions. In China, an enterprising tourist can find bargains in the tiny antique stalls or open markets, but the higher quality pieces are fast disappearing as the nouveau riche Chinese have started to collect it.

As the supply of silver adornments diminished in the United States in the 90's, my interest in the pieces increased. Finding little in the published literature, I turned to the dealers. I discovered that vendors, even those in Asian antique shops, disagreed with each other about the purpose or origin of any particular piece. I sought out museum curators. Once again, I encountered conflicting theories and opinions. I traveled to China many times and discussed the pieces with professors from the Academies. I found little agreement.

There is still much controversy among the experts because a lot of information was lost during the Cultural Revolution, but no one disputes the beauty and artistry of the authentic pieces. By combining various metalworking techniques with traditional Chinese symbolism, the Qing dynasty silversmiths created astonishingly intricate works of art that we are only now coming to appreciate.

Pleasing as they are to the eye, Qing dynasty silver pieces always went beyond the merely decorative. Their functions embraced three categories. The utilitarian pieces included grooming kits, needle cases, hairpins, combs, fragrance carriers, eating kits, and opium boxes. Another category denoted rank: fingernail guards, personal seals, earrings, and Imperial Court necklaces. The third group of silver artifacts satisfied superstitions: bells for scaring away evil spirits, locks for securing an infant to earth (and thus to life), babies for fertility, Hakka women for abundance, bracelets for warding off arthritis, qilins for insuring a son's success on his civil service examinations, and gods to aid every aspiration imaginable.

Many artifacts performed several functions at once. Silver gourds, needle cases, and fragrance carriers often embellished the grooming kits. Silver Hakka women, gods of wealth, babies, and other such charms assumed the form of needle cases. Silver bells, babies, and dragonfish typically dangled from grooming kits, qilins, and locks.

Dating Chinese silver pieces presents many challenges. It's easy to determine the era of a lock or needle case decorated with the two flags of the Republic, and scholars agree that Court necklaces were not worn after the fall of the Qing dynasty. Other pieces test the collector's knowledge. It is often impossible to distinguish a 1910 Qing needle case from a 1913 Republic piece. This book features photographs of Chinese silver adornments from both the Qing dynasty and the twentieth century, but the text concentrates on Qing cultural traditions only.

Identifying recent pieces and early reproductions is fairly simple since they are often bright, lightweight, crisp in detail, and often identical on each side. The first generation of reproductions lacks the worn features and telltale patina of genuine aged silver. For the newer reproductions, however, dealers have actually added an artificial coloration to suggest the Qing era. I am leery of a piece if I can't rub through the patina with the tip of my thumb and see the sheen of authentic silver.

Because they value the old patina so highly, serious collectors do not use silver cleaners. You will notice several highly polished items in this book: I was forced to purchase them in a scrubbed condition. I buffed most of the other pieces with a soft polishing cloth to enhance the details for the photographs, but I used a light touch, so they would quickly turn dark again.

The photographs illustrate different silversmithing techniques. The smith pierced designs for a three-dimensional effect. Granulation involved fixing minuscule dots of silver to a piece. For engraving, the smith cut into the metal the way a sculptor incises a piece of stone. In chasing, the smith used special tools to deftly hammer a design into the face of the silver. But it was with repoussé—wherein the craftsman created a relief image by laying a silver sheet face down on a bed of wax and then hammering into the back—that the Chinese artisans really excelled. The repoussé techniques, also called embossing, influenced metalworkers through the entire territory controlled by the Manchus from 1644 to 1911. Tibetan ga'us and Mongolian eating kits of this period often display the fine repoussé work found on the Chinese pieces.

Through their silver adornments, the various cultures that constituted China during the Qing dynasty bequeathed to us a significant and beautiful part of their civilization—along with enough questions to keep researchers occupied for years to come. While I have tried to be as scholarly as possible, I have come to reject some theories and views held by my colleagues. This book contains many speculations, but I hope that it will open the door to a systematic study and anthropological investigation of these wonderful pieces.

Illustrations in this chapter: page 10 (a minority necklace from the Kunming area, Ch 11); page 12 (a rope-chain necklace of coral beads, Ch 12); page 13 (a quilin carrying a figure wearing a long official gown of a "first candidate," Ch 4); page 14 (an amulet with the Heavenly Twins, Ch 8); page 15 (a symbolic lock with scallop design, Ch 2).

S outhwestern China, the mid-1700's. A small dusty town. Gaiyin Liu, the petite wife of a military officer, gingerly steps from her sedan chair and follows her mother-in-law and sister-in-law into the cramped fabric shop. She takes minute, painful steps on her bound feet, and the pearls dangling from her coral hairpins barely stir, a testament to her fine upbringing. She and the other women chatter as they examine the newest shipment: silks, needles of silver and brass, and embroidery threads of every shade and hue. Suddenly Gaiyin sees exactly what she wants.

Hanging from the corseted waist of an English missionary's wife—who wears no white makeup and has the largest feet Gaiyin has ever seen—the object glitters in a ray of sunlight. The fabric merchant sees the object as well, and asks to examine it. The missionary's wife unhooks the chain and slowly opens the hinged sterling case that holds her sewing needles, explaining that it was a farewell present from her family in England.

All the Chinese women crowd around and marvel at the shiny container, which makes the skillfully carved bamboo and wooden cases of the common people seem mundane by comparison. Although Gaiyin spends much of her time embroidering, her maid always stores the needles, securing them in a pincushion. A woman of the upper class would never think of attaching a bamboo case to her clothing, but Gaiyin immediately sees herself wearing a silver one as a personal adornment. The merchant studies the container, and Gaiyin smiles. She knows that he will soon instruct the local silversmiths to create such artifacts. On her next visit, she will be able to purchase such a treasure for herself.

The above scenario, though fanciful, is entirely plausible. Silver needle cases made their debut quite late in China. Engraved silver diamond-shaped needle holders hung from the waists of French women as early as the fourteenth century, but there is no evidence of silver needle cases in China until the 1700's. The technology was available—the Chinese had beautiful embossed and engraved silver bowls, plates, pitchers, cups, and even scissors as early as the Tang dynasty (seventh century)—but the inspiration was delayed. While a common woman always kept her expensive handmade needles

Opposite: *A Yao woman wearing a needle case*

safely inside a carved bamboo, wood, or reed case, a noblewoman didn't need to be so cautious: she could easily afford to replace a lost or damaged sewing tool. Needle cases entered upper-class households only after they acquired the features of expensive, finely crafted ornaments.

Beyond the missionary wife scenario, there is another way to explain the advent of silver needle cases in China. During the reign of Louis the XIV (1661–1712), a large Chinese ambassadorial group visited the French Court at Versailles to trade luxury items for iron ore. The aristocracy marveled at the beautiful Chinese silks, porcelains, jades, lacquerware, and ivory, and soon anything "Chinoiserie" was admired and desired. Eventually, Chinese faces and figures decorated the sewing paraphernalia of this period, such as the metal cases for scissors and needles. It is quite possible that the Chinese entourage also returned home with impressive French items, including silver needle cases.

By whatever means the first such container reached China, the concept eventually caught on with native silversmiths. Seeking to develop his own style, each craftsman must have experimented with embossing and engraving sheets of silver, which he formed and soldered into receptacles for both sewing and embroidery needles. The earliest type probably featured, beneath its outer silver sheath, a cylindrical or rectangular storage chamber, similar to the carved inner compartment of a bamboo case. The long inner container may have been a Chinese invention, since I know of no other country whose needle cases have this feature.

While the European silversmith attached a chain to the top of each hinged needle case, the Chinese artisan threaded the chain through the outer sheath and affixed it to the inner cylindrical compartment, so that the sheath could be raised and lowered along the chain. Perhaps this design was influenced by the Tibetan needle case, in which a leather sheath slides along a strip of yak hide. We'll probably never know for certain how the classic Chinese silver needle cases evolved, but we can explore the cultural influences and silversmithing techniques that make these artifacts so appealing today.

During the Qing dynasty, a young woman's future depended largely upon her expertise with a needle. A husband picked a wife not for her beauty, but for her mastery of embroidery. In the Qing dynasty, people felt that a woman revealed her inner soul through

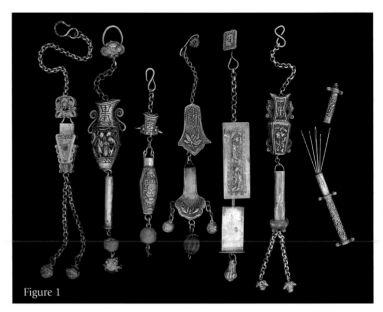

Figure 1

the intricacy of her stitchery.

From the age of seven or eight, a little girl practiced her sewing and needlework skills every day until she could produce the delicate stitches and complex designs. Her first endeavor was usually a small embroidered purse, and after much practice she advanced to quilt covers, pillowcases, tablecloths, tapestries, screens, curtains, door hangings, and clothing—all of which became part of her dowry.

Embroidery has a long tradition in China. From excavations in the caves of Zhoukoudian, we know that Paleolithic peoples used needles carved from bone and teeth to sew animal hides into clothing. Archeologists have unearthed chain-stitched embroidery covering clay vessels from the Western Zhou dynasty (1050–771 B.C.). They have also found fragments of cloth with chain-stitched designs in tombs from the Spring and Autumn period (770–475 B.C.).

By the fifth century B.C., brass and iron needles had replaced bone, and embroidered abstract designs had evolved into elaborate representations of plants, flowers, and birds, as well as certain animals thought capable of warding off illness and misfortune. During the Song dynasty, women worked with minute yarn-fibers and needles as fine as hair strands to fashion astonishingly delicate images.

In the Qing dynasty, the majority of young women were still not taught to read or write. They received instruction only in sewing, embroidery, and the creation of shoes. An impoverished

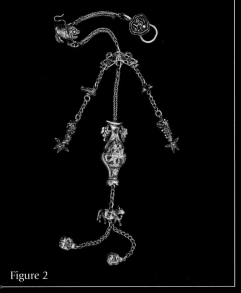

Figure 2

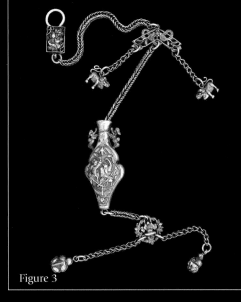

Figure 3

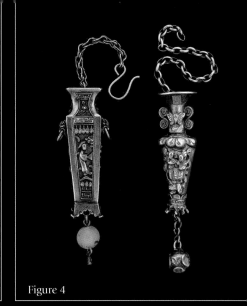

Figure 4

Figure 5

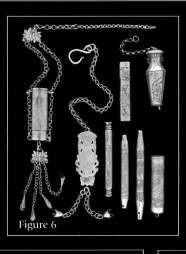

Figure 6

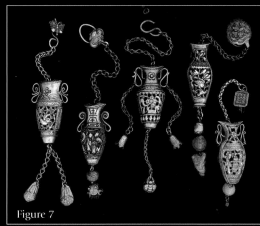

Figure 7

Figure 8

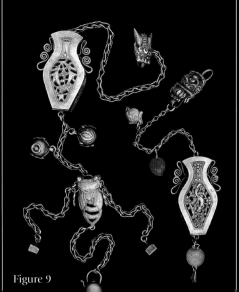

Figure 9

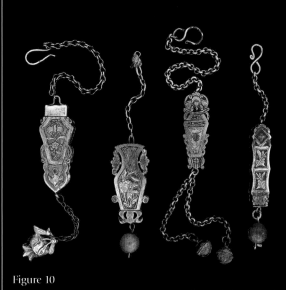

Figure 10

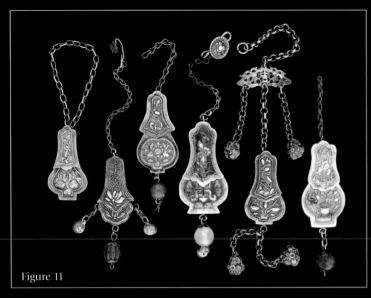

Figure 11

Figure 12

Figure 13

Figure 14

Figure 15

girl could supplement her family's income by selling finished embroidered pieces or by taking a position sewing for the wealthy. It was not unusual for an aristocratic family to employ thirty or more sewing women, and hundreds of skilled females worked in the Imperial embroidery workshops.

By producing fine stitchery, a peasant girl increased her chances of getting a good husband in an arranged marriage. Preparing a trousseau also enabled her to socialize with others of her gender. In the evenings, after dinner, the women of the household often sat on the *k'ang* platform and sewed, while the men smoked and talked.

For the upper classes, too, working with needles was a communal activity. Even though they hired poorer women to do the basic sewing, aristocratic women often sat together in their gardens or courtyards and passed many long hours chatting and embroidering. A pregnancy provided a great excuse for such gatherings to fashion complete baby wardrobes of the brightest silks and most intricate designs. Thick warm blankets, trousers, jackets, shoes, and tiny caps quickly took form.

The customs surrounding layettes varied from group to group. Among the Miao minority, a girl began to embroider elaborate hats, shoes, clothing, and quilts for her future sons when she was about fifteen. Carefully tucked away until she gave birth to a boy, the clothing was unpacked and displayed during the traditional first-month celebration banquet so that all could compliment the new mother on her fine embroidery skills.

Among the Han Chinese in the rural areas, it was the maternal grandmother's duty to provide the embroidered clothing for the first-month celebration. Because these peasant villages suffered from high infant mortality, the grandmother used appliqué and embroidery to provide the baby's wardrobe—hat, collars, vests, and shoes—with magical symbols, each such image intended to ward off evil spirits. The cosmological symbols yin and yang appeared frequently in Han layettes, as did the swastika, representing 10,000 efficacies and the resignation of the spirit found in the heart of Buddha. Many Han baby hats and baby shoes assumed the likeness of dogs or pigs, so that the spirits would think the child was only a common animal, not worth harming.

Throughout her life, a Qing dynasty woman underwent intensive training in fine embroidery, beginning with the small

Figure 16

purse she created at about age seven. This was not a purse as we think of one today, but a drawstring bag seven-and-a-half to ten centimeters in diameter. A woman hung this bag from a button of her dress, using it to hold incense. Once she perfected her craft, a girl would try creating the man's equivalent of the purse: a larger embroidered pouch hung from the belt as a container for eyeglasses, chopsticks, tobacco, pocket watch, fan, or money.

The creation of purses and pouches figured in Qing dynasty courtship rituals and marriage traditions. A young woman secretly fashioned a purse for her beloved. Before the wedding, she also created fine purses as gifts for all of her in-laws. The bride-to-be spent days and nights embroidering to meet this obligation.

But not all days and nights. During certain intervals in the Chinese calendar, needlework was actually forbidden. A woman could not sew or embroider during the first five days of a new year, when a moving needle might pierce the eye of Buddha. Tradition also proscribed using a needle on the third day of every month, when embroidering could cause a woman to become a widow. Needlework was prohibited on the second day of the second moon, when the hibernating dragon emerged from his long sleep: a moving needle might prick the awakening beast, causing the woman to develop a sore on her body corresponding to the dragon's wound.

Beyond these few prohibitions, a Qing era woman spent much of her life with needle in hand, bent over a rectangular embroidery frame. (Rectangular frames were preferred since a round frame could damage fine silk.) The Han Chinese still practiced footbinding in the Qing era, so it was easier for a Han girl to sit and embroider than to walk. Laboring day after day to perfect her skills, she rarely forgot that, upon her arrival in her new home, she would have to create a garment under the critical eye of her new mother-in-law and to embroider shoes for her husband's female relatives. Since a mother-in-law had complete control over her daughters-in-law, this must have created extraordinary anxiety in the young woman. Such tests filled a woman's life, and she was still trying to pass them at the birth of her first grandson, when she displayed the layette she had created for his first-month celebration.

Given the importance of embroidery in her life, it's not surprising that a silver needle case, often presented to a young girl as part of her dowry, was central to a woman's personal adornment in the Qing dynasty. The importance of these artifacts extended into the Republic era.

As I mentioned in the first section, a needle case typically consisted of an ornamental silver sheath fitted over a silver cylindrical compartment holding the instruments themselves, the whole arrangement suspended on either a chain or a silk cord, as in Figure 1. Before using the compartment, the owner would stuff it with human hair or cloth, so the needles would remain secure even when the cover was off. The sheath could easily be raised and lowered along a chain, which hung from the button of a woman's dress. In some Qing needle cases, the receptacle is not sheathed. Instead, a conventional lid fits over the compartment. It is interesting that the Chinese never employed either a hinged top or a screw top, both common in Europe, but remained faithful to the design of the bamboo cases.

The silversmiths employed engraving, chasing, or repoussé for the needle cases, or both repoussé and chasing. For the repoussé cases, with their striking, nearly three-dimensional relief, the artisan always decorated the metal before shaping it into the container, whereas chasing and engraving could be done after assembly. When we consider that the tiny figures, birds, and flowers had to be imposed on the hard metal with thousands of light hammer taps, we can begin to appreciate the incredible artistry of the more complicated pieces.

Hand-crafted to order by silversmiths throughout the empire, and covered with traditional images—symbols for fertility, harmony, wealth, longevity, and double happiness—needle cases assumed various forms, sizes, and hues. The color of the metal depended upon the quality of the silver. The higher the silver content, the brighter the shine.

The silversmiths' ingenuity was amazing. Figure 2 shows an elaborate enameled needle case that was obviously crafted for a wealthier patron. It displays most of the traditional charms: silver babies for fertility, fish for abundance, a pair of shoes for aging together, dragons for male vigor and fertility, a horse for perseverance and high office, a musical stone for good fortune, a plum blossom for longevity, and the ideal couple. A similar ensemble appears in Figure 3.

Many silver needle cases were obviously intended as dowry or wedding gifts. In Figure 4, the vase–shaped case on the left is embossed with a happy couple, fish for abundance, and an orchid and lotus, symbolizing eternal union. On the other vase we find pomegranates, representing the birth of many sons, surrounded by butterflies and bees, heralding abundant sexuality.

A carp and lotus blossom, expressing a wish for the couple to live in affluence for many years, appears on one side of the needle case on the left in Figure 5, while the reverse exhibits a peacock with chrysanthemums for many years of high rank. A deer and a cypress tree representing a wish for wealth and longevity decorate one side of the second artifact, while a magpie surrounded by plum blossoms promises marital joy on the other. The third case is unusual in that it contains all Eight Symbols of the Daoist Immortals. It also features a wave pattern representing a hope that the couple will rise in status, and a butterfly symbolizing longevity and marital happiness. On one side of the case on the right, the citron conveys a wish for abundant wealth, while the reverse pictures a plum blossom and two magpies for wedded bliss. The plum blossom, symbolizing longevity, is found on most Chinese needle cases.

Most of the vase-shaped needle cases featured elaborate repoussé with chasing, but some exhibit engraved patterns (Figure 6). Other cases display elaborate piercing for a three-dimensional effect (Figures 7 through 9). Whereas most of the needle cases appear rounded, a few feature a flat surface (Figure 10). Others highlight a decorated bottom half and a matching sheath that fits over the inner tube (Figure 11). Even more amazing is the great diversity in the girth of the needle cases (Figure 12).

Two-sided, four-sided, or hexagonal vases were among the most sought-after shapes for needle cases, but other forms ranked high as well. The symbolic babies in Figure 13 look identical at first glance, but upon closer inspection, individual details—facial expression, the cut of a jacket, the style of a neck lock, the decorations on the pants—make each infant unique. The backs vary as much as the fronts (Figure 14). The detailed, enameled baby in Figure 15 obviously belonged to a wealthy woman, whereas the simpler and older variations in Figure 16 undoubtedly cost far less.

Cicadas were highly esteemed because they symbolized immortality (Figure 17). The same insect was often used for a fragrance carrier, but we can easily tell one type of artifact from the other if we remember that a cicada needle case featured an enclosed lower torso, whereas a cicada fragrance holder incorporated decorative slits to let the perfume escape. Symbols of abundance—such as a fish with detailed scales (Figure 18), Hakka women (Figures 19 and 20), Liu Hai with his string of coins and three-legged toad (Figure 21), the God of Wealth (Figure 22)— were often commissioned as well. Sometimes a case incorporated an ancient coin from the Xin dynasty (Figure 23).

Elaborate repoussé designs often curved around a cylindrical needle case, giving the owner various views as she turned it (Figures 24 through 26). Some cases were six-sided, each facet different from the one adjoining it (Figures 27 and 28). Simple round or oblong paktong containers featured incised outlines of horses, mountains, trees, roofs, and scholars (Figures 29 and 30). As a special flourish, some silversmiths incised images on the inner tube (Figure 31).

Since a needle case hung from a button on a woman's dress, it required a tiny chain terminating in either an s-shaped hook or a metal ring. Silver qilin, bat, or butterfly plaques often hid the fastener.

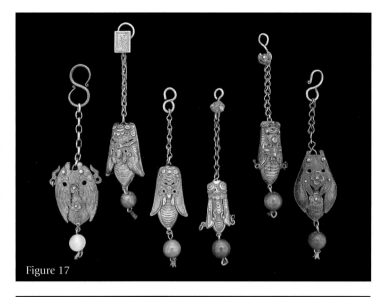

Figure 17

Figure 18

Blue, green, and yellow enamelwork was popular in the Qing dynasty and during the Republic era (Figures 32 and 33). Occasionally, all three colors appeared on the same needle case, but blue was evidently the preferred hue. Although many cases have lost their beautiful veneer through time and wear, some still display hints of this original splendor.

A woman of the Yi minority in Yunnan Province used a

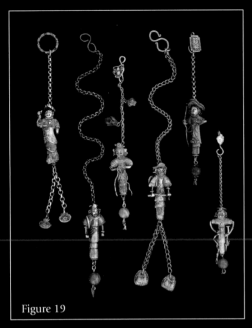

Figure 19

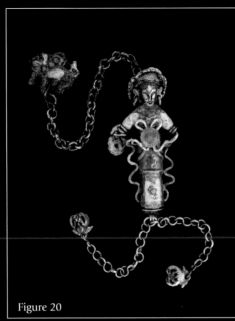

Figure 20

Figure 21

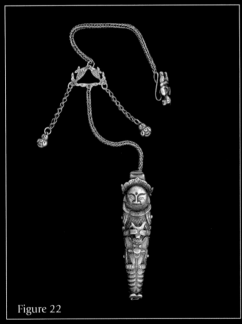

Figure 22

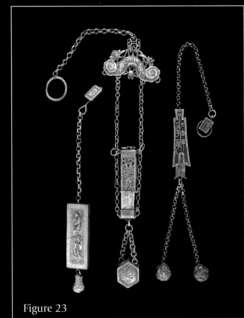

Figure 23

Figure 24

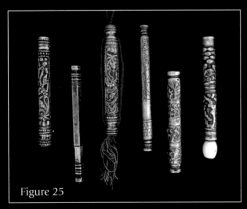

Figure 25

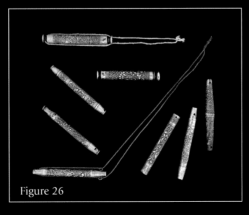

Figure 26

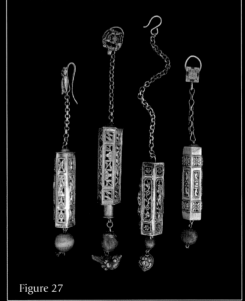

Figure 27

double-tubed needle case suspended from chains (Figures 34 through 36). She might have kept coarse sewing needles in one tube, fine embroidery needles in the other. For the more elaborate versions of this type, the smith added jade carvings, small opium boxes, and tiger teeth amulets. In Figure 37, we see a rare triple-tube and several double-tube needle cases, each with a single repoussé or engraved sheath.

Single needle cases from southwestern China often employed chains on both sides (Figures 38 and 39). One common type of Tibetan needle case hung from two cords of leather instead of chains (Figure 40). Both types of cases weigh a great deal for their size.

The Tibetans and the Mongols embedded turquoise or coral—either chunks or cabochons—into the silver on their needle cases, as shown in Figures 41 and 42. On the reverse of the Tibetan example (with the turquoise), we find a large nugget of coral.

Today, many needle cases are found as pendants on women's necklaces. In Figure 43 we have a piece probably cobbled together in the 1980's by a government worker (see the Introduction), and Figure 44 shows a newer assemblage found in the United States that includes the only gilded needle case I have ever seen. In each example, the artisan replaced the original chains with a strand of beads, making it impossible to raise the sheath and use the needle case.

Most of the needle cases currently for sale in China have tassels, or chains with small bells, dangling from the bottom. One rarely encounters a case with a bead. Private collections in the West, however, often include cases with old, carved, semi-precious stone beads—including agates, coral, and malachite—suspended from the bottom, along with non-standard amulets. These dangles, fascinating in themselves, were probably not added by the silversmiths. The small silver bells—especially the matching sets on double chains hanging from the bottom of a needle case—were surely in place from the first, since they functioned as charms against evil in Qing dynasty folk belief.

Another interesting aspect of some needle cases is their seeming uniformity, even though they were hand-crafted. Differences emerge only on careful examination. Figure 45 shows two sets of almost identical needle cases. Measuring them, however, we find that they vary slightly in their dimensions. On the first set,

the midpoint designs are slightly different; on the second set, the first case has a base and the second is enameled. Were these sets made by the same silversmith or in the same shop? This question merits further exploration.

In Figure 46, each smith stamped his hallmark on the side of the piece's inner tube. As we have seen, these artisans had reason to be proud of their work.

In the Introduction, I explained how I started collecting Qing dynasty silver after finding five needle cases in an antiques mall. The cases still fascinate me, partly because, as the daughters of Hungarian immigrants, several Hungarian-American friends and I learned sewing skills at the age of seven. For our practice sessions, our mothers and grandmothers would draw designs on scraps of cloth, and then we would embroider them. Eventually, we graduated to pillowcases, dresser covers, aprons, hand towels, and tablecloths. The finished products were carefully tucked into our cedar chests for our dowries.

Having spent much of my youth learning needlework, I am awed by the intricacy of Chinese embroidery, and I understand the pride and the pleasure the women must have taken in their creations. Holding a Qing dynasty needle case in my hand, I try to imagine the person who used it. Was she a young woman embroidering linens as I myself once did, or was she a middle-aged woman as I am now, anticipating the birth of a grandchild? Passing my fingers over the delicate repoussé, I feel a kinship that spans centuries.

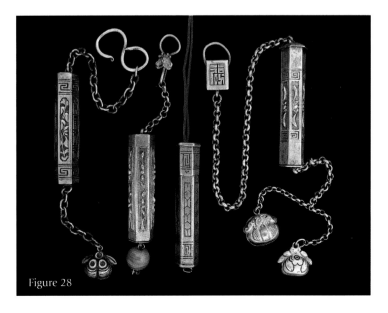
Figure 28

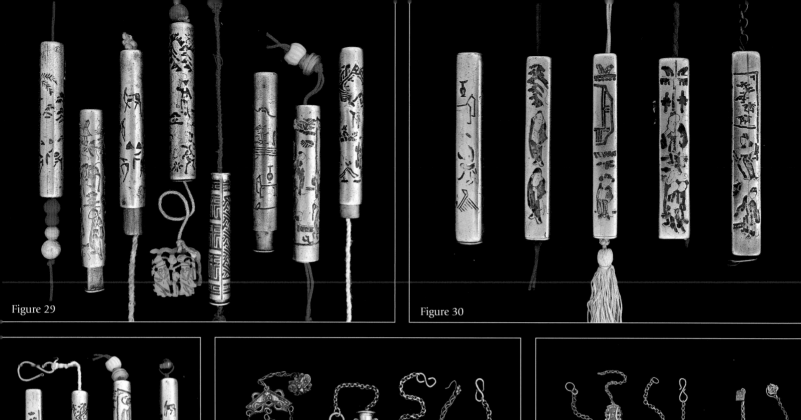

Figure 29

Figure 30

Figure 31

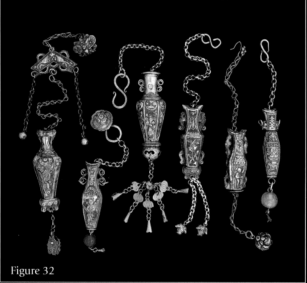

Figure 32

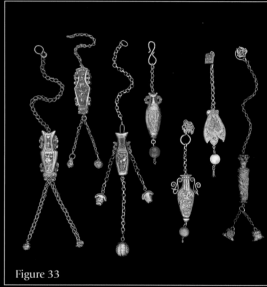

Figure 33

Figure 34

Figure 35

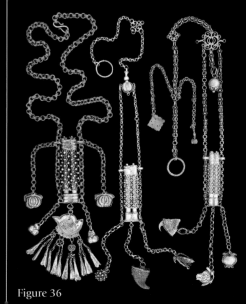

Figure 36

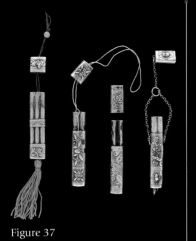

Figure 37

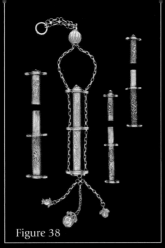

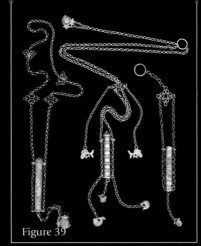

Figure 38

Figure 39

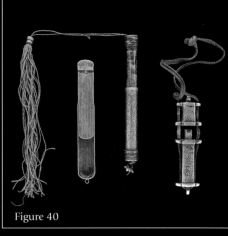

Figure 40

Figure 41

Figure 42

Figure 43

Figure 44

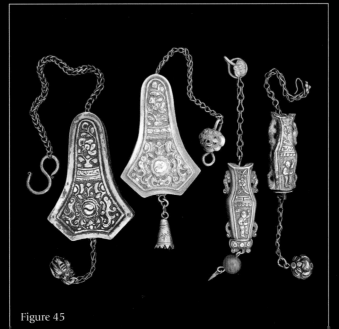

Figure 45

Figure 46

Symbolic Locks

During the Qing dynasty, folk beliefs permeated every level of Chinese society. Many common myths centered on demons from the land beyond. Evil spirits were always lurking around corners or hiding behind trees to snatch an unsuspecting child from his family. These spirits were especially hostile toward newborn sons, for the worship of family ancestors underlay the whole system of Chinese ethics.

Their belief in hostile supernatural forces enabled people throughout China to explain the high infant-mortality rate. To safeguard their children from evil spirits, families used all sorts of talismans and amulets. In some cases, friends contributed bits of string for a "hundred-family protection tassel" to be pinned to the child's clothes. In other cases, the parents wrote a spell on a piece of paper, folded it into a triangle, and fastened it to the infant's clothing. Or the parents encased a coffin nail in silver and then bent it into a bracelet or anklet. The most popular amulet, however, remained the silver padlock, hung around a baby's neck during the first-month celebration to ward off evil and "lock the child to Earth."

The idea of locking a child to Earth probably evolved from the traditional postnatal bathing ceremony. A newborn did not receive a bath until three days after birth, when the ritual was performed for a select number of close friends and relatives. In a wealthy family, the woman who nursed the mother lit incense sticks in a bowl of rice, and placed the bowl before the tablets of the ancestors. She prepared a basin of water for the baby's bath, then set one egg in the water for a boy, or two for a girl. She added a slice of green ginger, to be rubbed on the baby's navel to heal it. Alongside the bath, she arranged a bowl of warm water, a spoon, and a dish of red and white hard-boiled eggs. As the woman gently washed the baby, each guest took an egg and a spoonful of the tepid water, placing them in the bathtub. They chose either a red egg, which symbolized abundant good fortune, or a white one, suggesting the white hair of the elderly, which represented long life and good health.

Next, the woman in charge carried the rice bowl to the courtyard and allowed the incense to burn out. She also burned make-believe money and other paper offerings. Besides thanking the Goddess of Mercy, this tradition congratulated the ancestors for their newest descendant.

Opposite: A symbolic lock hangs around the neck of a young Han boy.

Following his first bath, the baby was dressed, and an actual, functioning lock—shackle open—was passed over its body from head to foot. As it touched the ground, the shackle was closed, ritually securing the child to earth.

The bathing ceremony contained great meaning, but even more significant was the first-month celebration, the *manyueh*. As the baby neared the one-month anniversary of its birth, the family's relatives and friends received invitations to the *manyueh*. Dressed in their finest clothes and adorned in jewelry, the guests paid their respects from early morning until late at night. Characters of joy decorated the courtyard, and in the homes of the wealthy, entertainment—a marionette show followed by fireworks—enhanced the festivities. Each guest brought a gift of clothing, jewelry, or money for the baby, all of which was duly chronicled by a designated registrar. Great feasting and merriment filled the day as the parents displayed the infant in an outfit especially embroidered for the occasion.

At a certain point in the celebration, either the father or a priest draped a symbolic silver lock and chain over the child's neck. In some areas, the lock hung from a silver neckring. If the family could not afford a silver chain or neckring, they substituted a red cord. Wealthier families occasionally used a gilded-silver lock. In Beijing, a first-month celebration was often held regardless of the baby's sex. This might explain why a few little girls are shown wearing locks in antique photographs (although most are post-Qing). In the more remote areas, the *manyueh* only followed the birth of a son.

Perhaps the most interesting lock was the "hundred-family protection lock" or *bai jia sau* (pronounced "buy jia swo"). Friends and family members would each contribute money toward the crafting of a unique lock that promised the baby their collective protection. This custom enjoyed special popularity in families where the parents had lost several children.

Qing dynasty citizens typically purchased ready-made symbolic silver locks in street stalls or in the silversmith's shops, but many customers evidently commissioned special pieces. Judging from the number that have survived, the scallop design seems to have been the most popular (Figures 1 through 22). Working within the confines of this style, the silversmith brought forth a tremendous diversity. The buyer had many choices: flat or

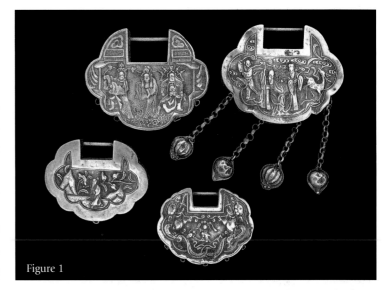

Figure 1

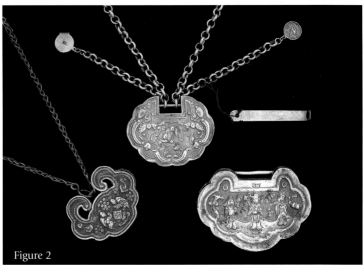

Figure 2

round, thick or thin, hung with dangles or dangle-free. Someone willing to pay more could have the lock gilded (Figure 6), or enameled (Figures 7, 8, and 22). It's interesting to compare the thin, delicate Han locks, which feature scenes from mythology, with the thick, heavy minority locks, bearing symbolism from the natural world (Figure 6).

Most of the locks consisted of two halves soldered together, and when you purchased an expensive lock, you were buying the silversmith's expertise in hiding the seam. Today, a visible juncture usually indicates an inexpensive lock, an inexperienced silversmith, or a piece from after the Qing dynasty. One major exception exists. The minority locks from the southwest used a design in which no amount of skill could hide the seam lines: these locks include a front, a back, and half a centimeter to slightly over a centimeter

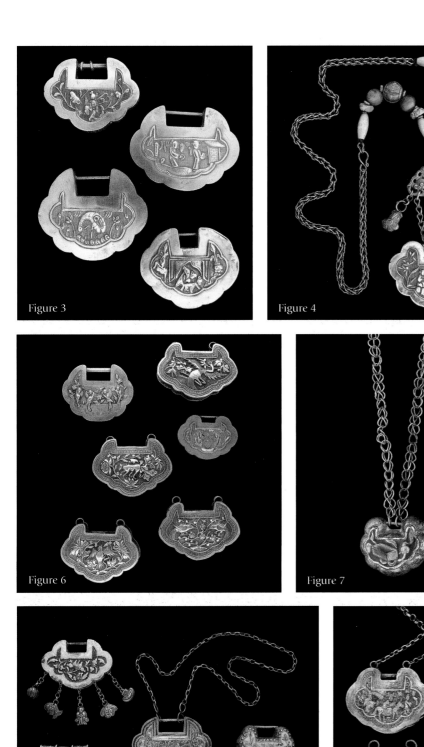

Figure 3

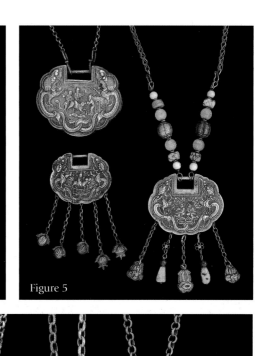

Figure 4

Figure 5

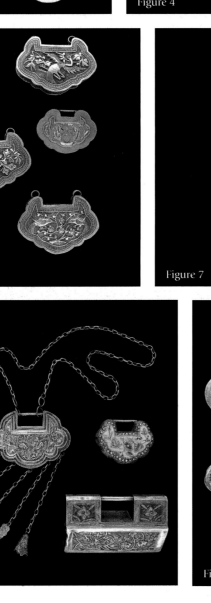

Figure 6

Figure 7

Figure 8

Figure 9

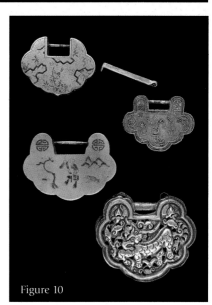

Figure 10

Figure 11

strip of silver between them (Figures 6, 9 and 10).

Some locks have no backs. When I first encountered this type, I wondered if the owner had broken off the rear half, but then I noticed that such a piece possessed a smooth outer edge. Obviously, a Qing silversmith produced backless locks as less costly pieces for his poorer patrons (Figures 13 and 14). Today these unique examples present us with an excellent opportunity to examine the reverses of repoussé locks.

Beyond the three-dimensional pendants, an artisan could repoussé a lock shape onto a flat sheet of silver, as in Figures 15 through 19. The little holes in most of these examples prompted me to imagine that these pieces were sewn to a child's clothing. Looking more closely, however, I noticed that the perforations usually appear along the bottoms only. Eventually, I found several flat locks with the dangles still attached to the bottom (Figures 17, 18, and 19). Today, a Miao woman often wears a huge flat silver lock, even larger than the one in Figure 24, dangling from a long chain or sewn to her clothing. Given the traditional symbolism on my flat locks, however, and the fact that most have no holes on the top, I feel that each probably hung from the neck of a young Han boy.

The dangles on the locks are as varied as the locks themselves. Many end in pomegranates, lotus blossoms, fish, monkeys and pigs, or a baby in a lotus. Particularly interesting to me are the leaves engraved with the most common Chinese surnames (Figures 19, 20, and 21).

The weight of a lock depended upon its style. Obviously, the solid locks weigh far more than the hollow or flat pieces. The sizes also varied greatly. Some locks measure just over two-and-a half centimeters, whereas others measure over ten centimeters wide and include rows of bell tipped chains along the bottom. The largest lock in my collection measures just over twenty centimeters across (Figure 24).

If a customer didn't like the standard scallop design, he could choose a plainer kidney shape (Figures 22, 23, 24, and 25), round (26 and 27), cylindrical (Figure 28), rectangular (Figures 29 through 33, and 36), multi-edged (Figure 34 and 35), hexagonal with a circlet of jade (Figure 37, bottom), or a butterfly (Figure 38). He might even select a Western padlock style with a silver leaf hiding the keyhole (Figure 37, top). But that was just

Figure 12

the beginning of the selection process. Once the buyer settled on the shape of the lock, he needed to choose the images to be embossed or engraved upon it.

Repoussé symbols of joy and good fortune, or scenes from mythology, the opera, folklore, and even novels, embellished the fronts of the more expensive locks. The Buddhist lotus (purity), the peony (wealth and distinction), and the plum blossom (longevity) enjoyed the greatest popularity. The mythological qilin, symbol of wisdom (Figures 9 and 10), with a rider in Imperial gown (Figures 5, 11, 13, and 34), embodied a wish for the baby's success on his civil service examinations, as did an official riding on horseback through a flag-waving crowd (Figures 9, 15, 16, and 29). The heavy, higher-priced locks often displayed artifacts associated with the scholar: chessboard, books, painting scrolls, musical instrument (Figures 10, 17, 20, 24, and 45). Locks featuring the three mythological deities called the Fu Lu Shou brought wealth, longevity, and happiness (Figures 2, 15, and 35), while Liu Hai played with his string of cash and his three-legged toad in a wish for wealth (Figures 1, 2, 10, and 16). A scene of the deities of the North and South Poles playing chess represented a fable in

Figure 13

Figure 14

Figure 15

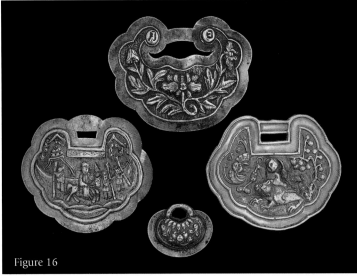

Figure 16

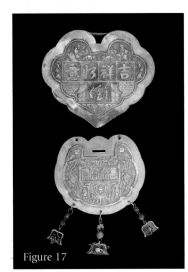

Figure 17

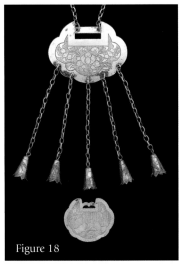

Figure 18

Figure 19

which they granted longevity (Figures 2, 6, and 30). The God of Longevity, with his long beard and elongated forehead, could be viewed as one of the three Fu Lu Shou, but he often appears alone with his staff, deer, and peach of immortality (Figures 1 and 11). The higher-priced locks often depict rare scenes. In Figure 5, Laozi, the legendary founder of Daoism, is shown riding his water buffalo toward the West, and meeting the border guard, with whom he leaves a collection of his work, at Hangu Pass.

The clothing on the silver characters adorning a lock offers clues to its age. A lock exhibiting men and women in long gowns dates from the Qing dynasty. Post-Qing examples depict human forms in long pants and short jackets. A man or woman of the Republic era rejected all adornment evoking the Imperial era, and so the newer silver items, even the symbolic pieces for children, embody this attitude.

Certain aspects of Qing symbolic locks merit scholarly exploration. A common type found today portrays two dragons, symbolizing male vigor and fertility, curling along the edges of the flat-topped locks (Figures 1, 2 and 5). Look for their feet and intertwining tails. The puffy variety of lock, on the other hand, often depicts twin dragonfish for perseverance and success in passing the civil service examinations (Figures 11, 15, and 23).

No matter what the border design, elaborate Chinese calligraphic messages adorned the backs of the average lock. In Figure 39, one lock conveys a hope that the baby and his descendants will prosper for five generations. Another lock offers a wish for the baby to enjoy one hundred years of life. Yet another inscription bestows literary talent (necessary for success in the civil service examinations). The most unusual message expresses a desire for the baby to live as long as the pine and the cypress, known for their longevity.

A silversmith employed either engraving or repoussé for a lock inscription (Figure 39). Sometimes, cursive characters squiggle creatively across a lock. In other cases, the characters appear controlled and formal. Occasionally, they constitute a perfect block similar to the ones on seals. Today, the calligraphy aids us in identifying the class of the owner. The rural pieces often exhibit simplified characters that are difficult for even the Chinese intelligentsia to decipher.

Many collectors assume that the elaborate repoussé designs

always faced forward, but in some instances the calligraphy predominated. The example in Figure 40 features hooks with butterflies and plum blossom leaves that probably attached the lock to an article of clothing. Note the gilded flamboyance of the characters.

Calligraphy style also helps us to date a lock. After 1949, the Communists simplified some characters so that more people could learn to read and write. Any piece containing these streamlined characters is probably a post-Revolution artifact. A piece that reads from left to right, or from bottom to top, also betrays a recent origin, for traditional Chinese is read either from right to left, or from top to bottom.

Figure 20

Figure 21

37

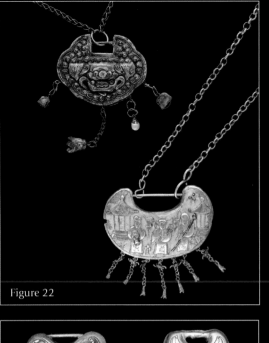

Figure 22

Figure 23

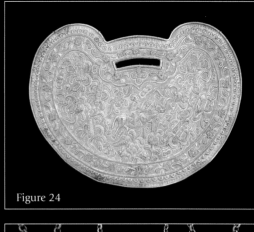

Figure 24

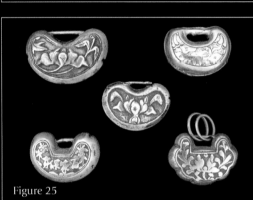

Figure 25

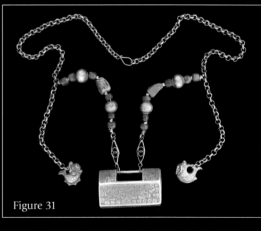

Figure 27

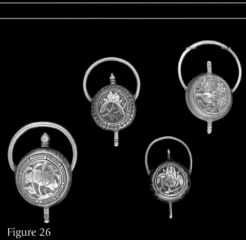

Figure 26

Figure 28

Figure 31

Figure 30

Figure 29

Figure 32

Figure 33

Figure 34

Figure 35

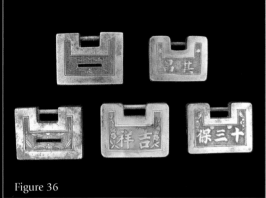

Figure 36

Figure 39

Figure 37

Figure 38

Figure 40

Figure 41

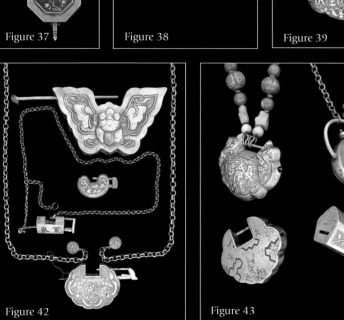

Figure 42

Figure 43

Figure 44

Figure 45

In addition to the calligraphic style, the symbolism on a lock often suggests its age. Even if a lock exhibits beautiful repoussé work, it does not date from the Qing dynasty if it displays the two flags of the Republic (Figure 41). The more modern artifacts also tend to combine images that were never grouped together on the traditional Qing locks.

As we see in Figure 42, a few locks actually functioned: the shackle opened with a key. The rectangular locks used a long, thin, flat key with one end curled up and notched at the tip. The drum-shaped lock has a small slit on the bottom to receive a flat key. Other keys were round. Figure 43 reveals the great diversity of keyhole shapes. It's clear, however, that a parent rarely opened even the most functional baby lock. Indeed, the shackle was often soldered shut. The artifacts' value lay in their symbolism, not their utility.

Today we often find a Qing lock adorning a necklace with coral, turquoise, bone, and carnelian beads strung along a silk thread between the lock and chain (Figures 4, 5, and 29 through 32). While the beads may qualify as antiques, they are not original to the locks. In the Introduction I described the way silver artifacts were turned into jewelry for sale to the West after the Cultural Revolution. This process always included adding strings of beads to the short chains, thereby turning the baby locks into pendants on adult necklaces. These mongrel pieces all exhibit similar bead patterns, making them easy to identify. Despite this destructive tampering, the locks themselves remain authentic Qing relics. Fortunately, many locks with their original chains still surface throughout China.

How can we tell if a lock chain is authentic? Note that in many cases, bells on chains dangle from the bottom of the lock. If the neck chain matches the bell chains, and all are still soldered to the lock, the entire assemblage is probably of a piece. Now, it's certainly possible that an active baby boy might have snapped his lock-chain, forcing his family to somehow restore it. But since any silver item cost a great deal, his mother probably had the chain repaired before replacing it. I believe that vendors of a much later period added random chains to orphan locks, for a necklace always commanded a higher price than a mere singleton pendant. I'm also certain that some vendors found it more profitable to deliberately remove an original antique silver chain from a lock

Figure 46

and sell the chain separately.

Occasionally, one encounters a child's amulet in which the lock is attached to a handsewn cloth neckring instead of a chain, the whole arrangement hung with dangles for good fortune. Such pieces are authentic. In Figure 44, the baby dangle represents a wish for sons, the three-legged toad stands for longevity, and the double fish symbolizes marital bliss. The lock itself depicts a magpie picking lotus blossom seeds, signifying a wish for the child to know the joy of passing his examinations. On the reverse, the Chinese script tells us that this was a hundred-family protection lock.

In Figure 45, another handsewn neckring holds a lock with images representing the four scholarly pursuits. On the reverse, Chinese characters express a desire for the boy to obtain high rank. The silver baby represents a wish for the child to further his line of succession. What about the donkey? In Chinese mythology, Zhang Guolao, one of the Daoist Eight Immortals, rode a magic white donkey one thousand miles a day, then folded it up and placed it in his gourd when he reached his destination. The donkey came to symbolize endurance. The whole necklace evidently wished the baby perseverance for a scholarly, prosperous future, as well as many sons.

Figure 46 strikingly resembles Figure 45, with the exception of the curled cord, a device also found on the lock in Figure 41. Did this cord represent the arcing horns of a cow? (Interestingly, cowhorns inspired the elaborate hairdos of Khalkha Mongol women). Or does it represent a *ruyi*: the wish-granting scepter of Chinese legend?

Besides chains and cloth neckrings, solid silver neckrings also served to suspend symbolic locks. A male infant, a boy in his teens, and a young woman wore such metal rings for special occasions. The Han Chinese, the Mongols, and the minorities, all used both plain neckrings and the more elaborately carved torques.

It is often difficult to tell if a lock was intended for a woman or for a boy. In Figure 38, we see a lock probably worn by a young woman at her wedding. Unlike the average baby lock, this piece opens. The large butterfly on the front symbolizes joy and marital happiness. On the back we have lotus blossoms, a bearded man with a staff, and a woman holding a flywhisk over a kneeling fgture.

The large, heavy, expensive lock in Figure 35 is easier to place in cultural context. The three Fu Lu Shou for longevity, wealth, and happiness adorn the front, along with a baby bearing a lotus (continuous birth of noble sons), a magpie (bringer of good news), a butterfly and plum blossom (longevity), a fungus (immortality), and a peach blossom plus peach bells (immortality). On the back, flanking a bat, we have a wish for longevity, prosperity, and nobility. I'm quite sure this lock adorned the neck of a teenage boy during the New Year celebration. The Fu Lu Shou rarely appeared on locks intended for infants or females, and only a boy would have been wished longevity, prosperity, and *nobility*.

Whatever its mass and value, a lock often exhibited the hallmark of the silversmith (Figure 47). Some locks might have two such stamps—one bearing the Chinese characters for "silver," the other bearing the smith's signature.

Occasionally, the silversmith added an extra safeguard to a child's lock. In Figure 2, the lock on the lower left contains a small bead to frighten away evil spirits. On a more mundane level, the clanging also helped the mother keep track of her wandering toddler.

Chinese culture is not unique in providing children with amulets. The Turks pin a blue and white glass eye on the newborn;

Figure 47

the Mexicans use a "deer's eye" seed; and the Palestinians deploy a green glass bead. Cowry shells are considered protective in El Salvador, claws and teeth in Nepal, coral in Yemen, and amber in Lithuania. Some cultures hang a small bag around the child's neck: a leather amulet in the Sudan, a blue knitted sack of garlic in Greece, a linen pocket of rue among the Pennsylvania Dutch.

Many such amulets derive from religious traditions. Not so long ago, a cross adorned a Protestant baby, a St. Christopher's medal dangled from the neck of a Catholic child, and the Star of David protected a Jewish infant.

What was once a strongly held belief in the Qing dynasty has today become a felicitous custom. Chinese peoples living in China, Taiwan, Hong Kong, Singapore, the United States, and many other countries still present a symbolic lock—sometimes a family heirloom, sometimes a reproduction—to an infant for his or her one-month celebration. Rectangular, oblong, drum-shaped, flat, fluffy, repoussé, or engraved, these talismans continue to fascinate, adorn, and protect.

chapter 3

Grooming Kits and Fragrance Carriers

A s the Han scholar-official slips into his navy-blue silk robe, he silently thanks the Buddha for all his blessings. Born in a poor village, he spent years studying the ancient Confucian texts and philosophical principles, ultimately passing a series of rigorous civil service examinations. Instead of a provincial post, he received an appointment in Beijing, where he enjoys high status, great wealth, and political influence.

Having buttoned his robe, the official wraps a sash around his waist and adds three embroidered pouches—for fragrance, tobacco, and his treasured watch—on one side, then his set of silver grooming tools on the other. He commissioned the grooming kit—earpick, tweezers, nailpick, two ornamental swords, jade centerpiece—from the best silversmith in Beijing. The jade was an indulgence, but he believes the stone imparts justice and wisdom, virtues he needs for his duties.

As his houseboy summons the rickshaw, the official slips into his studio to reread the poem he composed the night before. Beholding the fine calligraphy, he smiles in satisfaction. The servant now announces the arrival of the official's conveyance and hands him his six-sided black silk hat. Imagining his next literary creation, the official moves toward the front door amidst the tinkling of the grooming tools dangling from his sash.

Beyond the Great Wall, on the grassy steppes of Inner Mongolia, a wealthy young Chahar matron prepares to attend her cousin's wedding. Married to an aristocrat charged with guarding the Emperor's great herds of horses, cows, sheep, and goats, she wears her finest clothes and dowry accessories on special occasions such as this. Her two daughters, already dressed, gather around her in the felt yurt and help her into her red silk robe and a long sleeveless vest of brocade.

Giggling with excitement, the daughters plait their mother's long hair, drawing the ends into shoulder-length balls and binding them with coral strands. Atop her head they place a black cotton headband (which the matron inherited from her great-grandmother) covered with silver pieces encrusted with chunks of coral. Tiny coral bits dangle from the brow, sides, and back of the headband, and matching ornaments of silver and coral cover her ears.

Opposite: A Qiang man wearing a grooming kit.

The matron slips four large silver and coral rings onto her fingers, a bracelet over each wrist, and fastens a grooming kit to the top button of her del. The kit's centerpiece holds foxtail chains ending in a silver earpick, tweezers, and nailpick—a simple accessory compared to her husband's kit, which contains seven tools, but she loves it nevertheless. After a final check, mother and daughters compliment each other on their appearance and walk outside to the waiting horses and the men of the family, who will escort them across the steppes.

Fifteen hundred miles west, in a Qiang settlement in Sichuan Province, a farmer tells his wife that he is going to visit a neighbor to discuss grazing rights. To stay warm in the high mountain air, he dons his leather robe and hat trimmed with fur. After tying his long sash around his waist, he adds his elaborate silver grooming kit, emblematic of his status as an elder in the community.

Besides being essential to cleanliness, the kit will prove useful when he and his neighbor relax and smoke their pipes later that evening. He grabs his pipe and his tobacco pouch and exits his flat-roofed stone house, where his family stores grain on the top floor, lives on the second, and shelters their animals on the first. As the farmer makes his way along a narrow path in the fog, the clanging of his grooming tools blend with the sound of the distant yak bells.

South of Sichuan, in the province of Yunnan, a young woman of the Yi nationality prepares for the March Market. At the county fair and regional dance, unattached young men of the region will inevitably observe her. She fastens her finest embroidered skirt and adds a pink silk jacket with tight embroidered sleeves. A black sleeveless vest buttons over the jacket. She slips into her embroidered shoes and ties on her heavily embroidered short apron held up by a silver chain looped around her neck, knowing that every man will be examining her needlework.

After fastening her long hair into a bun, the young woman wraps a black cloth into a huge plate-shape around her head. She attaches silver flowers with dangling bells to the headdress, then fastens jade and silver earrings to her lobes. As a final touch, she hooks a silver grooming kit to a button on her vest. Beyond the traditional tools, this particular kit contains a fragrance holder

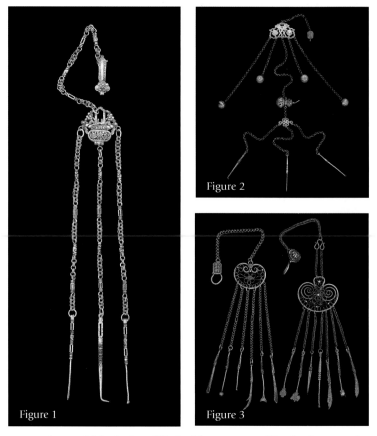

Figure 1

Figure 2

Figure 3

centerpiece, which she has filled with sweet-smelling herbs to make her more enticing, and two tiny bells on short chains to frighten away evil spirits. She smiles and coquetishly swings the grooming set to hear the jingle of the bells and smell the scented air as she fantasizes about a possible suitor.

Four different areas of China. Four different individuals, drawn from a myriad of possibilities, a diversity reminding us that the desire to present oneself as pleasing as possible—well groomed and exuding an attractive scent—was not confined to any particular region, class, ethnic group, or gender in Qing dynasty China.

The Chinese were not the first people to value grooming kits and air fresheners. After the excavations at Ur (part of modern day Iraq) in the early twentieth century, grooming tools of gold, probably fashioned for royalty, once again sparkled in the sunlight. Dating to around 3000 B.C., this particular kit included tweezers, a nailpick and an earpick. Nobility of the Indus civilization boasted grooming kits in the third millennium B.C., and sets containing nailpicks, tweezers, tattooing-needles, and earpicks adorned the Danes in the later Bronze Age, about 500-400 B.C. Archeologists

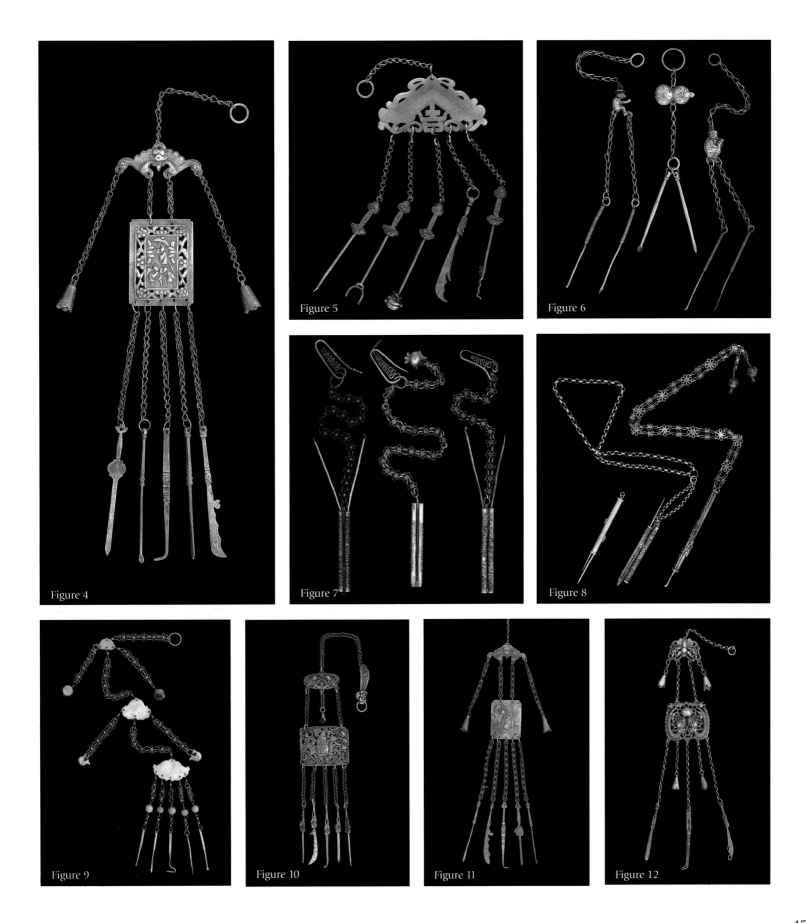

Figure 4

Figure 5

Figure 6

Figure 7

Figure 8

Figure 9

Figure 10

Figure 11

Figure 12

45

Figure 13

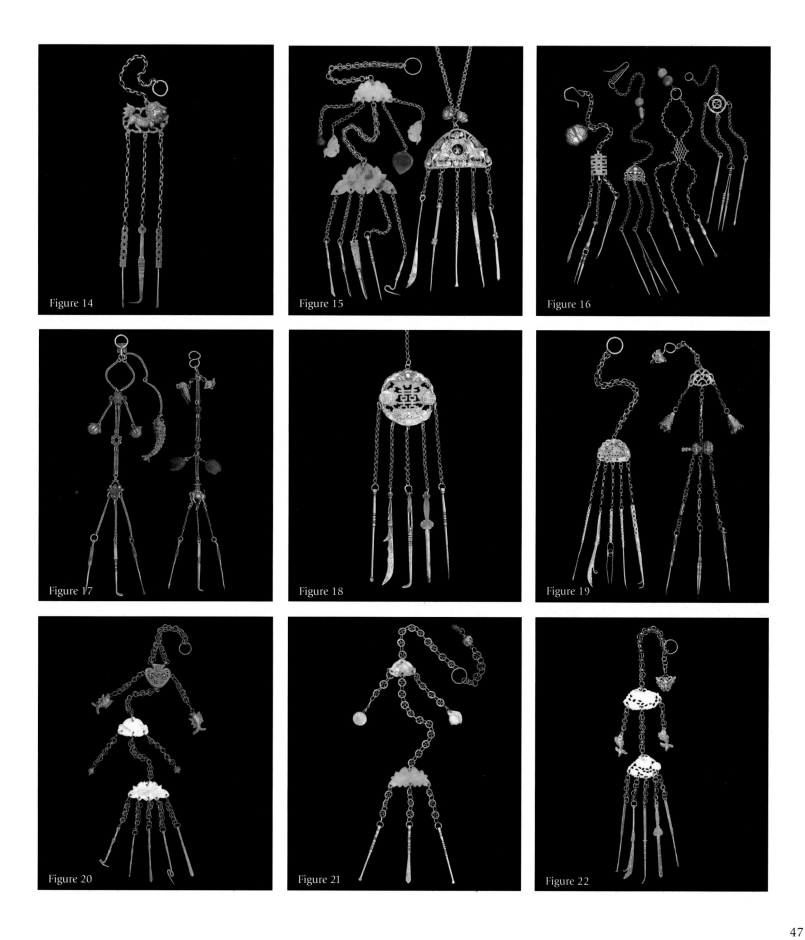

Figure 14

Figure 15

Figure 16

Figure 17

Figure 18

Figure 19

Figure 20

Figure 21

Figure 22

excavating a medieval Viking village beneath the modern city of Dublin found a ninth-century silver toiletry set containing tweezers, earpick, and a nail file.

In China, waist-hangings indicated status as far back as the Shang dynasty (1766-1121 B.C.), although the silver grooming kit appeared much later. The exact date of the first such set eludes us, but we know they were ubiquitous in the Qing dynasty.

Although many collectors refer to personal grooming kits as chatelaines, this designation is imprecise. The word "chatelaine" originally referred to the matron of a castle, then to her waist-hung keys. It did not signify other waist-hung ornaments until 1828.

In Chapter 10, as you will see, I use "chatelaine" to indicate the sort of large silver-and-leather clasp often hung from Tibetan and Mongol sashes in the Qing dynasty.

The classic Chinese personal grooming kit consists of an earpick, tweezers, and a nailpick, attached to an ornamental centerpiece. A man suspended his set from his waist sash. A Han woman hung her grooming kit from a button on her dress while some minority women attached theirs to their neckrings.

Each tool's function was straightforward. The owner used his nailpick to scrape away dirt from under his nails. His earpick removed excessive wax, but we now have to wonder how many people impaired their hearing this way. The tweezers were employed to pluck unwanted facial hair. For an upper-class woman, tweezers were also crucial to the application of makeup, which usually required the assistance of a personal maid. First, the maid would dampen the lady's face with towels. Next came a scrub and polish, followed by a thorough tweezing of all excess facial hair from forehead to neck. The maid was especially careful to groom the eyebrows.

While a three-tool set (Figures 1 and 2) was the norm in the Qing dynasty, I have seen kits with as many as seven tools (Figure 3). Six-tool and four-tool sets are extremely rare: even numbers were considered inauspicious and female in the Qing dynasty. Three, five, and seven are the usual numbers of items on a Chinese grooming kit. Today, many sets contain mismatched chains, dangles, and tools, evidence of their frequent and haphazard replacement. These mongrel assemblages are nevertheless genuine cultural artifacts—they enjoyed constant daily use in their owners'

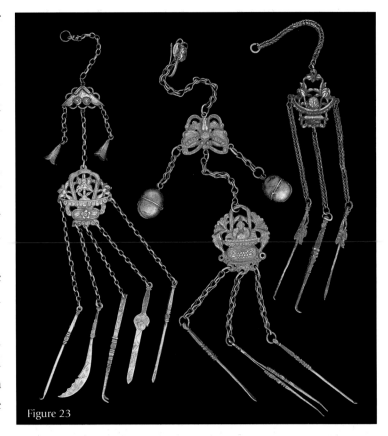

Figure 23

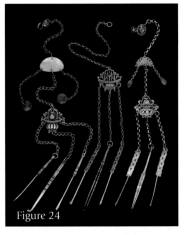

Figure 24

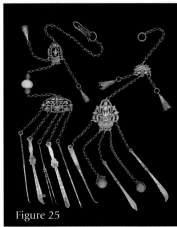

Figure 25

lives—and many collectors prefer them to the perfectly matched sets.

One or more miniature weapons, usually broadsword replicas, typically enhance the grooming kit worn by a man (Figures 4 and 5). In Daoism, the sword represents victory over evil and offers symbolic protection. In Buddhism, however, it holds a deeper meaning: as a symbol of wisdom, a tiny sword on a grooming kit cut away all doubts on the path to knowledge. A spear symbolized for Buddhists the piercing of ignorance; a trident

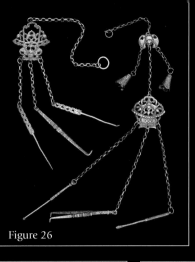

Figure 26

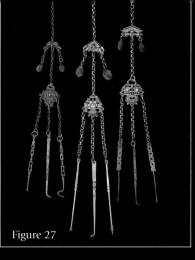

Figure 27

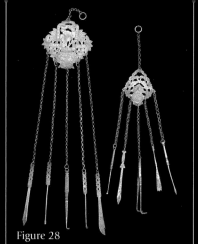

Figure 28

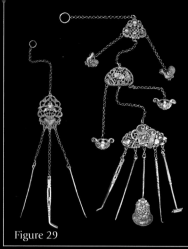

Figure 29

Figure 30

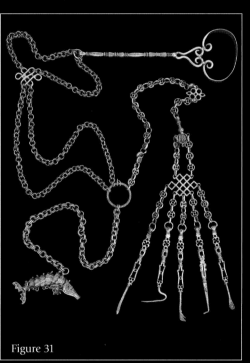

Figure 31

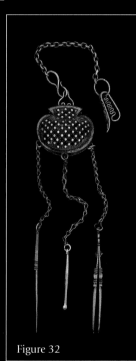

Figure 32

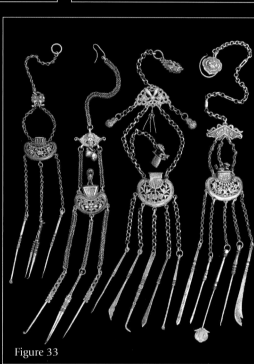

Figure 33

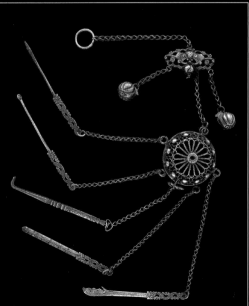

Figure 34

Figure 35

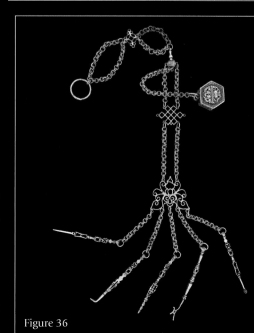

Figure 36

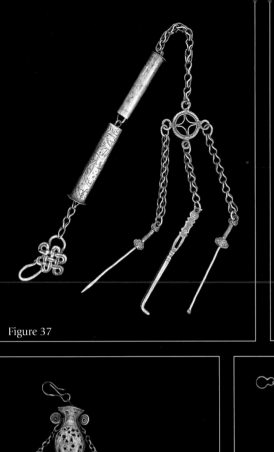

Figure 37

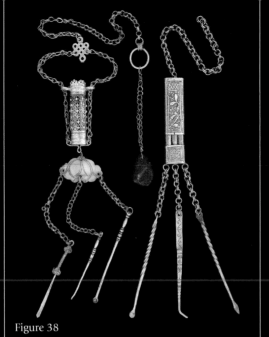

Figure 38

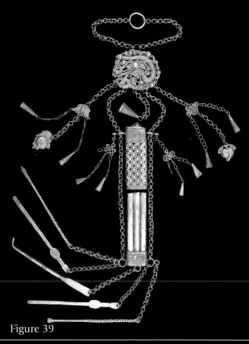

Figure 39

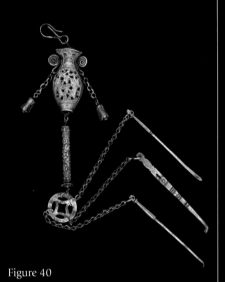

Figure 40

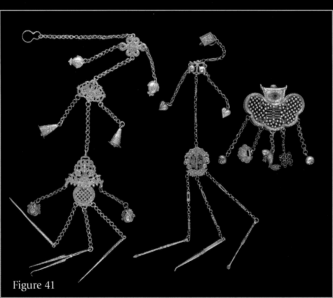

Figure 41

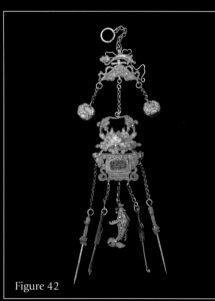

Figure 42

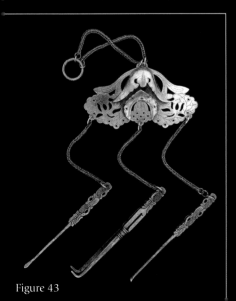

Figure 43

Figure 44

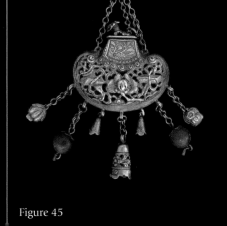

Figure 45

punctured the three poisons of ignorance, desire, and aggressiveness; a dagger penetrated hatred; and a club pounded out any corruption in one's karma.

Certain minorities used grooming sets containing only two tools—the earpick and the toothpick (Figure 6). In Figure 7, the nailpick and earpick lie in separate chambers of a single container and fall forward when you turn the receptacle upside down. Figure 8 offers some even more unusual pieces. In the example on the right, a tiny bearded man slides along a slot in the tube. When you push him down, the earpick appears; push him up, and the nailpick materializes. On the double tube, a silver flower decorates each side. Push one flower up to access the nailpick; push the other one down to use the earpick. The single engraved tube on the left of Figure 8 employs two knobs connected to two different tools, which both emerge from the bottom.

The shaft of every grooming tool gave the silversmith an opportunity to practice his art. Some shafts were engraved; others exhibited openwork, and others featured elaborate three-dimensional designs. Dragons, symbolizing male vigor and fertility, enjoyed the greatest popularity. Some dragons curled in two dimensions. Other shafts featured three-dimensional dragonheads with tongues that ended in tools.

The chain usually followed one of four designs: the circular belcher, the double loop, the foxtail, and the variable link with either small rosettes or symbolic coins between the circular links. A rarely seen fifth type—which intersperses the belcher circles with oblong openwork—links sculpted animals.

The chains and their accompanying tools varied dramatically in length. The grooming kit with the gourd centerpiece in Figure 6, which I purchased in Beijing, measures only sixteen centimeters from top to bottom, while the jade and silver ensemble in Figure 9, found in China's Yunnan Province, measures over sixty-one centimeters. The Inner Mongolians in the north wore elongated grooming kits, but the minorities in southwestern China boasted the most impressive sets of all: some women wore grooming kits extending from their necks to their waists, while the men had sets that dangled from their sashes to below their knees.

The central ornaments from which the utensils hung were sometimes incredibly elaborate, sometimes extremely simple, but they always held symbolic meanings. On one of the larger grooming sets from the Beijing area, we find a scholar riding on a deer, a symbol of wealth, and achievement (Figure 10). On others kits we find repoussé scenes from Chinese folklore (Figure 11). Still other silver centerpieces depict dragons chasing the pearl of potentiality (Figure 12), butterflies (Figure 13), lions (Figures 14 and 15), Chinese characters (Figure 16), and the endless knot (Figure 17).

The grooming tools of a high-ranking official often hung from an intricate jade carving fixed inside a silver rim. In Figure 18, the double happiness carving and the bats suggest that the kit was a wedding present. A smaller gilded-silver grooming kit encases a piece of jade in Figure 19.

In southwestern China, jade centerpieces carved in the shape of a lotus blossom—symbolizing redemption, purity, and fruitfulness—often adorn the minority sets (Figures 20 and 21). Most specimens are sculpted from solid jade and feature a lotus, but a few exhibit a pierced design (Figure 22). Many of the southwestern grooming sets include beads of carnelian and amber, prevalent in this region, dangling from chains.

The basket, signifying abundance and prosperity, is perhaps the most common design for a centerpiece. At first glance, the baskets look the same, but if you study the examples in this chapter, you will discern much complexity and variety. The baskets in Figures 23 through 25 contain silver flowers, fruits, butterflies, and even a baby. The baskets in Figure 26 both incorporate bat motifs. Some baskets appear woven from reeds, while others feature a five-petaled plum blossom, symbolizing the Five Gods of Good Fortune (Figure 27). Although most baskets are modeled in high relief, some are completely flat (Figure 28).

The symbolism on a grooming kit tells us much about the owner's status. In the example on the right in Figure 29, we see an umbrella for nobility, books and a painting for wisdom, a *ruyi* for the granting of wishes, a sword to dispel ignorance and evil, and a rhinoceros horn for good health. The prevalence of double symbols—bats for happiness, roosters for male vigor and reliability, coins for wealth, lotus flowers for purity amidst corruption— suggests that this was a wedding present. Further evidence lies in the magpie and the plum blossom designs, denoting marital bliss, on the painting scroll.

Besides the three basic tools, the symbolic armaments, and

Figure 46

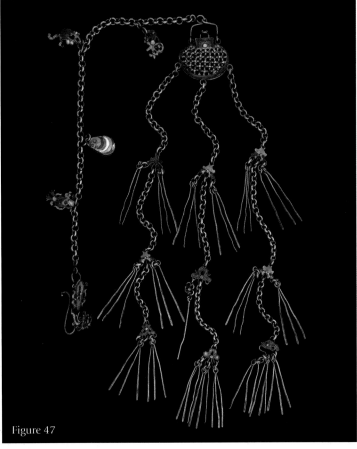

Figure 47

the centerpiece, a grooming kit often incorporated other items, both utilitarian and symbolic, including personalized seals, religious charms, incense spoons (Figure 29), mustache combs (Figure 30), and tongue scrapers (Figure 31). The set in Figure 2 features a silver gourd to hold medicine or snuff, while the kits in Figures 32 through 34 incorporate containers for herbs or perfumed cloths. The Shanghai Museum labeled a centerpiece similar to the one in Figure 35 as a southwest minority powder receptacle. The small box in Figure 36 held opium.

Figures 37 through 40 show needle cases combined with grooming kits. Unique engraving appears on the sheath in Figure 37, which also includes the symbol for wealth. In Figures 38 and 39, sheaths cover three tubes instead of the usual two. Figure 39 actually has two centerpieces—the triple-tube needle case, and a large centerpiece with a dragon on one side and an official on the other. Figure 40 depicts one of the most unusual needle cases I have ever encountered. Elaborate repoussé covers the tube, echoing the intricacy of the vase-shaped sheath.

As with all Chinese silver, the quality and color of the metal in the grooming ensembles vary considerably. Occasionally, you'll find a gilded kit, probably made for members of the aristocracy (Figure 41). The piece in Figure 42, also fashioned for the wealthy, was most likely covered with real kingfisher feathers. At the other end of the spectrum, darker sets—a lower quantity of silver—adorned the less affluent during the Qing era.

One function of the grooming kit had nothing to do with personal appearance. The tools could be used as probes to determine whether a portion of food was rancid or poisoned. If the inserted silver turned dark, the food was probably contaminated. The emperor's entourage routinely used silver in this way. Besides tasting each dish beforehand, the royal eunuch would place small pieces of silver in the bottom of the dish and then check to make sure they had not changed color.

Grooming tools could also serve as tobacco-smoking implements. In Qing dynasty China, both men and women used tobacco, considered medicinal. They might have employed the tweezers to transfer the tobacco to the pipe bowl, the earpick to tamp the tobacco down, and the nailpick to clean the bowl.

Missionaries returning to America brought stories of the Chinese employing grooming tools in their opium-smoking customs. I would guess that some opium smokers used the earpick to heat the narcotic over the open flame—though a real opium spoon has a larger bowl and a longer handle. The nailpick would have served well for cleaning an opium pipe.

The Mongols harbored a particular fondness for grooming kits and created some of the most unusual specimens. This fact might surprise readers who've heard that the Great Khan banned bathing and clothes washing. The prohibition had nothing to do with disdain for grooming or hygiene, however. Rather, the Khan knew that if a thunderstorm arose while his soldiers were scrubbing their bodies or garments by a lake or river, they would often become terrified, run into the water, and drown.

I have not been able to identify the centerpieces in Figures 43 and 44, but a breast ornament with a similar centerpiece was found in an Inner Mongolian monastery. We must remember that Inner Mongolia was part of Qing dynasty China. Chinese silversmiths often traveled with the Mongols to make artifacts for them, and monasteries throughout the area received silver gifts from the faithful. It's entirely possible, therefore, that the items we see in Figures 43 and 44 are Chinese—although Mongol artisans were certainly capable of such craftsmanship. The Henning Haslund-Christensen expeditions of 1923 and 1936 to Mongolia brought back many examples for the National Museum of Denmark.

In recent years, many collectors of Qing dynasty silver have specialized in the traditional grooming kit and its many variations. The original kits—solid, heavy, and meant to last—are the more highly prized (as opposed to the recent replicas, which feature chains of shiny silver that never tarnish, or lightweight tools that bend easily). Despite years of repeated use, the authentic antique grooming kits are still as functional and beautiful as the day they were made.

For the Chinese, making a favorable impression has always involved not only looking your best, but also emitting an agreeable fragrance. Among Han women, the custom of footbinding aggravated the normal human problem of body odor. Because the unwrapping process was so painful, Han women washed their feet only once or twice a month. The silk clothing of the wealthy made them vulnerable as well. Such garments could not be laundered, so they often smelled of stale perspiration.

No wonder the Ming and Qing dynasty peoples used

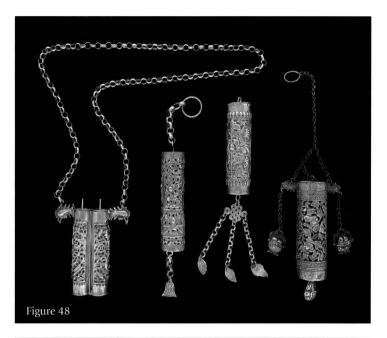

Figure 48

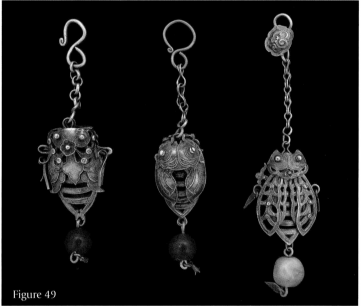

Figure 49

embroidered sachet bags filled with herbs or some perfume-soaked material. Besides improving your own scent, a fragrance carrier helped to conceal unpleasant smells in the environment. The urban streets of Qing dynasty China reeked of open sewers, people who rarely bathed, animal droppings, and sidewalk markets.

As the silversmith's art spread through China, wealthy patrons commissioned solid metal fragrance carriers to replace their sachet bags. The most popular style mimicked the classic kidney-shaped embroidered drawstring purse (Figure 45). Flowers, Buddhists symbols, and scholar's symbols were the most common

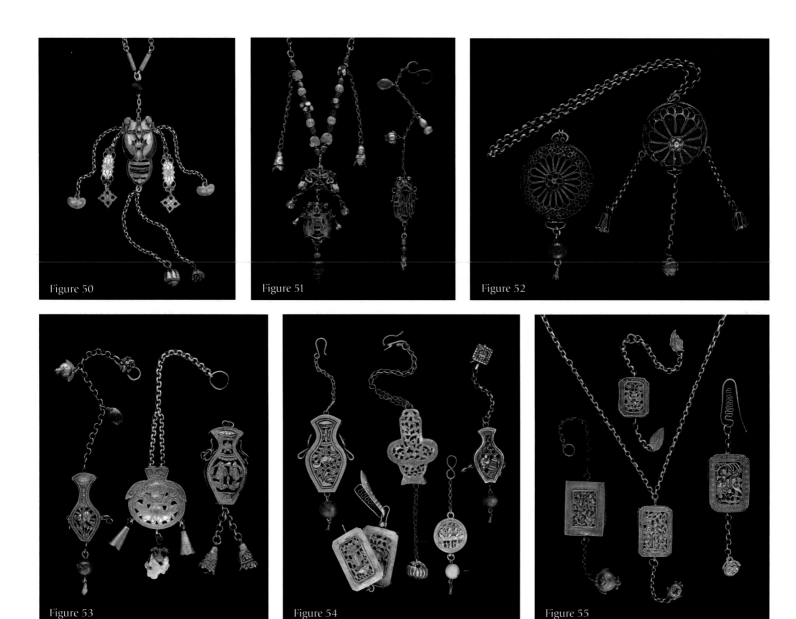

Figure 50

Figure 51

Figure 52

Figure 53

Figure 54

Figure 55

decorations. The smith would subtly perforate these designs, allowing the fragrance to escape and freshen the air around the wearer. The larger type of carrier, measuring up to seven centimeters, was probably used by men, for it often included symbols of the Eight Immortals or the symbols for the scholar. The smaller type, probably used by women, measures less than four centimeters, and is usually embellished with flowers.

I suspect that some of the carriers in my collection were originally grooming kit centerpieces, especially when I see lugs and dangles at the bottom (Figure 46). It's possible, however, that the silversmiths simply used the exact same style for both types of carriers: centerpieces and singletons.

Figure 47 shows the most unusual purse-style fragrance carrier I have ever seen. An impressive fifty-eight centimeters long, this piece must have been worn by a member of the aristocracy or possibly even a member of the Imperial Court. On the bottom, silver dangles appear beneath two rows of enameled lotus blossoms. Above the carrier, we find an enameled *ruyi* hook and other enameled charms. To open the carrier, you must first disconnect the purse handles, then spread the sides.

Judging from the large number we find today, I would say that cylindrical tube-shaped fragrance carriers achieved great popularity during the Qing dynasty (Figure 48). Most measure six to eight centimeters in length and one-and-a-half centimeters to three centimeters in width, and most contain an inner rod. Sometimes the owner rolled fragrant paper around this rod; sometimes he surrounded the rod with perfume-soaked cotton. In both instances, the enswathed rod strengthened the fragile casing, easily bent because of the air holes.

Another popular carrier assumed the shape of a cicada, symbol of resurrection. Similar to the cicada needle case, the cicada fragrance carrier is pierced along the insect's abdomen to allow the scent to escape (Figure 49). Colorful enameling covers many such pieces, so they must have been favored by the nobility (Figures 50 and 51). Over time, many cicada fragrance carriers evolved into centerpieces on necklaces, and thereby ceased to function as air fresheners.

Circular, filigreed fragrance carriers were often fashioned from the very darkest silver. In Figure 52, one carrier still contains the original cotton, sandwiched between pieces of red and gray cloth. The other carrier, boasting a more complex design, probably also held cloth-wrapped, perfumed cotton.

The vase-shaped type of fragrance carrier—see Figure 53—is often mistaken for a needle case. Instead of having a central tube for needles, however, such a container features a top that raises to admit the perfumed cotton. Naturally, it also has air holes. The purse-shaped item in the middle of Figure 53 features a top that slides along the chain, as in certain needle cases, but the perforated bottom identifies it as a fragrance carrier.

Many repoussé fragrance carriers were probably not opened frequently. Consider the examples in Figure 54. On the two vase pieces, as well as the circular carrier, the loop holding the chain passes through both top lugs. The user had to detach the loop before raising the front, which remains hinged to the bottom via the lug on the other end. Obviously, the owner needed a perfume that lasted a very long time. An alternative is represented by the elaborate basket-shaped carrier. Because it has two loops and two chains—one attached to each of the lugs—the front is easily raised from one end. The carrier in the lower left is notable for the small silver post atop the front section. To secure the front to the back, the owner slid the small round flower over the post.

The rectangular type of fragrance carrier, common in the Shanghai area, has a silver sliding door on the side to give access to the cotton (Figure 55). Such a carrier is smaller and more fragile than the rectangular piece in Figure 54, whose heavy clasp suggests that it hung from a man's belt. The more delicate carriers were probably worn by women and some also hung from the curtains around an enclosed platform bed.

The Qing dynasty silversmiths had a wonderful gift for combining functionality with beauty. They held to this ideal even in the seemingly mundane domain of personal hygiene products. In the hands of these great craftsmen, devices for grooming and deodorizing acquired such elegance and grace that they were destined to become treasured family heirlooms. These unique artifacts have come down to us having survived the busy lives of government officials, the spirited dances of minorities, treks across remote mountains, and galloping rides over the Mongolian steppes. It is now our task to preserve them for the enjoyment of our descendants.

Qilins

The evolution of the mythological qilin—from paragon of wisdom to symbol of fertility—remains one of the mysteries of Chinese folklore. Initially a benevolent creature of great wisdom, the qilin (pronounced "cheelin") gradually developed into the Chinese equivalent of the Western stork; the creature brought sons with the talent to become high officials or scholars. A Qing dynasty woman who hoped for industrious offspring owned a silver amulet depicting a mounted qilin: the rider was either an infant, the Goddess of Fertility, or a young man in the robe of a successful civil service examination candidate. Male progeny wore the qilins bearing candidates to insure their own success on the examinations, or the riderless qilins for wisdom.

Sometimes called a "unicorn" in Chinese literature, the qilin boasted a dragon's head bearing one to three fleshy horns tipped with white hair, a scaly body shaped like a deer's, the hooves of a horse, and the mane and tail of a lion. More than three-and-a-half meters to four-and-a-half meters tall, the qilin had a bare chest, extending from neck to tail. As a vegetarian, it avoided stepping on any living insect and only consumed grass that was already cut. The qilin walked with a regal gait, and its musical voice suggested monastery bells. Fluffy clouds often surrounded the beast. It was one of the most colorful animals in Chinese mythology: when embroidering a qilin, the artist used red, green, violet, yellow, and blue.

Embodying both the male and female elements, the qilin lived two thousand years, and hence it became a longevity symbol. It always lived alone. Whenever it appeared, flocks of animals followed reverently. An avatar of endurance, the qilin could travel up to ten thousand *li* in a day.

The qilin may have originated in an actual animal now extinct, but many feel it's a romanticized version of the giraffe. In 1414, the eunuch Commander Zheng He led the Ming fleet to the coast of Africa and returned with a giraffe as a tribute to Emperor Yongle. Word of the gift spread quickly, and these rumors probably sparked the legend of a mythical beast who honored wise rulers. Like the imaginary qilin, of course, a giraffe has a gentle disposition, great height, and a regal gait, and it never eats meat. The giraffe also possesses a deer-like body, a lion-like tail, hooves, a fleshy horn, and a pelt of variegated colors. The Somali name for giraffe is *girin*, which to the Chinese might

Opposite: A qilin hangs around the

As the embodiment of wisdom and cosmic harmony, the qilin supposedly appeared only when the empire achieved perfect balance under a just and benevolent ruler, or on the eve of the birth of a great sage. Chinese writers claim this magnificent creature materialized during the times of Emperors Yao and Shun, and it was also reportedly seen by the mother of Confucius during the birth of her son.

One popular legend ascribes the Chinese alphabet to the qilin. The story begins as Fuxi, the first legendary Emperor, is walking along the Yellow River. Suddenly, the qilin rises from the water and swims toward shore. Fuxi sits down. When it reaches the Emperor, the gentle creature drops to the ground and puts its head in Fuxi's lap. On the qilin's back, the Emperor sees strange signs, which he memorizes. As the wind increases, the qilin returns to the water, and the Emperor inscribes the strange symbols in the sand with a stick. Rushing back to the palace, the Emperor scratches the signs into the soil and asks his wise men to decipher them. The advisors retire to discuss the matter, and before long, they have created China's first written language. Aided by this new communication medium, the Emperor then wages war on weaker countries for many years, and so the qilin never comes back. His advisors finally inform Fuxi that the qilin is staying away because it wanted its gift to be used in the service of beauty and peace, not power and greed.

Along with the dragon, the tortoise, and the phoenix, the qilin belongs to the quartet of Four Mythical Creatures. The dragon reigned over the east and influenced the spring by determining rainfall quantities. The tortoise, symbol of longevity and endurance, controlled the north and provoked the harsh winter. The beautiful phoenix, representing happiness and warmth, appeared only when the country was at peace; its province was the south and the joys of summer. The qilin, ruler of the west, facilitated the autumn, time of maturity, and fulfillment. Together, the four animals brought order to the universe.

In their paintings, the Buddhists often portrayed the qilin carrying the Book of Law on its back or in its mouth. During the Qing dynasty, the court robe badge of the highest-ranking military officials displayed an embroidered qilin. A woman who was granted an audience at Court wore a skirt trimmed with qilins. When a young man of intellectual promise reported to the capital to take

Figure 1

Figure 2

his examinations, he found paper qilins decorating the walls of the room where the tests were administered. During the Qing era, all young couples prayed for intelligent sons who could rise above their parents via the civil service, and they did everything within their power to circumvent the divine dictum that a family must go from peasant to high position and back to peasant again in seven generations. Thus did embroidered qilins hang on the walls of many houses, inviting the mythical animal to bless the family with a distinguished son. During the lantern festival on the fifteenth day of the first month, people acquired paper lanterns bearing the figure of a boy riding a qilin, presenting them to friends while saying, "I wish you may be blessed with a talented son."

Figure 3

Figure 4

Figure 5

Figure 6

Figure 7

Figure 8

Figure 9

Figure 10

Figure 11

Figure 12

With its presumed powers over fertility, the qilin played a major role in Qing dynasty nuptials, especially the type that bore an infant or the Goddess of Fertility on its back. After putting on a red silk gown embroidered with dragons, the young bride would slip a thick veil over her face, top it with a wedding crown, and leave her parents' home in the red and gold sedan chair hired for the occasion by the groom's family. Amidst bursting firecrackers and the thundering drums of rambunctious musicians, four men bore the chair to the groom's home. Paper cutouts of the Chinese "double happiness" character, bats for good fortune, and the prancing qilin decorated the gate and courtyard. The carriers deposited the bride in the reception room, where she found paper qilins adorning the feast cakes. The nuptial chamber featured illustrations of the Goddess of Fertility holding a baby and astride a qilin. Among the wedding gifts, there was sure to be a silver qilin and rider, as if the bride needed yet another reminder that her primary role in the marriage was to conceive numerous successful sons.

A relative or good friend presented a qilin amulet to a young boy to help him do well on his examinations. Naturally, this would be the sort of qilin that bore a successful civil service candidate, not an infant or the fertility goddess. Because a boy started to prepare for his examinations at the age of eight or nine and continued studying into his late teens, he might have worn a small qilin during infancy, a medium one during boyhood, and a large one in adolescence for special occasions.

On the Qing dynasty silver amulets found today, the qilin assumes many guises. It appears both with and without a figure on its back. The simplest form, often seen on the jewelry of the south China minorities, is the riderless qilin. Scaly and bushy tailed, it sports two horns, horse's hooves, and either dorsal spines or the carapace of a tortoise. This type of qilin probably symbolizes wisdom, benevolent justice, and longevity. In Figures 1 and 2, compare the differences among the silvery scales, manes, tail, and backs. Moveable tongues, such as we see in Figure 1, show up on the older pieces, which may also feature moveable ears, whiskers, and tail. Each silversmith used a different technique for rendering the scales. The artisan who created the high-quality amulet in Figure 2 saved on time and silver by leaving the reverse flat and undecorated. Figure 3 offers an unusual specimen,

Figure 13

probably a Buddhist qilin, which carries the Book of Law on its back.

The infant-bearing silver qilin is less common than the riderless style. Dressed in a *doudou* (infant apron), the baby usually clutches a lotus blossom, symbolizing the Chinese word for "continuous." The combination of the baby, lotus, and qilin equaled a wish for the continuous birth of noble sons. Figures 4 and 5 reveal the front and reverse of an open-backed qilin. By contrast, repoussé covers the front and back of the qilin in Figure 6. In both Figures 4 and 6, the baby grasps the qilin's horn for balance.

The rarest style shows the Goddess of Fertility on the back of the qilin. Dressed in long robes, with her hair pulled up into a bun, the goddess is frequently shown carrying a baby. In Figure 7, she appears wonderfully benevolent, and this figure might be Guanyin, the Bodhisattva who evolved into the giver of children. In Qing dynasty China, after a month of marriage, a bride's parents presented her with a statue of Guanyin, a censer for burning incense, and a pair of candlesticks. These gifts formed the personal altar where the young wife prayed to Guanyin for the blessing of sons. Some parents possibly also gave their daughter a silver Guanyin riding a qilin.

Figure 8 shows two qilins from the minority cultures. Notice the large, bare feet on each child, and the silver lock on his neck.

Swords flashing, the character on the qilin in Figure 9 seems prepared to meet any foe, but that is a Western interpretation. If we remember that in Buddhism, swords cut through doubt on the path to knowledge, we realize that this amulet depicts a young man overcoming ignorance to succeed on his civil service examinations. In the same photograph, the back of a qilin's head becomes a lotus in bloom. The small qilin hangs from a red cloth neckring similar to the ones we saw holding locks in Chapter 2.

The commonest type of silver qilin carries a figure wearing the long official gown of a "first candidate," a young man who placed first when he took the civil service examinations in the capital (Figures 10 through 40). Because of the robe, such a rider is often incorrectly perceived as female. Unlike the Goddess of Fertility, a candidate is never portrayed carrying a child, but he usually grasps a lotus blossom, and occasionally the *sheng*—a reed mouth organ—whose sound is similar to the word for giving birth. For some reason, a candidate on a qilin will often have holes in his mouth and eyes; perhaps these openings suggested the child's ability to speak and read well. Every candidate wears shoes and flowing robes.

Qilins adorned members of almost every social class, and the wealthier patrons commissioned special effects. In Figure 10, two symbols for double happiness link the matching chain to the heavily-gilded qilin, and five types of fruit symbolizing fertility hang from the bottom. (I believe this piece was intended as either a wedding present or wedding jewelry). In Figure 11, we find astonishingly moveable parts: tongue, eyes, ears—even whiskers. A wealthy client could also ask a silversmith to enamel a qilin. Since only the Imperial family could wear yellow robes, the person who commissioned the piece in Figure 12 had very high expectations for the recipient.

A qilin needn't be enameled, however, to qualify as an exhilarating work of art. In Figure 13, the rider's robe flaps in the

Figure 14

wind as he gallops toward success. Amazing details grace the robe, the saddle, the animal's body, and the candidate's face. Another exuberant silversmith fashioned the elaborate amulet in Figure 14. Surrounded by clouds, qilin and rider seem to fly through the air. Many wonderful flourishes—including moveable whiskers—adorn the qilin in Figure 15. The rider, with a serene expression and elaborate robe, gallops forward carrying an enameled wish-granting *ruyi*.

Each silversmith prepared various dangles to hang on chains beneath the qilins: bells to frighten away evil spirits, fruits for fertility, lotus blossoms for purity, dragonfish for perseverance, as well as silver leaves and gourds. The silver gourds in Figure 16 bear some of the most common surnames in China. Quite possibly, we are looking at a catalogue of the families who collectively purchased the gift.

In Figures 17 and 18, we encounter necklaces created when a government worker added beads and a qilin to a chain. These pieces are not as inauthentic as other government-sponsored assemblages. In the Qing dynasty, every qilin indeed hung on a detachable chain. Originally, however, these qilins probably enjoyed much heavier chains than the ones we see here.

A very wealthy young boy received the three-dimensional qilin in Figure 19. Composed of several pieces crafted separately and then soldered together, this qilin actually stands on its own legs.

Figure 20 depicts two qilins and candidates from the Republic era. One wears a twentieth-century hat, the other a suit. Both bear flags, often found on pieces from this period.

The huge qilin in Figures 21 and 22 measures eleven centimeters across. Front and back, the silversmith gives us a fully rendered animal bearing the traditional civil service candidate with his *sheng* and lotus. As we can see, the artist hallmarked his creation on the robe. It's actually quite unusual to find an artist settling for a plain back, or merely etching a back (Figure 23 and the reverse in Figure 24).

Qilins and their riders vary in size from just over four centimeters in width to well over eleven centimeters. Other differences are equally dramatic. To suggest embroidery, some silversmiths employed elaborate floral designs (Figures 15, 26, 27, 34, and 37), while others preferred to use Chinese symbols for longevity (Figures 23 and 27). The artisans might give the candidate a scalloped collar (Figures 29, 30, 36, and 38), or a large lock and torque (Figure 28). While one smith would leave the candidate's head bare (Figure 18), another might adorn him with a military commander's hat (Figure 10).

We also find physical and personality differences among the candidates. Many appear obese, which might suggest the prosperity of one who passed his civil service examinations and became a scholar-official. In Figure 28, one candidate is heavy jowled and overweight, while the other flaunts his protruding stomach. In Figure 29, the rider on the left sits tall and proud, while one man in Figure 31 appears short and stooped over. Beyond these varying postures, most candidates smile with joy.

Like the candidates who ride them, the qilins are astonishingly diverse—hardly a surprise, since each silversmith worked entirely from his imagination, not from a real animal. The simplest appear almost primitive, while the most expensive boast incredible detail (note especially the scales), but all are

Figure 15   Figure 16

depicted in motion. A qilin's legs are either wholly elevated or touching clouds, leaves (Figure 35), or flowers (Figure 36). In some cases, the symbols of a scholar lay nestled in the clouds (Figures 29 and 37). On other amulets, we find coins in the clouds (Figures 30 and 31) or a dropped *sheng* (Figure 33). The silversmith usually gave the qilin an open mouth with a protruding tongue. One to three horns embellish its head: the most common number is two. In many qilins, we see flames—symbolizing the renewal of love and virtue in the kind and wise ruler—shooting across the animal's flank.

The silver content of the qilins is inconsistent, giving us great variety in color. The ones with less silver appear very dark, while others shine like sterling.

For a buyer with limited resources, a silversmith might repoussé a qilin and rider onto a flat sheet of silver to hang from a chain (Figure 40). Some even pierced these two-dimensional creations for greater effect.

Why did the qilin ultimately evolve into a fertility symbol? I have a pet theory. If Confucius's mother indeed saw a qilin while delivering her son—who became one of the wisest and most influential men in the history of China—some people may have decided that a qilin amulet would possess the power to guarantee at the very least, a scholar or wise administrator. We may never know the real answer to this riddle. Whatever the truth, the silver qilins of the Qing dynasty remain among the most impressive and wearable artifacts of the period.

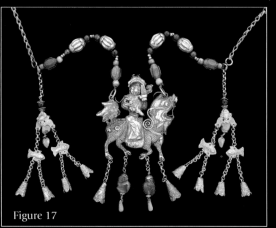
Figure 17

Figure 18

Figure 19

Figure 20

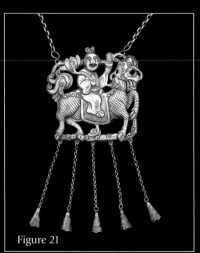
Figure 21

Figure 22

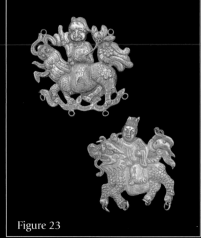
Figure 23

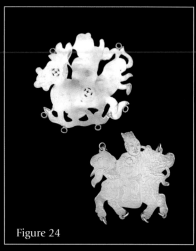
Figure 24

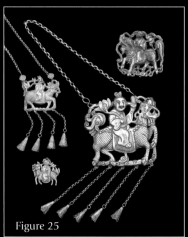
Figure 25

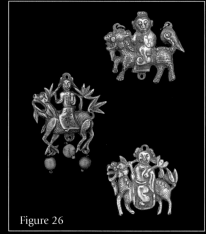
Figure 26

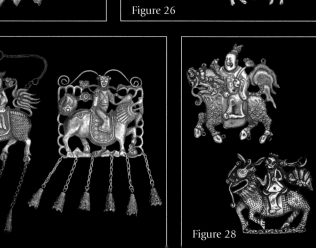
Figure 27

Figure 28

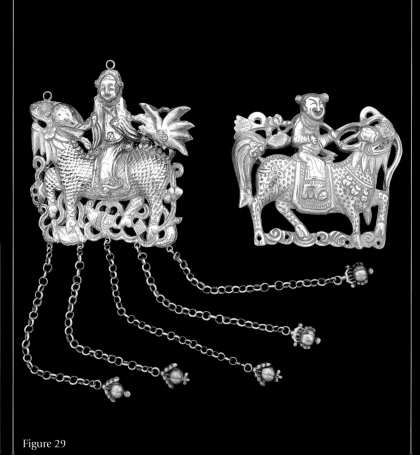
Figure 29

Figure 30

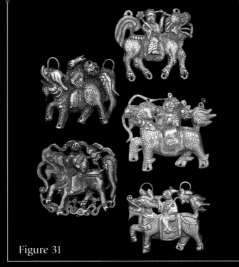

Figure 31

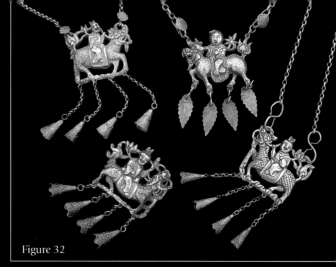

Figure 32

Figure 33

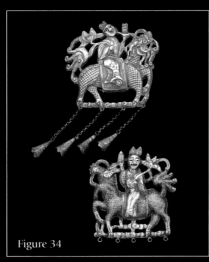

Figure 34

Figure 35

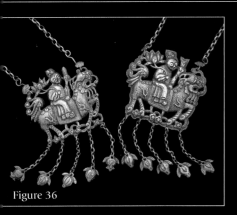

Figure 36

Figure 37

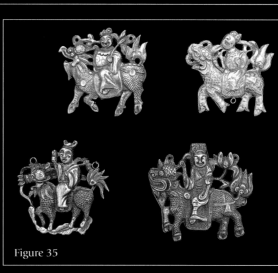

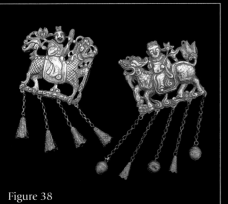

Figure 38

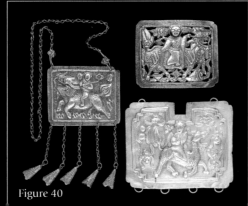

Figure 40

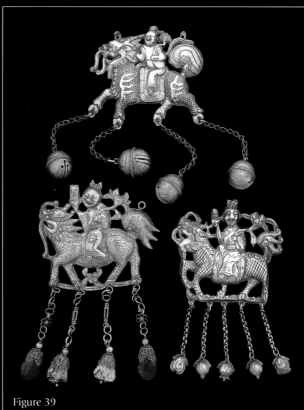

Figure 39

In a small hut on a mountainside in southwest China, the old grandmother's arthritic knees throb as she paces the floor holding the feverish baby, trying to soothe him. It was a hard birth, and her daughter-in-law, exhausted, dozes fitfully. The baby's father, anguished over his new son's peril, has drunk himself into a stupor with his brothers. Her duty done, the midwife has left, and the other family members have withdrawn, certain the infant will die before morning.

But the grandmother does not give up hope. With each painful step, she prays for the newborn's life. Should he die before receiving his animal name and a silver collar, tradition would deny him a funeral, as if he were never born. The baby wails as if evil spirits are wrenching his tiny body. The grandmother holds him tighter. She forces some herbal medicine down his throat, and finally he grows quiet. The grandmother fears the worst, but at least she can feel his chest rising and falling. "Sleep, my little one, and gather your strength," she whispers, settling into a chair to begin the long vigil.

As the sun climbs over the eastern mountains, the light touches the baby's face, and he opens his eyes. The grandmother kisses his forehead, now cool to the touch, and gives prayers of thanksgiving. Her daughter-in-law stirs and asks for the baby. The grandmother gladly presents him for a feeding.

Waking her son, the grandmother tells him the good news. "Now hurry to Auntie Ming and tell her the baby lives," she says. "We will have his naming ceremony today. Since Ming is the foster mother, she needs to buy the collar this morning. Now go!" She pushes her son out the door and watches him stumble toward the village, mumbling in his half-sleep. The grandmother smiles, knowing she can rest at last.

Huiling sits in a circle on the *k'ang* platform bed with her three friends as they embroider dark material for the upcoming festival. She has reached a marriageable age, fourteen, and the others compliment her on her fine stitches and creative designs.

At last a young man can court her, but Huiling harbors little hope. Unless Huiling makes some display of wealth, no man will notice her. This year her family lacks the funds for even a simple neckring. Her sickly mother has needed expensive herbs, and the drought has withered the harvest.

As their needles spread creative designs over the plain material, one girl begins to describe her new neckring. A friend jabs her in the ribs and an uncomfortable silence follows. They all know.

When it grows too dark to see the fine stitches, Huiling's friends bid her farewell. Soon her two younger brothers come bounding into the house, followed by their father, who has been clearing the fields. Huiling lights the candles and notices that her father carries an object wrapped in cloth. To her surprise, he presents it to her.

"Open it, open it!" her brothers cry in unison, unable to contain their excitement.

Unfolding the flaps, Huiling finds a flat silver neckring decorated with engraved flowers and vines. Her mouth drops in disbelief. "But how?" she asks, turning toward her mother.

"Your father sold the pig. Vegetables are better for us."

"And your mother had the silversmith melt down her bracelets," her father hastens to add.

"What do I need with such things at my age?" says her mother. "Now you will get a good husband."

Huiling slips the circlet around her neck. Her mother fastens the hook. Tears of joy trickle down Huiling's cheeks as her brothers bring the mirror.

Wenfeng waits patiently as his personal servant braids his long queue. The servant then helps him into an exquisite blue silk gown, wholly befitting the fifteen-year-old son of a scholar official.

The fragrances of twenty dishes waft into Wenfeng's room from the kitchen. Cries of joy ring through the house as each member of the extended family arrives for the Lunar New Year celebration. All will offer homage before the ancestral tables, then retire to the dining room for the annual feast. After the huge meal, the elders will pass out envelopes of money. Having paid off all his debts, Wenfeng will save his portion for his journey to Beijing, where he will take the civil service examinations.

In the soft glow of the gas lamp, Wenfeng's servant lifts the glass top from a presentation case and removes a gilded silver torque, a gift from the young man's grandfather. A heavy lock hangs from the ring, which is encrusted with tourmaline stones. The servant slides the torque around Wenfeng's neck. The lock almost covers his chest. Wenfeng runs his fingers over the face of the lock:

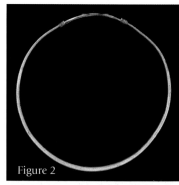

Figure 1

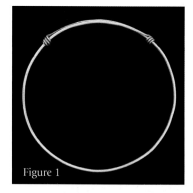

Figure 2

Figure 3

a repoussé scene of a young man riding a qilin through a cheering crowd. After the evening's celebrations, the torque must be returned to his father's safe, but from this night onward, Wenfeng will think often of the mounted man: a successful civil service candidate heading home after triumphing in his examinations.

A circlet of silver. During the Qing dynasty, a minority foster mother, equivalent to a Western godmother, faithfully bought a silver collar for her foster son's naming ceremony to protect him from evil spirits. Within certain ethnic minorities, people adorned their bodies with neckrings holding locks and pendants. Other

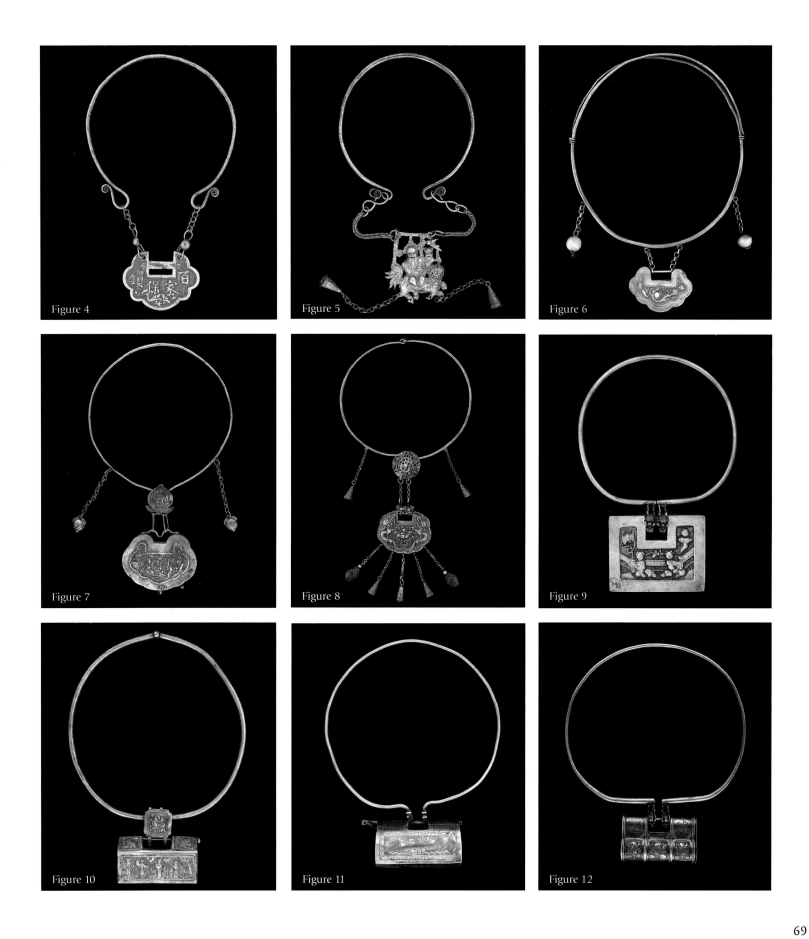

Figure 4

Figure 5

Figure 6

Figure 7

Figure 8

Figure 9

Figure 10

Figure 11

Figure 12

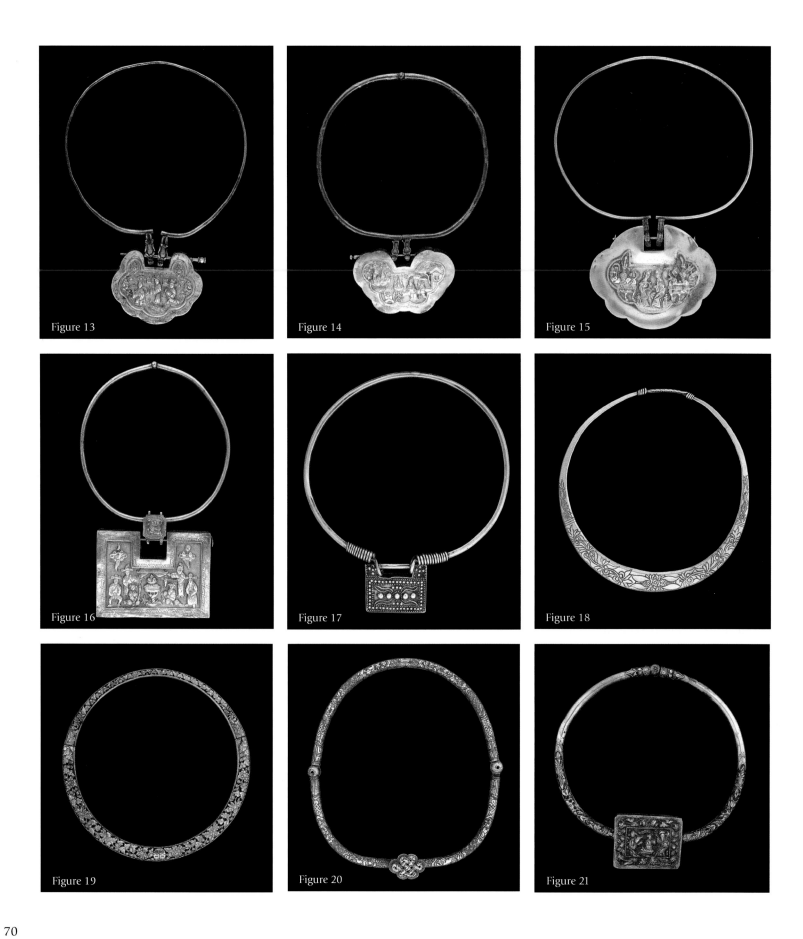

Figure 13

Figure 14

Figure 15

Figure 16

Figure 17

Figure 18

Figure 19

Figure 20

Figure 21

minorities favored torques—engraved and repoussé neckrings—as did the Han aristocracy. It is truly amazing to see what the Chinese did with so simple a concept as a circlet of silver.

Infant Collars

Hung around the neck of an infant son, a simple silver ring represented a dog collar. It functioned to fool malicious apparitions into perceiving the male heir as nothing but a worthless animal. Some of these collars fell into the "one-size-fits-all" category. Another type featured a sliding clasp, so that the collar "grew" with the child. The example in Figure 1 expands from fourteen to nineteen centimeters.

The Highland tribespeople placed a silver ring over a newborn infant's neck in a special ceremony that culminated in the child receiving the name of an animal guardian. Besides protecting him from illness and evil spirits, the collar signified that the child had entered the human world. If the baby died before he could be presented with such a token, the parents dispensed with a funeral, for they believed the child had never actually left the prenatal spirit world.

After a son outgrew a non-expandable baby collar, it was melted down and refashioned into a larger neckring that would fit him. This practice probably accounts for the fact that few simple infant collars appear on the market today.

Neckrings

One variety of silver collar—the neckring—functioned to hold an elaborate lock, qilin, or protective pendant. Four styles are prevalent. In one type, the neckring features an opening at the bottom with the ends turned back to hold the chain for the lock or pendant (Figures 4 and 5). In the second style, one end of the ring fits into a tube behind the centerpiece (Figures 7 and 8). The third variety features a strip of silver soldered to each end of the neckring and then recurved, forming a hook for the lock (Figures 10 and 16). The shank of the lock passes over the strips and hangs from the arc. A thick centerpiece plaque with two holes in the top and bottom hides the strips themselves and completes the ensemble. The fourth, and possibly most popular, style of neckring features tips with double dragons—symbols of fertility—who seem to hold the shank of the lock in their mouths (Figures 9 and 12 to 15).

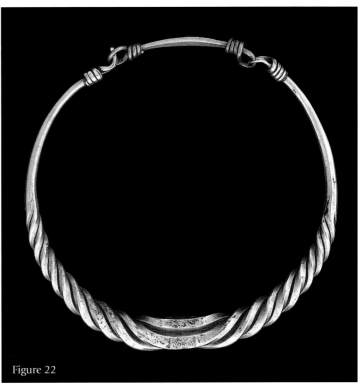

Figure 22

Neckrings adorned babies and young boys in many minority groups, as well as the Han majority. Some examples, such as the one in Figure 3, include an elaborate chain with a large symbolic counterweight on the back. One has to wonder how a baby ever slept with such a cumbersome thing around his neck. This particular neckring opens by removing the lock. The inside diameter is only thirteen centimeters.

In the next two illustrations, we find neckrings that gave the wearer more flexibility. In Figure 4, a simple flat "hundred-family protection" lock connects to a chain beneath the neckring. It was most likely presented to the infant at his first-month celebration. Figure 5 shows the smallest neckring I've ever seen. The inside diameter is only ten centimeters. On the bottom, we see the lion—a guardian against evil—carrying Wen Shu, the Buddhist God of Wisdom, who dispelled ignorance. The young boy probably represents the fortunate recipient of this piece: the pendant embodied a wish that he would pass his civil service examinations. The bottle gourd on the pendant added a wish for fertility and protection from illness, while the plum blossoms conveyed the hope for longevity.

It is often difficult to tell whether a large neckring originally adorned a boy, a young minority woman, or a young man. While messages and symbolism help to identify the original wearer of a lock, we can't speak so confidently about an accompanying neckring, because Chinese silver dealers often interchange the locks. When I visited a popular antique shop in Beijing in the summer of 1997, I found a wonderful torque but I didn't like the lock. The dealer offered to sell me any lock in the shop as a replacement.

In Figure 6 we see a lock depicting a dragon for virility and Imperial authority. The back of the lock features a wish for "one hundred years of life." A silversmith obviously crafted this lock for a male child, but we cannot be sure that it originally appeared on this neckring. Figure 7 shows a neckring that we know a young woman wore on her wedding day, because it includes a double happiness centerpiece. This circlet is small, but bear in mind that young girls were often married by age fifteen during the Qing dynasty. The lock depicts a woman seated on a chair, a bearded man in a cone-shaped hat, and a child seated between them. The inscription on the back reads either: "may an emperor be born in this house," or, "an emperor has been born in this house."

The small neckring in Figure 8 probably contains most of its original components. The bells on the neckring match the bells hanging from the lock. This exquisite item measures only sixteen centimeters; a lion sprawls across the centerpiece and the lock depicts a qilin and rider with a wish for wealth, longevity, and nobility.

The twin *Hehe erhxian*, representing harmony and wealth, cover the large square lock in Figure 9. The shackle actually opens. As usual, one twin holds the lotus, and the other holds a box of treasures. A string (or possibly a cloud) emanates from the box along with a bat for happiness. A fungus for longevity hovers beneath a coin for wealth. On the reverse, an engraved fish among lotus blossoms brings a wish for affluence year after year.

Figures 10 through 12 illustrate plain neckrings fitted with rectangular locks of various shapes and designs. The first lock offers a repoussé scene with three people and the four symbols of the scholar; the second employs engraving to portray a baby with a lotus blossom for the continuous birth of noble sons; and the third—a "hundred-family protection" lock—wishes the recipient wealth and good fortune.

The lock in Figure 13 appears to show a woman sitting in a chair fanning herself, an official standing over a longevity symbol, and a young scholar with a queue carrying books as he runs. On the reverse, we find wishes for longevity, wealth and honor.

An unusual butterfly-shaped lock dangles from the neckring in Figure 14. Two people appear in the clouds in the upper left-hand corner. One character holds a rope proclaiming (or promising) the birth of a noble son. The smaller figure is carrying books. On the right side of the altar, another small character waves the umbrella of spiritual authority over the larger figure. A pine tree for steadfastness and longevity straddles the rocks, and a building—either a temple or a house—and another tree fill the right side. The back is plain but has three holes shaped like coins symbolizing wealth.

The lock in Figure 15 portrays a couple enjoying blissful harmony: the woman plays a stringed instrument for the man, and the tables on either side abound with symbols of scholarship and wealth. Double happiness symbols, a bat, and a pair of dragons cavorting with pearls sprawl across the back. Considering all these clues, we can assume that a silversmith crafted this lock, and possibly the neckring, for a wedding.

An elaborate rendering of the twin Hehe appears on the huge (15.5 centimeters by 11.5 centimeters) lock in Figure 16. The twins flank an altar before a temple. A bowl of fruit sits on the altar and a plate of lotus blossoms adorns the base. Several additional characters, possibly some Immortals and other mythological heroes, complete the tableau, as the fungus of longevity rises above them.

Because it is welded to the circlet, we can be sure that the lock on the minority neckring in Figure 17 is original. One side unhooks to open the neckring, but the other remains fixed.

Torques

Collectors commonly refer to elaborately decorated neckrings as torques. Rare before the Sui dynasty (A.D. 581-618), torques became more popular in the Tang dynasty (A.D. 618-907). Many of the neckrings found in royal tombs—whether of pure gold or gilded silver—feature a flattened, chased design.

Evidently the Tang style influenced the Qing silversmiths, especially those who created artifacts for the Miao minority. In Figure 18 we see engraved flowers on a torque that weighs 181

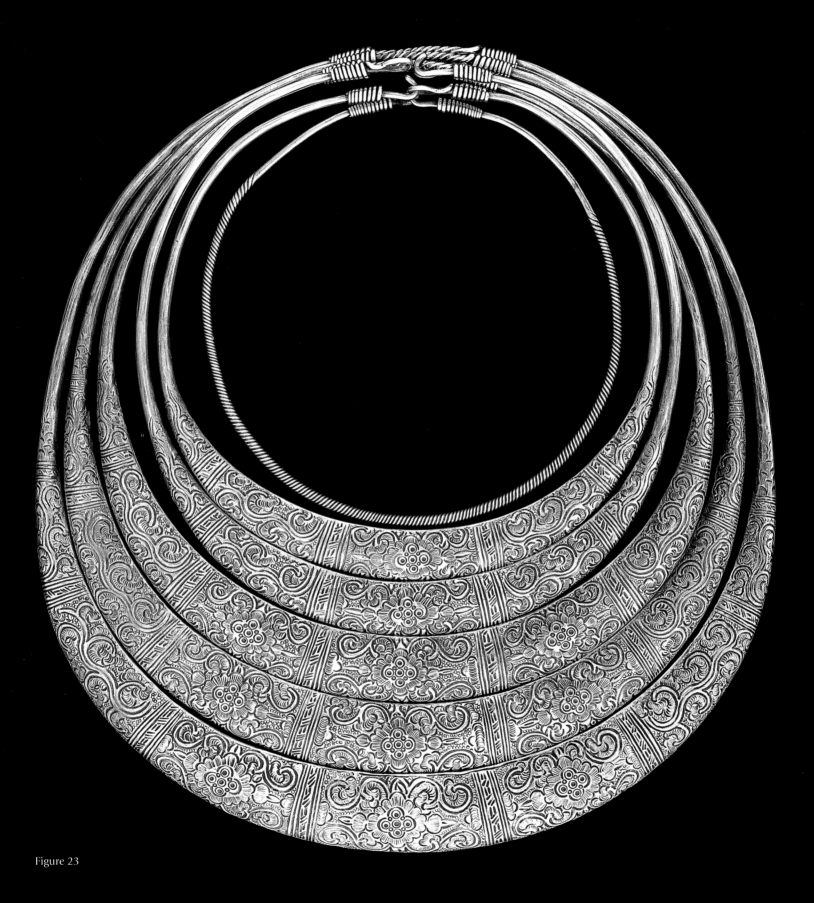

Figure 23

grams. Obviously a wedding piece, it includes double fish—symbolizing marital harmony, double abundance, and sexual pleasure—hidden in the central leaves.

Figure 19 depicts a single torque covered with pierced floral designs. The diameter is only 12.9 centimeters: it would have encircled a very thin neck. The symbolism fails to tell us whether this piece belonged to a girl, a woman, or an elderly woman. Whoever the owner, she obviously came from a wealthy family.

In Figure 20, many clues tell us that the torque hung around a woman's neck on her wedding day: the endless knot centerpiece for longevity, the repoussé babies carrying lotus flowers, the additional longevity and double happiness symbols.

Three repoussé figures adorn the centerpiece of the blue enameled torque in Figure 21. One person kneels before a bearded old man with a staff, as another person stands behind him with the flywhisk of authority. The old man seems to be passing a scepter or a *ruyi* to the kneeling person. Representations of various flowers beautify the ring itself.

Today, torques still adorn the Dong people in the Guangxi Province of southwestern China. During the Lunar New Year, every unmarried Dong man puts on a heavy, thick, twisted neckring, such as the one shown in Figure 22, which weighs a hefty 244 grams. An unmarried woman will wear an elaborate headdress, earrings, bracelets, and several long or short torques.

The New Year festivities celebrate the heroic woman soldier Xing Ni, who died in battle over 1,000 years ago fighting for the Dong people. After firing canons and guns in Xing Ni's honor, the Dong men in every village offer gifts of glutinous rice, pickled peppers, and grilled pork to the eligible young women of their choice. Each newly formed couple then engages in a delightful custom: they publicly sing love songs to one another, thereby testing their compatibility before the whole community.

Even heavier than the Dong neckrings are the multiple torques of the Hmong Miao, who formed one of the largest contemporary minority groups in southwest China. Beyond dispelling evil and insuring safety, such pieces enhanced the beauty and announced the wealth of a young Miao woman. Because tradition dictated "the more silver ornaments a young woman wears, the wealthier and more beautiful she becomes," parents spared no expense in

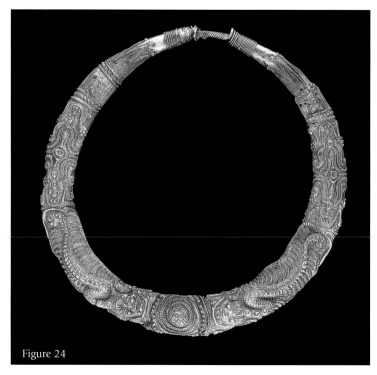

Figure 24

adorning their daughters with silver. One Miao woman might have worn up to fifty different silver ornaments weighing six to nine kilograms. This convention persists among the Miao in the present day. In Figure 23, the six torques collectively weigh an unbelievable 2,681 grams, almost six pounds. Engraved with popular floral and geometric designs, this set was obviously an ordeal for any woman to wear. It did, however, send a clear message concerning the size of her dowry.

The repoussé minority torque in Figure 24 is actually hollow. The double dragons chasing the pearl dent easily, so I doubt that the owner wore this piece every day. The reverse is plain, but heavily dented: someone repaired it in two places with blobs and bits of silver. The slit in the middle of the back reveals the artisan's technique. He used repoussé to create his design on a flat sheet of silver, then folded the plain sides back and soldered them together. Despite its faults, the piece remains an appealing example of the silversmith's craft.

The torques of the wealthiest Han noblewomen and adolescent boys were among the most substantial silver pieces ever created in Qing dynasty China. We recognize them today by their sheer size. Most of the locks measure ten to eighteen centimeters in width. In Figure 25, engraved plum blossoms and other longevity symbols amble across a heavy torque intended for a boy.

On the lock, repoussé lotus flowers and bats surround the Fu Lu Shou—the three mythological figures denoting happiness, good fortune, and longevity. In the surrounding engravings we notice the symbols of the Immortals and a wish for longevity, wealth, and nobility. Large, noisy bells hang from the bottom to dispel evil spirits.

The pendant in Figure 26 consists of a double happiness symbol filled with miniature couples and the Eight Buddhist Symbols. Above this massive artifact, which measures twelve centimeters across, we find a centerpiece featuring a bat for happiness plus the God of Longevity riding his deer—a rebus for the Fu Lu Shou. Additional longevity symbols decorate the torque itself, undoubtedly created for a wedding.

Symbols of long life cover the torque in Figure 27. The lock features a mother with a baby: this woman might represent Guanyin bringing a son, while a bearded man bestows authority with his flywhisk, or else a scene from a drama. Two guards stand by with their long swords. The centerpiece displays a lion for protection.

The repoussé scenes on the more elaborate torques often suggest allegories. In Figure 28, we find tableaux that seem to illustrate the path from youth to old age. One half of the torque shows a man in a house, a young boy presenting something to a seated character, a person beneath a large lotus stalk and blossom, a couple in bed, and another couple. The other half offers a couple (or perhaps a man and a child), a couple in bed, an old man under a lotus flower, and a couple standing before a temple. The lock is not so overtly allegorical. On the front we see a central figure surrounded by three people with fans. The *ruyi* above the characters stands for the granting of wishes. The plum blossom brings longevity, and the peony adds wealth and distinction. On the back of the lock, we find an inscription for wealth and good fortune.

In Figure 29 the repoussé figures are actually cut out and appear in high relief on the torque. We find a carp (abundance), a lotus blossom and stalk (representing past, present, and future), a couple in a house, a female with a lotus bud (fertility), a male with a flywhisk (authority), the God of the South playing chess with the God of the North, a young man being fanned, and two magpies above two dragons. On the lock, the characters might

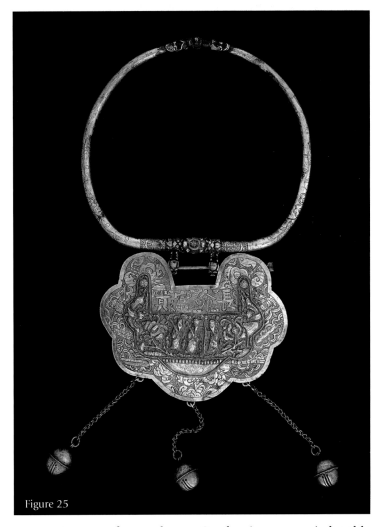

Figure 25

represent a scene from a drama. On the rim, a magpie heralds good news, fruits bring fertility, and a rat promises wealth. On the back we find various characters inhabiting a house-like structure.

Double flowers, fruits, and bats adorn the torque in Figure 30, whose lock features an unusual setting. This might be a scene from mythology, an opera, or a fable. After considering the large, rounded ears and the seemingly hairy legs of the seated character at the right, I decided he might be the Monkey King from *The Journey to the West*. In this novel by Wu Chengen, a monkey accompanies a pilgrim to India in search of the sacred Buddhist texts. Ultimately, the monkey is deified. Thereafter he controls evil spirits and grants believers health, protection, and success.

In Figure 31 an unusual torque displays male and female characters, fruits and plants (fertility), and magpies (joy and marital happiness). The double peaches and plum on the enameled centerpiece represent immortality and longevity. The lock

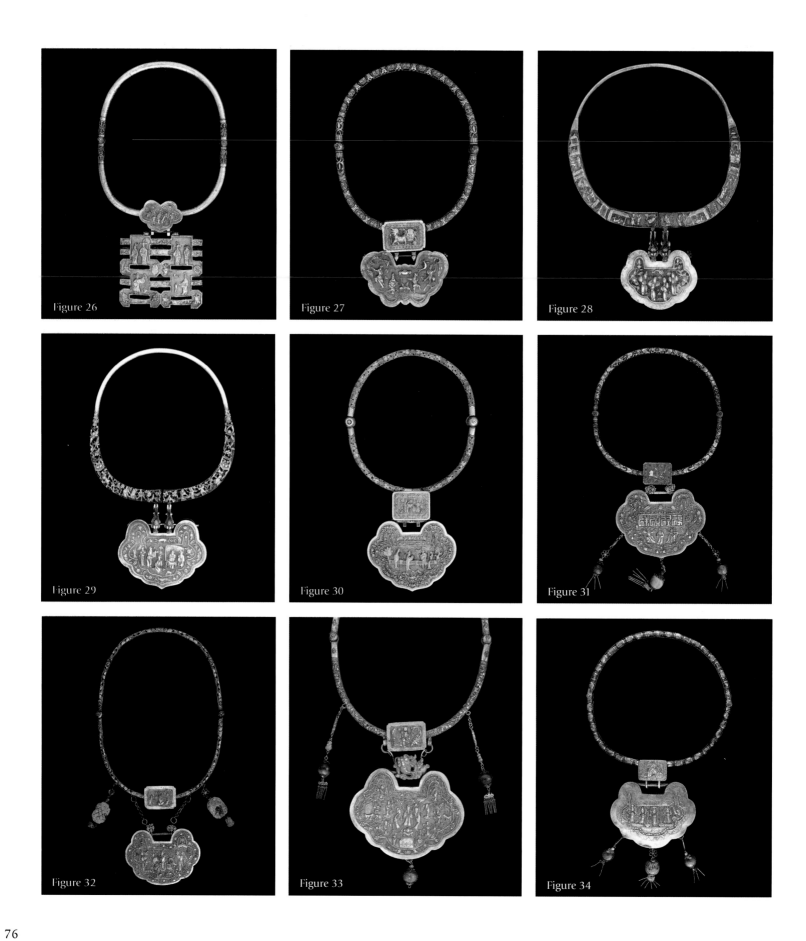

Figure 26

Figure 27

Figure 28

Figure 29

Figure 30

Figure 31

Figure 32

Figure 33

Figure 34

represents a scene from a Chinese play entitled *The Yellow Crane Tower* and also includes the symbols for a scholar. I believe a silversmith created the lock for a young man and it now hangs on a wedding torque, which originally had an enameled lock to match the centerpiece.

On the lock in Figure 32, admirers holding umbrellas of respect and swords of authority honor a successful civil service candidate astride a mythological qilin. The antique carved turquoise beads suggest that a wealthy Inner Mongolian might have worn the torque, but these may not be original to the piece. The torque is covered with repoussé flowers, and the centerpiece includes a young person kneeling before a character who anoints with a flywhisk.

The largest torque in my collection appears in Figure 33. The circumference is twenty-nine centimeters, while the lock measures seventeen centimeters in width. Covered with engraved floral designs, the torque features a centerpiece depicting Liu Hai, God of Wealth, with his three-legged toad and string of cash. A silver carp (abundance) dangles from the centerpiece: it holds a lock portraying the three Fu Lu Shou (longevity, good fortune, happiness), plus the Eight Immortals, the patron saints of the Daoists who represent the quest for eternity. Two magpies (marital bliss) with plum blossoms and a chrysanthemum (longevity) surround the center, which includes ancestral tablets and a tripod holding fruit on a trunk. This tableau also includes vases filled with plum blossoms, and the four symbols of a scholar. On the back we find a lotus with an engraved inscription: "May your house be filled with wealth and nobility." Sons of noblemen wore such locks on special occasions, well into their adolescent years.

The gilded torque in Figure 34 is my most elaborate such discovery. Inlaid with green tourmaline, the torque terminates in a centerpiece depicting Liu Hai and his three-legged toad. Measuring fourteen-and-three-quarters by twenty centimeters, this gilded lock depicts figures resembling the military characters in a Peking Opera. On the reverse, we find the God of Longevity, a figure kneeling before an Immortal with a flywhisk, and a wish for gold and jade. Old carnelian and turquoise stones dangle from the bottom of this lock, probably worn by a wealthy adolescent boy.

Collars, neckrings, torques: of all the hundreds of artifacts discussed in this book, the silver circlets are perhaps the hardest to appreciate through the photographs alone. These pieces demand to be touched. I have no doubt that Qing dynasty people spent many hours running their fingers along the endlessly curving contours, sensing the circlets' magical, religious, emblematic, and aesthetic power. It is a power we can still feel today.

Talismans Against Misfortunes

The inhabitants of modern industrialized nations face many hazards. Air pollution, automobile accidents, airplane crashes, insane gunmen, and mutating viruses make our lives less than peaceful. Qing Chinese peoples also occupied a dangerous world, but the threats were largely ascribed to a supernatural domain. Infertility, premature death, illness, marital discord, sudden impoverishment, and failure on civil service examinations all bespoke the displeasure of the gods or the intervention of wicked spirits. To appease the deities and banish the demons, the Chinese deployed an astonishing variety of talismans, amulets, and charms. In the Qing dynasty, many such tokens assumed the form of silver adornment.

Babies

The most important duty of a wife in Qing dynasty China was to give her husband a son. This boy would continue the male succession and perhaps bring honor to the family by passing his civil service examinations and becoming a high government official. A daughter left to join her husband's family when she married, but a son remained with his parents and brought his wife home to care for his mother. A couple with a son felt financially and emotionally secure in their old age—and even after death—for males alone could perform the rites of ancestral worship.

Until the birth of a son, a married woman in a Chinese household was little more than her mother-in-law's servant. Following this momentous event, however, the wife rose to a position of equality. The whole family showered respect and admiration upon her, whereas the birth of a daughter occasioned only disappointment. Most pregnant women, from peasants to princesses, prayed to Guanyin, the Goddess of Mercy, for the blessing of a son.

Considered the wisest man after Confucius, the sage Mencius insisted that the worst impiety was having no son to bring food and sacrifices to one's tomb after death. Mencius also sanctioned the drowning of a new female infant if a poor family already had several daughters. If the wife remained barren at age forty in the Qing era, a husband felt free to marry again. If the second wife produced children, they regarded the first wife as their mother. Even the Imperial household followed

Opposite: A baby talisman adorns a Gaoshan woman.

this custom. When the concubine Cixi bore the Emperor a son, the Empress Cian became his official mother and fully guided his upbringing.

Even Chinese cuisine reflected the desire for male heirs. Every traditional New Year's dinner included steamed or fried *chiao-tsu*: ingot-shaped dough balls filled with meat and vegetables. On the balls, the cook stamped the character *tsu* meaning "many sons." The menu also included lotus seed soup, or *lien-tse*, which means "successive sons."

As her first step in guaranteeing the safe birth of a son, a Han Chinese woman wore an anatomically correct male-baby amulet, fashioned from silver, on a tiny chain or cord of silk. A tiny moveable penis adorned the more elaborate babies (Figure 1). Others simply had the hint of the male genitalia, peeking below the edge of the baby's triangular apron, his *doudou* (Figures 3 and 5).

Most of the silver amulets in Figures 1 through 5 portray an infant boy carrying a lotus blossom. Both the fronts and the backs of the babies are fully rendered (Figure 2). In Figure 4, several babies are depicted walking, which might signify either their early arrival or their rapid advancement in life.

Chinese craftsmen also fashioned baby amulets in ivory, brass, and gold. One expert I consulted in China informed me that ivory babies, fastened together on elaborately knotted cords, hung on marriage beds during the Ming dynasty, and they are still called "little Ming babies." Another authority told me that a wife wore a single baby—whether of silver, ivory, brass, or gold—on her undergarment from the day of her wedding until the birth of her first son.

A Han Chinese bride's mother or sister-in-law often presented her with a silver baby amulet as a wedding gift. This practice also existed among the other minorities. The wife might also attach the baby to a chain dangling from a grooming kit or a needle case. Figure 6 presents an exception. Because of its huge size, I believe this amulet hung from the sash of a wealthy man who desired a successful son. The teapot, too, represents fertility.

In Figure 7, we see a large baby (for fertility), connected to a tortoise (for longevity, strength, and endurance) via an auspicious red cord. This artifact is actually an infant's rattle: both pieces have beads inside them. The singleton baby is also a rattle. The amulet showing the lion and the front and back of identical boys probably

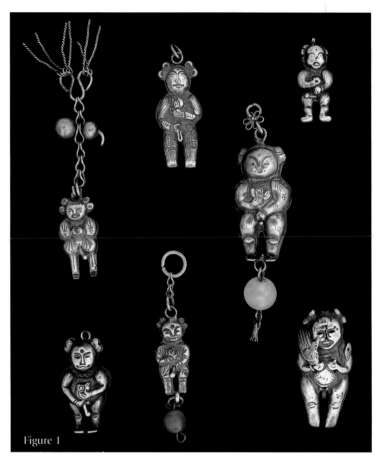

Figure 1

refers to the legend of the fifty-year-old man whose wife bore male twins as a reward for his piety.

Women enjoyed much more respect among the Imperial Manchu than among the Chinese. The Manchus did not bind the feet of their young girls or women, and even though she could not perform ancestor worship, a Manchu household welcomed a baby girl. A daughter ranked equally with her brother and ahead of his wife. Her father could not dispose of her property without her consent, and she could remain single or marry later in life if she desired. Manchu daughters and wives might have worn silver babies, but such amulets did not carry the misogynist baggage of Han culture.

I've never seen a Qing silver amulet depicting a female infant, nor do I expect to find one. The scholar Elizabeth Cooper tells us of a Chinese historian who was asked why one encountered so little writing about the women of China. The historian looked puzzled for a moment, then said, "The women of China! One never hears about them. I believe no one ever thinks about them, except perhaps that they are the mothers of Chinese men!"

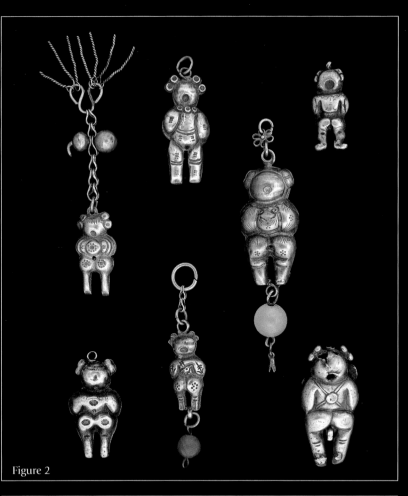

Figure 2

Figure 3

Figure 4

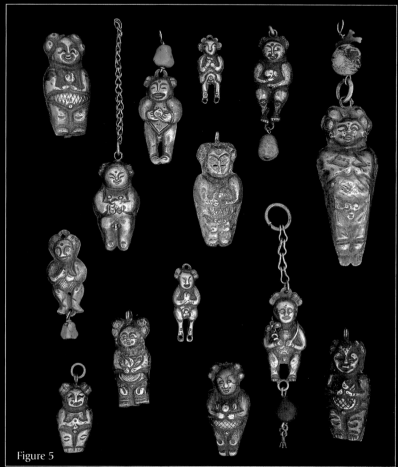

Figure 5

Figure 6

Figure 7

Figure 8

Figure 9

Figure 10

Figure 11

Figure 12

Figure 13

Bells

Bells clanged, tinkled, jangled, and bonged throughout the history of China, one of the first civilizations to make and use such instruments.

In the earliest dynasties, a bell lacked a clapper. Struck with a wooden staff to summon citizens to hear Imperial edicts, a bell also brought soldiers to attention. A Chinese shaman sacrificed animals to sanctify bells with blood, and a ceremonial chair glittered with silver bells. An official ringer struck a bell at midnight and upon the death of a dignitary, and a frame of sixteen bells chimed during Confucian ceremonies.

By the Qing dynasty, Chinese mothers adorned their babies' ankles and clothes with small silver bells, high officials hung silver bells from jade amulets, and the minority women wore strings of silver bells—all to ward off evil spirits.

During the one-month ceremony, parents tried every possible means to protect their children. Friends and relatives usually presented a newborn baby, especially a male, with a silver bell (Figures 8 and 9). Red thread—a lucky color—secured the bell to the baby's ankle or wrist. Certain minority groups adorned babies with metal anklets, or bracelets, holding several tiny bells to frighten away evil spirits, for such demons were always waiting to sicken or even kill a newborn. This custom was also utilitarian: the mother could keep track of a toddler by his jingling. The boat people of southern China especially valued the infant bell. A sudden silence warned that a child might have fallen overboard.

Large silver bells and bells fashioned into tiger heads, functioned as baby rattles (Figures 10 and 11). The tiger heads bear the symbol for "king." As a male "yang" symbol, the tiger represented courage and could dispel demons. Such rattles were presented to newborns as much for protection as amusement.

Adults also wore small bells attached to needle cases, grooming kits, symbolic locks, neckrings, amulets, qilins, hairpins, and fragrance carriers. Since the Chinese word for bell stands for "hitting the mark," bells represented success, as well as safekeeping.

The Jingpo women who resided in the thickly wooded mountains of Yunnan wore the largest number of bells. Weighed down with as many as seven chains hung with bells, a woman felt safe from demons as she traveled through the dense forests.

Figure 14

Among the Mongols, bells also served a symbolic purpose. Occasionally, a bell replaced the Wheel of Law icon on the end of a chain. The Wheel of Law was one of the Eight Buddhist Symbols that symbolized the contraction of the Universe and led a disciple to nirvana.

In Qing dynasty China and well into the Republic, silver bells hung from the corners of the roofs of sedan chairs, heralding the approach of a wealthy man or woman. Four-sided bells, shaped like seals, sparkled from the conveyance of a high official (Figure 12). A more rounded type of bell bedecked a noblewoman's chair (Figure 13). Bells on chains held back the curtains surrounding the passenger compartment (Figure 14). Other bells clattered against the chassis, alerting pedestrians to make way and scattering evil spirits. A sedan chair for a moderately rich man might have two pairs of bells (Figure 15), while an official's conveyance would boast as many as eight pairs.

Sexual experimentation was widely accepted in Qing dynasty China, since Confucianism never challenged the idea that sexuality was normal and healthy. Tiny silver Burmese bells, *mianling*, containing gold beads or grains of sand, became sexual stimulants when inserted into the vagina or under the foreskin. Because any exotic sexual practice was regarded as protection against evil, Qing people had an additional motivation for wearing Burmese bells.

Not all Chinese sexual customs were benign. Footbinding, of course, is the most notorious example. Such mutilation strengthened a woman's thighs and tightened her vaginal muscles, so that her husband would feel that he was deflowering a virgin every time. A woman tried to make the best of her encumbrance, hiding small bells in the heals of her tiny lotus slippers to attract attention at festivals (Figure 16).

Although Qing society found many uses for bells, we find only three basic designs. The first is the open mouth bell, which tinkles when the clapper swings back and forth, hitting the inside surface. Such bells proved particularly popular with the Mongols, who hung them from their jewelry. If a Mongol lost the tools from his grooming kit, he might transform it into an amulet by adding small bells to the ends of the chains.

The second type of bell is the crotal: a sphere or spheroid enclosing pellets of copper, wood, or clay (Figure 8). A slit in the bottom releases the sound when the bell is shaken or swung. Popular with the Han and the minorities, crotal bells were given to babies at the first-month celebration. The larger ones gained popularity as baby rattles (Figure 10). Crotal bells also hung on sedan chairs (Figure 15).

The third type of bell, a variation on the crotal, was made in one organic shape or another (Figures 17 and 18). Especially popular were the peach and the lotus, but one also finds other fruits and flowers plus infants, lions, ducks, monkeys, dogs, roosters, teapots, purses, and dragonfish. These images were charged with meaning. A peach-shaped bell symbolized longevity. A lotus, infant, pomegranate, or teapot bell conveyed a wish for fertility. The dragonfish represented success, whereas a pair of ducks portended marital bliss. Roosters, dogs, and lions protected from dangers of all kinds, natural and supernatural.

Many types of Qing silver adornments assume the shapes of animals and vegetables. But only the functioning bells actually exorcised demons. If a silver bell didn't jingle, it held no power over the supernatural world. It was merely an ornament, worn for its symbolic meaning.

Bottle Gourds

The fruit known as the bottle gourd, sometimes the white-flowered gourd, lent itself to many utilitarian and symbolic functions in Qing dynasty China. Dried and hollowed out, the fruit served as a container in most households, and in south China, the boat people tied hollow gourds to their children to keep them from drowning, should they fall overboard.

Owing to its swelling contours, which the Chinese felt suggested a pregnant woman, as well as its many seeds, the bottle gourd came to symbolize fertility. An association with wealth arose from the Chinese characters for gourd, *hulu*, which form a homonym for "good fortune." In ancient times, old men used hollow gourds as water containers, and so the gourd also came to signify longevity.

Equally important was the fruit's relationship to healing. In the ancient stories of the lame Daoist Immortal Li Tieguai, patron saint of the sick, hollow bottle gourds always held magic potions, which flowed out to revive the dead, trap demons, or vanquish foes. In the mundane world, bottle gourds held medicine in herbalist shops, whose signs often featured a picture of the fruit.

On the summer solstice, May 5, the waxing yang surrendered to the yin, and evil vapors brought misfortune and illness. As this day progressed in Qing Chinese villages, elaborately decorated dragon boats raced down the rivers. Reaching the finish line, the crews cast paper offerings into the river so that evil influences would float away. But this was not enough. Gourd-shaped paper lanterns also hung in gateways, so that the fruit's symbolic vapors could combat diseases and demons.

As a talisman to secure fertility, wealth, longevity, and healing, a miniature silver bottle gourd was either attached to a chain, hung in the center of a grooming kit, or worn as a toggle to counter-balance items suspended from the sash (Figure 19). The more elaborately decorated pieces had removable stoppers. The gourd could be either plain silver, gilded, or enameled (Figure 20). Whether solid and heavy, or filigreed and light, each bottle gourd challenged the silversmith's powers of representation.

A variation on the single gourd, the double gourds represented the unity of Heaven and Earth (Figure 21). Most of these pieces did not open. The purely decorative stoppers always faced in opposite directions: this design might have referred to the yin-

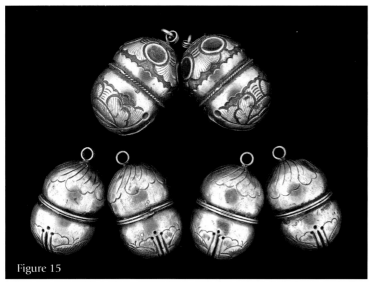

Figure 15

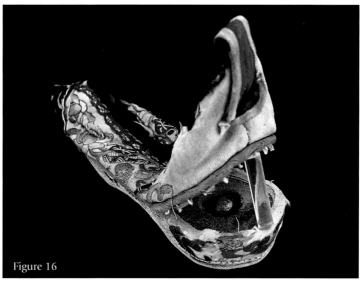

Figure 16

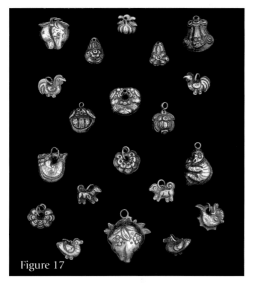

Figure 17

Figure 18

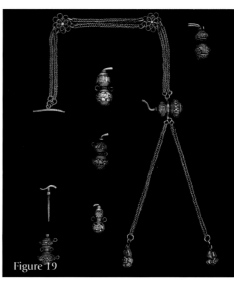

Figure 19

Figure 20

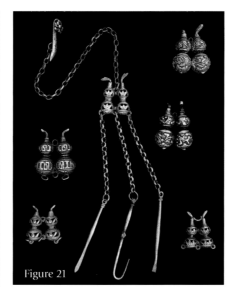

Figure 21

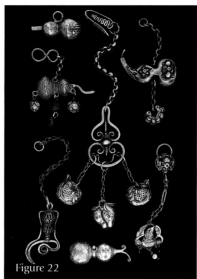

Figure 22

yang principle, or to the gourd's power to dispel evil coming from any direction.

The silver gourd intended as a medicine container did have a removable stopper, which terminated in a tiny spoon. Often these spoons resemble those found in snuff bottles, and certain silver gourds clearly served to hold both pharmaceuticals and snuff. Indeed, many still contain traces of white powder.

Aside from the tiny stopper, the most interesting aspect of a silver bottle gourd is the symbolism embellishing its surface. On the bottom, a gourd typically displays either the longevity symbol or the yin-yang. Repoussé or engraved designs cover the rest of the artifact; the orchid for love and beauty, the plum blossom for longevity, and the lotus for purity in the midst of corruption were especially popular. Arabesques swirling across a silver gourd reflected a wish for "ten thousand generations of sons and grandsons." Lotus and plum blossoms adorn the enameled bottle gourd in Figure 23, and the motif is repeated on the two musical stones.

Silver gourds often displayed the Four Attributes of the Scholar (books, scroll paintings, chessboard, and lute) or some combination of the Symbols of the Eight Immortals (fan, sword, bottle gourd, castanets, flower basket, bamboo cane, flute, and lotus). The bottle gourds in Figure 24 (left) are notable for three reasons. They are part of a single amulet; they are lightweight and hollow; and their bottoms feature plum blossoms instead of the usual yin-yang or longevity symbol. One occasionally finds a chain with as many as five or six different gourds, evidently strung together by the owner.

A Qing dynasty silver gourd could easily become a bell amulet to dispel evil spirits (Figure 24, right). Such bells contained metal pellets to create the reverberation and slits on the bottom to release it.

Animals

To secure safety, prosperity, conjugal bliss, fertility, and longevity—in short, the essential human desires—a Qing dynasty family depended on silver animal amulets. Animals have always been extraordinarily meaningful to the Chinese, with many creatures becoming the centers of cults.

In the Cult of the Ox, the animal symbolized spring, strength,

and domestic bliss. Fertility rituals among certain minorities involved not only sensual dancing to drums, but also bullfighting. Men and boys wore a silver ox as a symbol of fertility, both agricultural and human. Most amulets were hung singly, but sometimes, we see an ox with its calf (Figure 25). The amulet in Figure 26 shows an ox plus a vase for peace, a basket for abundance, a dog for protection, and a teapot and gourd symbolizing fertility. Occasionally, one finds a male child riding an ox while playing a flute, a Buddhist metaphor for having attained nirvana through the realization that salvation lies within (Figures 27 and 28). The ox is the true self, which the boy pacifies through contemplation. Reveling in his new knowledge, the boy makes joyful music as he returns home astride the beast he has mastered.

Another popular creature found on animal amulets is the donkey (Figures 29 and 30). Often hung incorrectly by today's jewelry dealers, with his feet down, he should be displayed with hooves in the air to represent the white donkey of Zhang Guolao, one of the Eight Daoist Immortals, whom we first met in Chapter 2. Most conveniently, when not using his white donkey, Zhang Guolao could fold up the animal and drop it into a pouch or bottle gourd. Before hitting the road, he simply sprayed his donkey with water from his mouth, and the animal would magically grow. A symbol of endurance and perseverance, this mythic beast could carry Zhang Guolao one thousand miles without resting.

In Qing culture, the horse symbolized speed and endurance. For their Mongol patrons, silversmiths depicted each horse with bells around its neck, since the nomads bedecked their real horses with silver bells. The horse also represented a wish for high office, since officials were the only ones allowed to ride horses. In Figure 31, the two horses with chain bridles represent the Tibetan windhorse, who was thought to dispel demons, illness, and misfortune, even as he bestowed positive personal energy on the wearer. The mounted silver candidate wished the fortunate recipient endurance and success on his civil service examinations.

The goat, symbolizing peace and retired life, is hard to find in silver, and the two examples in Figure 32 are delightful. Since the Qing Chinese made no distinction between goats and sheep, the goat and rider might signify filial piety.

Although not indigenous to China, lions became common images after ambassadors from Central Asia presented several specimens to the Imperial zoo. Pairs of carved stone lions soon stood guard at the entrances to temples and official buildings, defending Buddhist law and symbolizing courage, energy, and wisdom. The male always appeared on the right, toying with an ornamental ball, while the female, to his left, cuddled her cub. A silver male lion with its ball frequently adorned a baby boy's hat or hung around the neck of a young boy. The lions on the left and in the center of Figure 34 look as if they might have hung from a man's sash. In Figure 33, the lions' heads and tails rotate and pivot by themselves when worn, while the ears and tongues move on the pieces in Figures 35 and 36.

Rats decorated knot picks and earpicks (Figure 37). In the Qing dynasty, packages were wrapped in cloth and tied with string, ending in elaborate knots. A Chinese person used the pick to help him undo the knots or cut the string with the serrated back of the rat. A popular gift for a young man going to take his civil service examinations, a rat pick supposedly helped him untie the knots in the questions. The first sign of the Chinese zodiac, the rat symbolized wealth: for the Chinese, a rodent scratching at night suggested someone counting money. Merchants naturally favored adornments depicting rats. In southern China, some minorities believed that the rat brought rice to mankind. Others saw such rodents as avatars of longevity, since they were so hard to eliminate.

A symbol for longevity, immutability and steadfastness, the tortoise appeared frequently in Qing silver pieces, often as a pendant. The silver tortoises I've discovered are quite large, and plum blossoms—another longevity symbol—cover their feet (Figure 38). In Chinese mythology, the tortoise concealed the secrets of Heaven and Earth. The twenty-four rim plates of a tortoise's shell were often identified with the twenty-four divisions of the Chinese agricultural calendar. The animal's upper shell symbolized Heaven, while the underside represented the flat disc of Earth.

The pig, with its rapid maturation and strong reproductive powers, symbolized prosperity, fertility, and virility (Figure 39). In Qing dynasty China, pig-shaped money receptacles became the ancestors of today's "piggy-banks." To insure prosperity, peasants placed papercuts of pigs on their houses. Candidates for civil service positions consumed braised pig's feet before the examination. The bridegroom's family often presented the bride's family with a pig as a fertility symbol, and every wedding feast

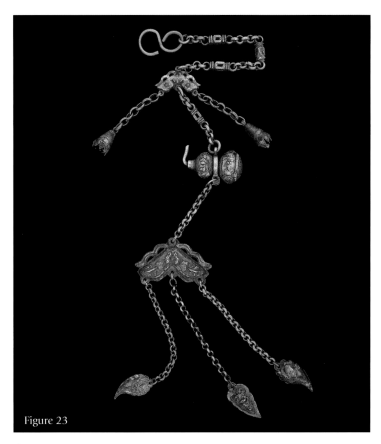

Figure 23

featured at least one pork dish.

The rooster, tenth creature of the zodiac, provided protection, since its crowing frightened away demons. A family often placed a white rooster on a deceased person's coffin. Widely regarded as a symbol for reliability and courage, since it never failed to crow at sunrise, the rooster also represented achievement, fame, and male vigor. Each silver rooster in Figure 40 was probably worn by a man or boy for protection from evil spirits and success in his endeavors.

The duck also figured in many silver amulets. Mandarin ducks, always shown in pairs, symbolized marital fidelity and happiness (Figure 41). A singleton duck, worn as a talisman against evil, probably bespoke a Buddhist owner.

A dog amulet also brought protection, since it could frighten demons with its bark and bite (Figure 42). On the summer solstice, paper dogs symbolically bit evil spirits when they were thrown into rivers during the Dragon Boat Festival. Paper dogs also protected the dead, and the insane were washed with dog feces to expel demons. Among the Yao minority, the dog was always venerated as the forefather of the race, and today Yao

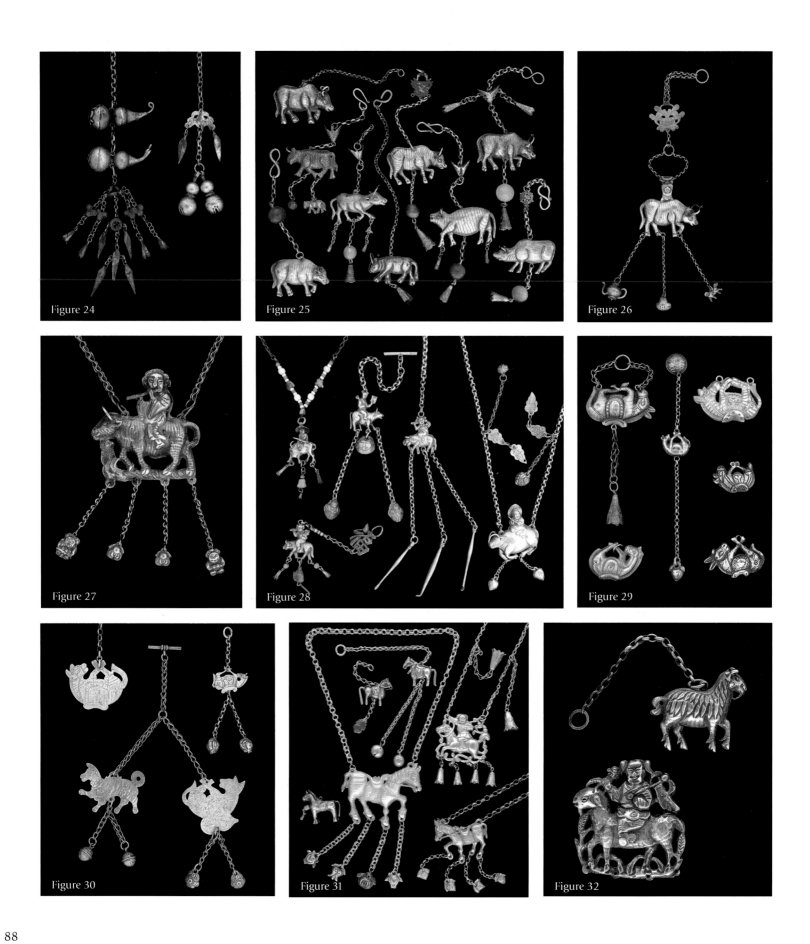

Figure 24

Figure 25

Figure 26

Figure 27

Figure 28

Figure 29

Figure 30

Figure 31

Figure 32

children still wear hats shaped like dogs to deter evil spirits. Many silver dog amulets resemble the popular Pekinese breed.

The fish symbolized abundance, wealth, and fertility, because the word for fish is phonetically identical to the word for "surplus" or "excess" (Figure 43). A pair of silver fish, representing connubial bliss and harmony, enjoyed popularity as a wedding present. A fish with a boy on its back brought a wish for numerous high-ranking sons. Because a fish swims upstream against the current, it became an avatar of scholarly success, often adorning the knot picks given to civil service examination candidates (Figure 44)

The three-legged toad in Figure 44 symbolized longevity and the unattainable, but it also had a deeper meaning. Supposedly, this creature lived in a deep well, breathing poisonous vapors. One day Liu Hai, a Minister of State destined to become a benevolent Daoist deity, lowered a fishing line baited with gold coins into the well. He lured, caught, and destroyed the toad. The Chinese interpret this fable to mean that: "money is the fatal attraction which lures men to their ruin."

The monkey was revered as a god in southern China, and many temples were built in his honor, for he could bestow health, protection, and success. The most famous monkey of all is certainly Sun Wukong, the Monkey King. In 1592, Wu Chengen wrote a novel, *The Journey to the West*, in which the Monkey King accompanies the Buddhist pilgrim Xuanzang to India, coming to his rescue many times. In Figure 45, I believe the character in the center is Sun Wukong. Worshipped by Buddhists, the Monkey King proved a favorite amulet of the sick and unsuccessful.

In Chinese folklore, a solitary animal conveyed one meaning—we've discussed many of them—while an animal with an official on its back conveyed quite another. The mounted pig in Figure 46 presented a young boy with a wish for prosperity, virility, and good fortune. In Figure 47, the official on the dog and the official on the rooster guaranteed protection and success on civil service examinations. The official on the rat surrounded by grapes represented wealth and fertility.

The idea of wearing an animal image for purely aesthetic reasons was alien to the Chinese imagination. So dangerous was the world, so proliferous its demons, you treasured your silver animals primarily for their talismanic powers. The tortoise and toad forestalled death. The donkey, lion, and the horse embattled

lassitude and melancholy. The goat thwarted senility. The ox, pig, and fish prohibited shortages. A monkey fended off illnesses. A rat averted poverty. A pair of ducks prevented marital strife. The dog, cat, rooster, and duck dispatched wicked spirits. Not bad for a few ounces of silver.

Figure 33

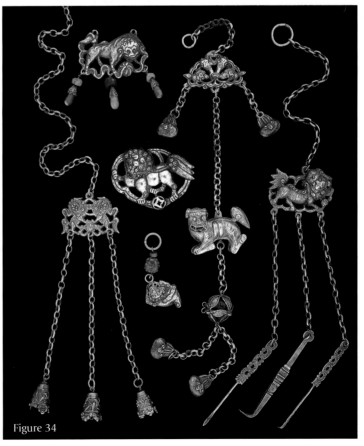

Figure 34

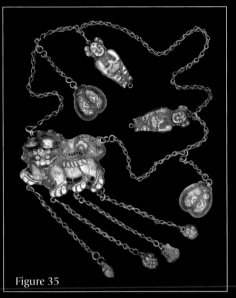

Figure 35

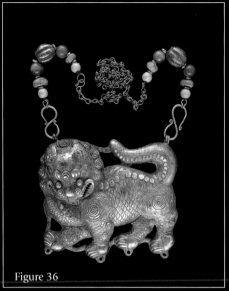

Figure 36

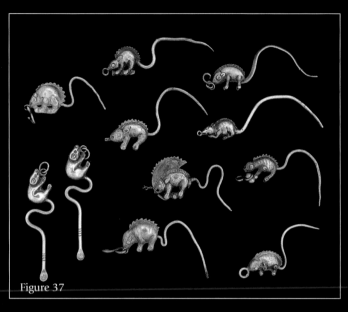

Figure 37

Figure 38

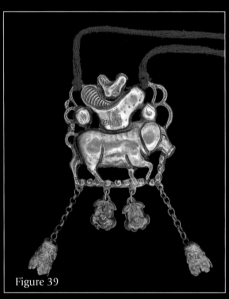

Figure 39

Figure 40

Figure 41

Figure 42

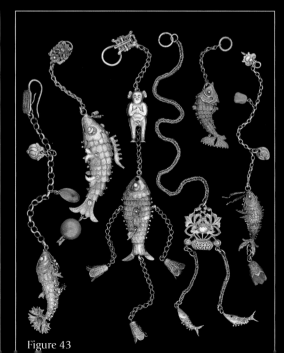

Figure 43

Figure 44

Figure 45

Figure 46

Figure 47

Rings, Earrings, and Bracelets

Yinzhi puts down her embroidery and fingers the perforated thimble ring, which her mother contributed to her dowry two years earlier. The large lotus on the top conceals the utilitarian underside. "The finest for the finest," her mother had said upon presenting the ring to Yinzhi. "You will need exceptional items now that your father has arranged for you to marry into the wealthiest family in town."

Yinzhi's eyes fill with tears at the sweet memory as the baby kicks in her stomach. She misses her family so much, but according to custom, cannot visit them again until the fifth day of the New Year.

"Why do you dawdle?" Yanfang, her mother-in-law, scolds as she bursts into Yinzhi's room without knocking. Her gray hair, pulled back into a bun, gives her features a pinched look.

Yinzhi lowers her head and pushes the needle back through the silk. "I'm working on the baby's jacket," she says.

Her mother-in-law grabs the frame. "The stitches are too big. You're ruining good material." Then she sees the thimble ring. "That ring is wasted on you. Your husband should sell it. I'll tell him."

Yinzhi's sister-in-law, Bingbing, a younger but equally tyrannical version of her mother, enters the room without acknowledging Yinzhi. "The silk merchant has arrived," she informs Yanfang.

"Tell him I'll be right there."

Yinzhi knows that Bingbing is about to acquire expensive bolts of silk for her wedding trousseau. But Yinzhi will receive nothing, not even the remnants, for she is "so beautiful" that she looks good in "any old thing."

"I am trying not to displease her," thinks Yinzhi, "but it is impossible." The criticism never stops, no matter how hard Yinzhi tries. If she complains to her husband, he always—in filial piety—takes his mother's side.

"Weddings!" says Yanfang, "Babies! It's all too much, but at least I'll have a grandson to pay tribute to me when I am gone."

Opposite: A Han woman wearing earrings and bracelets (as well as a wedding torque).

"It could be a granddaughter," Yinzhi murmurs, fingering the ring for courage.

"Never! This house will have a grandson," Yanfang insists on her way out.

Yinzhi twists the thimble ring as she offers a silent prayer to Guanyin. "Please give me a healthy baby," she pleads, "And I know I should want a son, but please make this one a daughter who will be just as kind as my mother."

At the Shenyang Palace in Manchuria, Liujing leaves the Buddhist shrine in the Pavilion of Continuing Thought and makes her way back through the moongate and into the corridor. As one of five consorts chosen to accompany the Emperor on his pilgrimage—he is paying homage to his ancestors—Liujing hopes to have the honor of pleasuring him this evening.

The heated floors of the palace feel warm beneath her embroidered slippers as Liujing moves along a row of alcoves filled with lanterns that turn night into day. She passes enormous porcelain vases, paintings by famous artists, and cabinets inlaid with jade and ivory.

"Liujing," a voice calls, and she turns to see Juwen, the chief eunuch. Instantly, she knows that the Emperor, after examining a tray of papers bearing the concubines' names, has selected her. "Come."

Without a word, she follows him as they enter an anteroom where by day the Emperor and his consorts practice their calligraphy, read, and relax. An inkstone, brush, paper, and two inksticks—one black and one red—lay on the table. Only the Emperor can use the red.

Beyond lies the dressing salon, where Liujing's clothing and accessories await, along with the litter that will bear her to the Emperor's bedchamber. As Liujing enters the room, eunuchs and handmaidens strip her down, bathe her, and help her into a silk gown and elaborately embroidered slippers. Sitting before the mirror, Liujing relaxes as Juwen undoes her long hair and combs it until it shines. Satisfied, he sweeps the hair into an elaborate hairdo atop Liujing's head and adds kingfisher hairpins encrusted with pearls and coral. From a carved ivory jewelry box, he removes a gilt silver ring and a pair of gilded kingfisher earrings. Liujing proceeds to adorn the ring finger

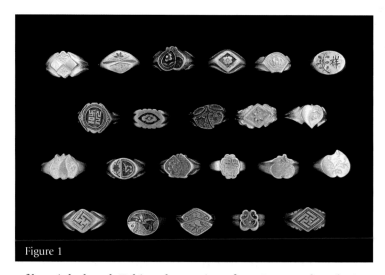

Figure 1

of her right hand. Taking the earrings from Juwen, she admires the tiny coral butterflies on the kingfisher plum blossoms, and shakes the dangles. They make her smile. "The Emperor is waiting," the eunuch urges.

Liujing attaches the earrings to her lobes, then dabs jasmine on her neck and over her breasts. Covering her with a silk shawl, the handmaidens lead Liujing to the litter.

The eunuchs lift the litter and bear it down the corridor past walls of carved wood. Soon Liujing arrives at the Emperor's bed, cloaked in flowing curtains dotted with embroidered fragrance carriers. As she delicately steps from the litter, Liujing prays that she will conceive tonight—and that, this time, she will be allowed to keep the infant.

Meilin shivers with excitement as she hears the servant call, "They're coming! They're coming!" She rushes to the window with her sister and her mother to watch the middlemen march down the street. Behind them, coolies carry casks and crates of betrothal gifts hanging from poles balanced on their shoulders.

"The bracelets will tell you everything," her sister, younger by a year, reminds her. "If they are unique and expensive, your husband will treat you well."

"That's an old wives tale," her mother insists, but Meilin hears the excitement in her tone as well. "Just remember, the middlemen will report your every reaction to the Liu family. Now, where are your father and brothers?"

The three women hurry to the sunny anteroom, seating themselves on couches as Meilin's father and two brothers enter

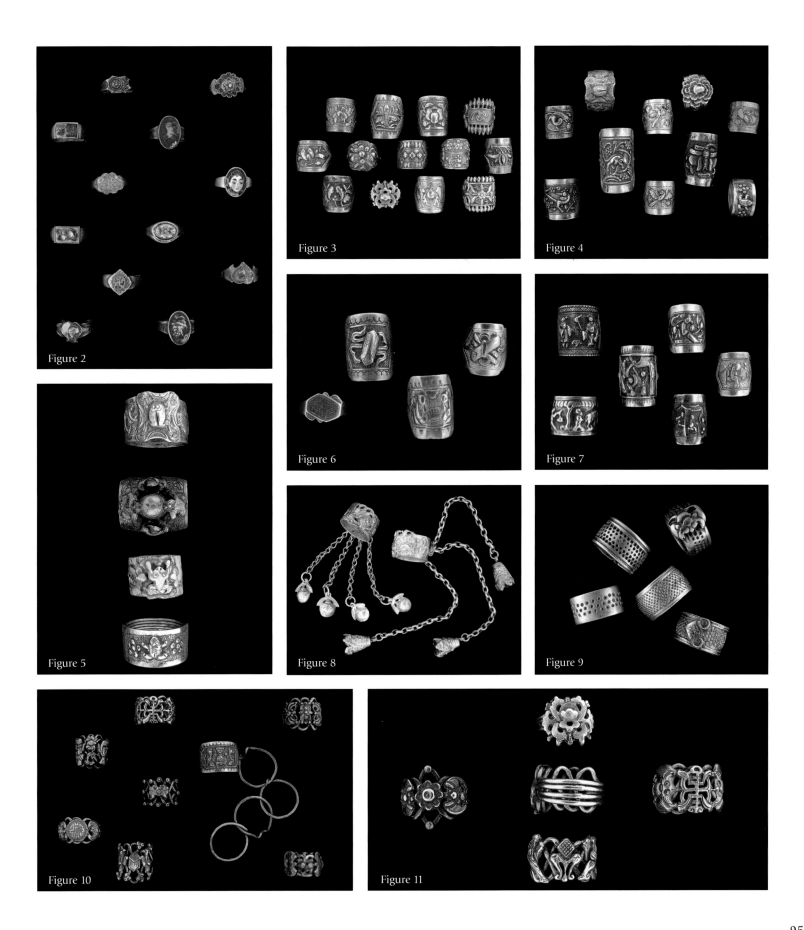

Figure 2

Figure 3

Figure 4

Figure 5

Figure 6

Figure 7

Figure 8

Figure 9

Figure 10

Figure 11

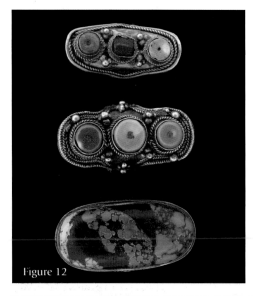

Figure 12

Figure 13

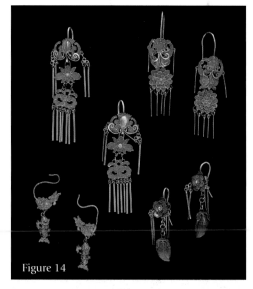

Figure 14

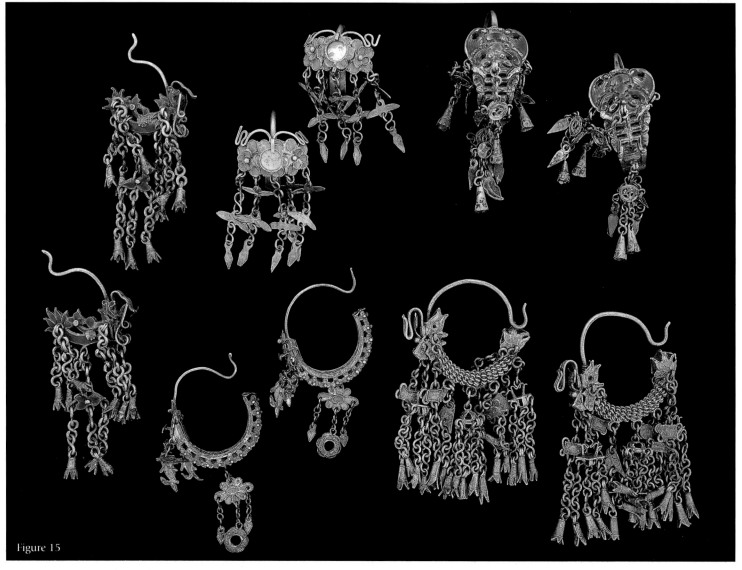

Figure 15

and stand behind her. Meilin sits up straight and her father pats her shoulder.

A servant shows the middlemen into the room. One carries the tray with a piece of red paper stating an auspicious wedding date determined by a diviner through astrological means. Behind them come the coolies with pairs of live mandarin ducks and squawking geese in cages. Other coolies tote red lacquered boxes filled with dragon and phoenix cakes, and still others bring garments of flowered silk to be worn at the ceremony. Meilin and her family nod approvingly at every item. Bouquets of flowers, kegs of wine, and tins of expensive tea soon fill the room, but there is no sign of any jewelry. Meilin tries to hide her disappointment. Suddenly one of the middlemen grins and, drawing from his wide sleeve an object wrapped in red silk, hands it to Meilin.

Meilin can feel the anticipation in the air. She unties the elaborate knots of gold string, slowly unfolds the red silk, and gasps. Inside rests a pair of wedding bracelets crafted in solid silver, with blue and green enameling highlighting the flowers of the different seasons combined with the longevity symbol. "Put them on," her sister whispers, but Meilin's hands are trembling so much that her sister has to lean over and help her. Once the bracelets are in place, Meilin rotates her wrists and watches the silver glitter in the sunlight. "I love them, I love them," she blurts out, then remembers her manners and smiles politely. The middlemen smile as well.

"Tell the Lius that we are very pleased," says Meilin's father. The middlemen nod, and back toward the door.

Utilitarian mementos. Status symbols. Ritual tokens. In the Qing dynasty, rings, earrings, and bracelets were far more than ornaments. For this society, such pieces emanated promises and longings—meanings largely forgotten after the architects of the Cultural Revolution impounded the native silver artifacts and buried them in warehouses. Fortunately, many paintings and photographs have survived that enable us to associate these diminutive but beautiful artifacts with particular periods, customs, ranks, classes, and ethnic groups.

Rings

From the earliest days of Chinese civilization, a royal concubine reportedly received a silver ring each time she spent the night with

Figure 16

the Emperor. Throughout the lovemaking, she wore the ring on her right hand. Upon being discharged, she switched the ring to her left hand. If she became pregnant, she earned a gold ring.

By the Qing dynasty, even common women could afford simple rings, and these have survived in plain silver (Figure 1) or in a slightly more elaborate enameled form (Figure 2). The designs were spare: fruits, fish, flowers, animals of the zodiac, double happiness symbols, and the swastika.

More intricate imagery covered the rings of wealthier citizens. On such pieces, we find detailed flowers (Figure 3), animals and birds (Figure 4), and the ever popular frog for fertility (Figure 5).

Each specimen in Figure 6—rings featuring engraved stacks of books—might have been owned by either a man or a woman. Since wealthy, privately educated women were writing and publishing poetry as early as the seventeenth century in China, it's entirely possible that they wore rings bearing literary themes.

Rings engraved with theater scenes, often referred to as "opera rings" represented a unique tradition (Figure 7). According to published sources, traveling Peking opera companies sold such rings as souvenirs of their performances.

Long chains with bells or charms dangled from some Qing dynasty rings (Figure 8). Since bells were thought to exorcise evil spirits, these rings served both a decorative and utilitarian purpose.

The Chinese referred to thimble rings as *dingzhengu*, which literally means "the band that pushes the needle from below" (Figure 9). A thimble ring fit around a woman's middle finger. She used it to nudge the needle upward from underneath the embroidery. Since a Qing dynasty needle featured a framed round eye, the silversmith would punch tiny holes—sometimes mere indentations—into the ring. The eye-frame could fit into any given hole, stabilizing the needle. Some rings endured so much use that the indentations almost disappeared.

Atop the typical thimble ring, we usually find a flower. A more expensive thimble ring will weigh more, offer finer detail in the floral design, and often contain the silversmith's hallmark. A less expensive version—little more than a band of thin silver (with holes for the eye frame)—will necessarily feature a flatter flower.

The thimble ring is the most unusual such Qing dynasty artifact, but the puzzle ring is the most intriguing (Figures 10 and 11). Behind the central emblem, we find four linked circlets that can unravel to form a small chain. Common themes on the emblem include the God of the North playing chess with the God of the South, bats with a flower, and bats with the longevity symbol. Apparently, a puzzle ring denoted the army unit to which a soldier belonged.

Puzzle rings provided the basis of an army drinking game. Each soldier would disassemble his ring on the table. At the signal, the soldiers would put their rings back together. The last one finished had to drain his glass. One can imagine the raucous laughter in the barracks as the soldiers slowly lost their dexterity.

A puzzle ring owner often used a vertical, thin band of silver to keep the circlets from separating. Alternatively, he might secure them with old string, or solder the circlets to the emblem.

A Tibetan man during the Qing dynasty preferred an enormous chunk of turquoise or a row of coral cabochons in his silver ring. In Figure 12 a deep black matrix colors the blue-green

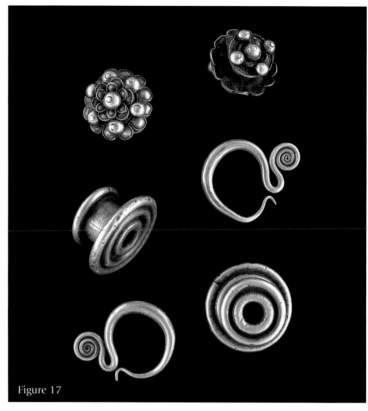

Figure 17

turquoise of a specimen weighing fifty-five grams. For stability, as well as extra decoration on the coral and silver rings, the smith pounded a silver nail through each of the original stones. Coral is not indigenous to this part of Asia, so the Tibetans relied on traders, who sold the stones on strands. A strand could be worn as jewelry, or each bead could be removed and encased in a silver ring.

The "saddle ring" slipped over a Tibetan man's queue. He might wear just one, or as many as a dozen strung on a padded cloth band encircling his head. In Figure 13, a silversmith added coral centerpieces to the repoussé geometric designs on the two rings, but turquoise beads enjoyed equal popularity.

Earrings

For three thousand years, dynasties came and went in China, influencing the personal adornment of each period. But no matter the dynasty, members of the nobility in ancient China wanted their status symbols buried with them for use in the afterlife. This religious belief has yielded a bonanza for archeologists.

A typical specimen is a pair of pounded gold earrings—curvilinear in shape, with a handcarved turquoise bead on each shaft—discovered in a Shang Dynasty tomb from the thirteenth

Figure 18

century B.C. The Zhou dynasty (1100-256 B.C.) prescribed specific ornamentation for every rank and class, with the aristocracy naturally favoring gold: gold rings, earrings, bracelets, belt hooks, and hair ornaments emerge routinely at Zhou excavations. Gold and gilt bronze earrings have also surfaced at royal burial sites from the Liao dynasty (A.D. 907-1125).

When artisans began working in cheaper metals, such as silver, brass, and copper, adornment became available to government officials and the moderately wealthy, including the merchant class.

By the Qing dynasty, most women could afford at least one pair of earrings. Members of the Imperial family still preferred gold, supplemented by various grades of Manchurian eastern pearls. The quality of the pearls depended on the rank of the wearer. A Manchu woman often wore three earrings in *each* ear. The piercing process must have been extremely uncomfortable; quite likely the women used acupuncture to mitigate the pain. In time, Han customs from the Central Plains influenced Manchu women, and many started to wear a single pair, one per ear.

Besides their solid gold earrings, the royal concubines often wore gilded-silver earrings decorated with kingfisher feathers, beads (coral, jade, and tourmaline), and different grades of pearls. They favored one of two basic types—*erh-huan* (without dangles) and *erh-chui* (with dangles).

The Han aristocracy harbored an idiosyncratic attitude toward earrings. The scholar Tsao Hsingyuan believes that elite Han women rejected earrings so as to avoid association with the lower classes and the minorities. By the Ming dynasty, however, they'd obviously overcome this prejudice, since we find both gold and silver earrings in their tombs. Figure 14 shows several sets of gilded-silver earrings, trimmed with kingfisher feathers, that a noblewoman might have worn.

In contrast to the Han, the women of the southwestern ethnic minorities favored large earrings (Figures 15 through 19). The longest pair, probably Yi, measures 14.5 centimeters (Figure 16). The thick Miao earrings in Figure 17 have 2.6 centimeter cores that fit into the ear holes, and they weigh a remarkable sixty-two grams *each*. This same illustration shows two other types favored by Miao women—floral earrings and silver circles with the curled tips—while a Bai woman treasured the silver and jade disk earrings in Figure 19. It's important to remember that each minority did not wear its own group's jewelry exclusively. Photographs of women from the fifty-five minorities reveal a remarkable diversity in bodily adornments.

The vendor who sold me the two smaller pairs of earrings in Figure 19, and the two pairs of dragon earrings in Figure 20, said they are antiques from Qing dynasty tombs. This may or may not be true. Dubious stories accompany many artifacts on the Chinese silver market. I only know these earrings are old and were probably worn by Han women.

No matter what the style of an earring, local customs determined its use. A Han Chinese mother often pierced one of her infant son's lobes and inserted a tiny earring, thereby fooling the demons into thinking him a worthless girl. Another intriguing tradition derives from the fact that a woman could wear only silver jewelry while in mourning. Among the Han, this proscription took an unusual form: a grieving woman slipped white thread in her ears instead of earrings for the first hundred days of mourning. After that, a woman could wear silver earrings, but she rejected gold or jewels until the full grieving period had elapsed. Manchu women also eschewed gold during mourning, wearing tiny silver earrings instead.

Bracelets

Predictably enough, during the Qing dynasty, members of the Imperial family and the nobility favored not only gold rings and earrings but also bracelets of gold or jade, often studded with pearls, kingfisher feathers, and semi-precious stones. The wealthy Han aristocracy, Mongol, and the wealthier minority women, by contrast, wore silver bracelets. They loved circular bangles, open-ended bracelets, and chainlink bangles. Some received solid silver bracelets as a betrothal gift. Suitors in the minorities often chose hollow bracelets with beads inside for their intended. In many cases, designs covered the whole ornament; other pieces displayed designs only on the open ends. While a Manchu woman donned only one or two bracelets at a time, a minority woman might slide four to eight on each arm. Longevity symbols, scholar symbols, bats, and certain traditional flowers enhance the Han bracelets. Many southwestern minority pieces exhibit a fertility emblem: one or two coiling dragons chasing the pearl of potentiality. They also include the double fish for marital happiness, as well as flowers (though not the varieties found on Han pieces).

Today, we typically find Chinese silver bracelets in pairs, which is in fact how a prospective bridegroom presented them—through the middleman—to his betrothed. When the card proposing the marriage arrived at the bride's house, it was typically accompanied by a pair of bracelets and various articles of food—typically a pair of mandarin ducks and special cakes—and other costly gifts such as the fabric for the wedding dress. The hopeful groom's family spent as much as they could on the elaborate bracelets. Judging from the illustrations I've seen, a woman wore one on each wrist. In Figure 21 we find a pair of typical oval Han bracelets, each with unusual enameling. Flowers and longevity symbols adorn the edges. In Figure 22 a pierced pair—probably from the Miao minority—combines the double fish for marital happiness with the lotus for purity, fruitfulness, and protection. The bracelets in Figure 23, another typical minority set, contain tiny beads to scare away evil spirits. Stylized dragons—symbols of fertility—twist and turn across the surfaces, chasing that elusive pearl. Dragons likewise adorn the Miao bracelets at the top of Figure 24. Engraved dragons swirl across the heavy set in the middle, also Miao, while the longevity symbol and bats stand out in high relief on the hallmarked Han pair.

The Chinese of the Qing dynasty believed that rattan cured, or at least alleviated, arthritis and gout. They often combined this material with silver in their bracelets. After 1860 the silversmiths used the fresh water variety, though they called it "deep sea rattan." In Figure 25 rattan-and-silver bracelets display repoussé, engraved, and cutout designs. Longevity symbols and flowers abound on these pieces, which made them suitable gifts for elderly women.

A Qing dynasty Chinese person wore a jade-and-silver bracelet for both good health and protection. If the bracelet shattered in a mishap, the owner felt fortunate: but for the bracelet, she believed, her wrist would have broken instead. The jade-and-silver piece in Figure 26 features repoussé symbols for the scholar. It may have belonged to a wealthy woman educated at home.

The chainlink bangle in Figure 27 depicts those ubiquitous dragons, playing with their pearl. Extremely flexible, this type of bracelet also surfaces in gold and copper. A smith could leave the silver plain, or enamel it for his more prosperous customers.

Normally crafted for baby girls, the small silver bracelets from the Qing era still retain their charm. The examples in Figure 28—expandable for long-term wear—measure four to five centimeters in diameter. Figure 29 depicts various bangles with the dragons-and-pearl motif. It's fascinating to note how each silversmith treated this same basic theme.

The extra wide minority bracelets (measuring up to three centimeters) in Figure 30 feature unusual designs with the double fish, eternal knots, crabs, bats, lotus flowers, geometric designs, scholar's objects, and—possibly—chrysanthemums. Figure 31 displays the widest bracelet in the book. Probably Miao in origin, it measures 4.5 centimeters in width and features the dragons-and-pearl motif. The narrower bangle, also Miao, accentuates the animals of the zodiac in high relief.

One especially peculiar style from this era suggests two thin single bracelets soldered together, but each such piece is really a single bangle crafted to look like two. In Figure 32, the three bangles have beads inside. The open-ended specimen does not.

In Figure 33 we find eight heavy bracelets, all solid silver. The most substantial weighs ninety-five grams. Some display twisted silver; others braided. The smiths covered some with chasing, but left others plain with engraved designs on the ends. Crafted for various ethnic groups in different regions, they all share the same open-ended design.

Rings, earrings, and bracelets served as both utilitarian ornaments and as status symbols in the Qing dynasty. The wealthier the person, the more such items he or she owned. An affluent woman often commissioned a silversmith to enamel or gild her silver pieces, or inlay them with kingfisher feathers. The peasants treasured the one or two pieces they owned. We know these accessories filtered down from generation to generation because we find them not only in Qing dynasty paintings and ancestral portraits, but also in more recent family photographs. As I fasten on my earrings, slide bangles over my wrists, and slip rings on my fingers, I realize that women's appreciation of these adornments hasn't changed in centuries. Our contemporary pieces are less utilitarian and more ornamental than those of Qing China, but our desire for such subtle beauty remains a constant.

Figure 19

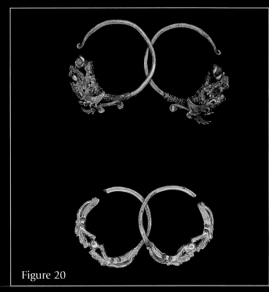

Figure 20

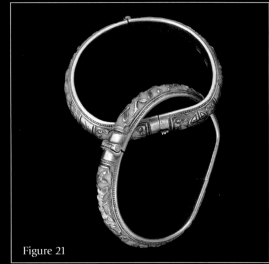

Figure 21

Figure 22

Figure 23

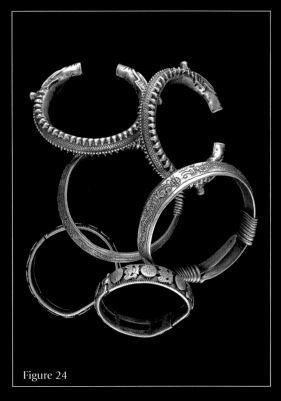

Figure 24

Figure 25

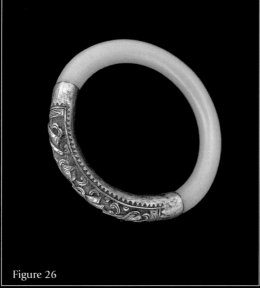

Figure 26

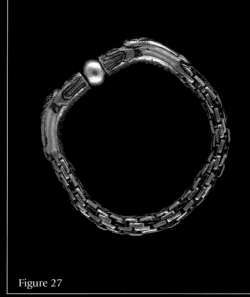

Figure 27

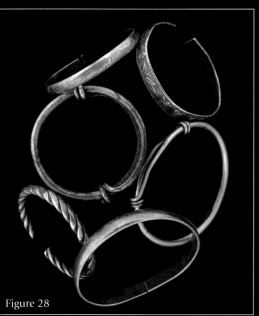

Figure 28

Figure 29

Figure 30

Figure 31

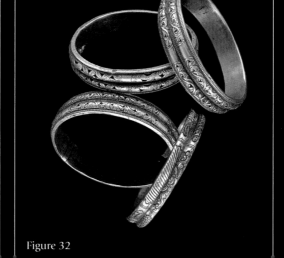

Figure 32

Figure 33

104

chapter 8

Amulets for Security and Success

T he different ethnic groups of Qing dynasty China shared the same aspirations. Everyone desired a happy marriage, success in business, enough money, good health, and a long life. To secure these blessings, the Chinese made special offerings to the gods—and they relied on the power of amulets, especially silver amulets. Thousands of these pieces have survived the ravages of time. Today they tell us about an age when people believed they needed the help of the spiritual world to thrive.

Gods of Wealth

The worship of the Gods of Wealth blurred the distinction between materialism and mysticism in China during the Qing era. While the origin of these deities remains unclear, we know that they inspired great reverence and adoration.

One could not enter any sort of Qing commercial establishment—shop, market, office—without finding Gods of Wealth displayed prominently, for these images were thought to bring success in business. At home, meanwhile, a woman routinely offered devotions to the wealth gods, praying to them for money and for sons who would attain official rank. These deities received particular attention during the New Year holidays, when the head of the household needed to settle all debts before the year's end.

An artist created wealth gods in all media: wood, jade, bronze, gold, silver, paint. The painted images typically depict both the civil God of Wealth, in his official gown, and the military God of Wealth, in his uniform. Silver amulets usually show the military God of Wealth only. The smith represented him as an ancient warrior wearing a coat of armor over a war-robe consisting of a round collar, a helmet, iron trousers, and traditional combat boots. He normally carried a silver ingot.

A wealthy woman of the Qing dynasty could wear an elaborate silver needle case embossed with the military God of Wealth in full regalia (Figures 1 and 2). Incredibly intricate, such needle cases were clearly beyond the means of a poor woman. They probably hung from the waists of the affluent wives of merchants, military officials, or scholars.

Opposite: A member of the Han wearing the Eight Trigrams.

An amulet depicting the military God of Wealth might also have hung from the sash of a man. In Figure 3, the silver God seems to be carrying a pouch of money instead of an ingot, but he still wears a modified suit of armor.

The silversmiths depicted Liu Hai—an official minister in the Jin dynasty who became a Daoist deity—as a man or small boy playing with a string of coins and accompanied by a three-legged toad. We first encountered Liu Hai's legend in Chapter 6: how he beguiled the toad with coins and thus taught humankind the hazards of greed. But the story exists in another form. In the second version, the toad becomes Liu Hai's servant—bearing him wherever he wishes—not his victim, and Liu Hai emerges as a benevolent money-giver, and ultimately as a God of Wealth. No longer a poison-breathing monster, the toad in version two ultimately achieves the status of longevity symbol. In a coda to the legend, we learn that, whenever the toad escaped down the nearest well, Liu Hai always lured him out with his string of coins. This suggests that for the Chinese, wealth added to one's longevity.

Liu Hai often appears on a baby lock or on a pendant that hung from either a hat or an apron. In Figure 4, we see him with his strand of cash and his famous toad. On one amulet, Liu Hai tries to control the toad. On the other, he succeeds in riding him.

The *Hehe erhxian*, or Heavenly Twins, often depicted as young boys carrying a lotus and a covered round box, received homage from every merchant who sought harmony in his enterprise. Sometimes called the *Hoho erhxian*, they secured wealth and amicable business and marital partnerships. The *Hehe* with the chains in Figure 5 obviously hung from the neck of a young boy. The specimen with a single loop at the top might have been sewn to either a hat or apron.

The God of Longevity

Shouxing, the God of Longevity, is a stellar deity from the constellation Argo. Easily recognized by his elongated bald skull and white beard, he usually carries the peach of immortality and a staff made from the fungus of life. Often mounted or leaning on a deer, Shouxing resides at the South Pole, the region of life. The immortality peach from the orchard by the palace of Xiwangmu, the Queen Mother of the West, gives him his powers. These mythic peach trees bloom every 3,000 years, and the fruit

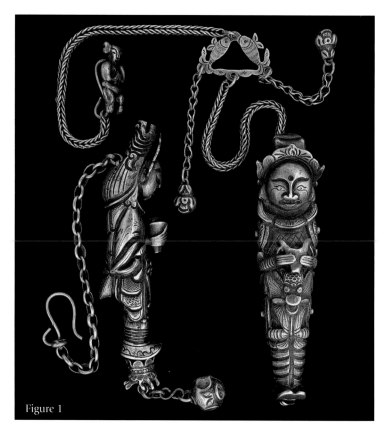

Figure 1

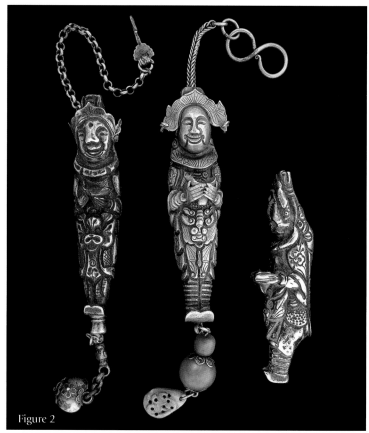

Figure 2

Figure 3

Figure 4

Figure 5

Figure 6

Figure 7

Figure 8

Figure 9

Figure 10

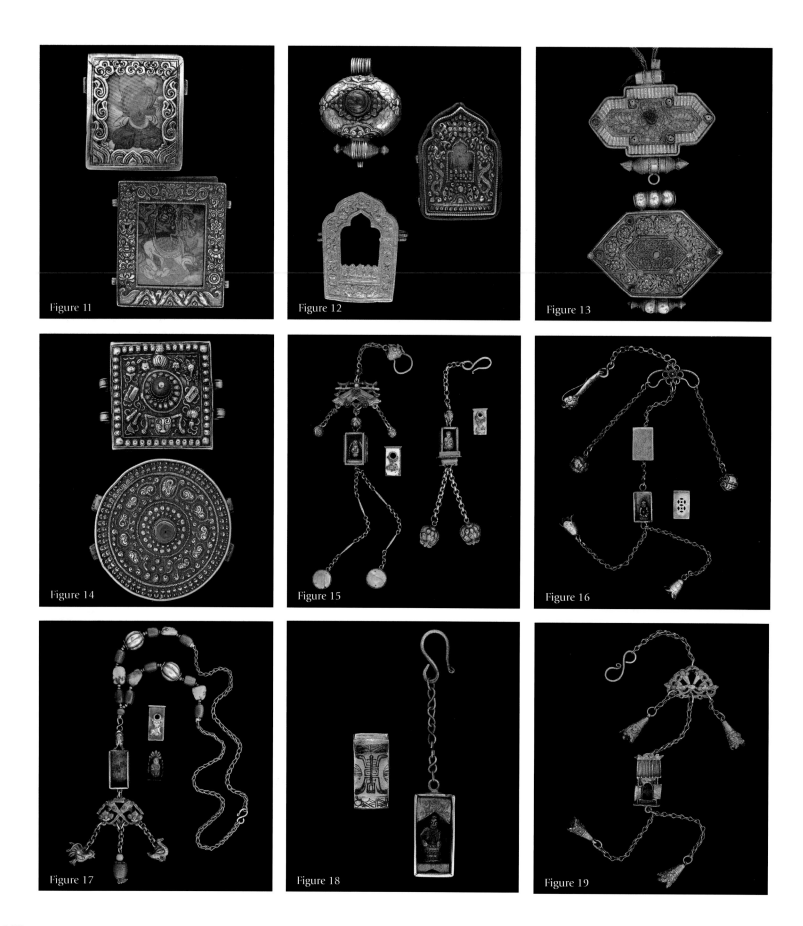

Figure 11

Figure 12

Figure 13

Figure 14

Figure 15

Figure 16

Figure 17

Figure 18

Figure 19

takes another 3,000 years to reach maturity, but the ripe peach enables the eater to live forever. At harvest time, Shouxing and the Eight Immortals enjoy a banquet to celebrate the birthday of the Queen Mother of the West and to rejuvenate themselves.

In Qing era China, a silver amulet of the God of Longevity was an appropriate gift for an infant, a child, a couple at a wedding, or an older individual—especially the head of the household. Not surprisingly, Shouxing appears on numerous hat adornments and pendants from this period (Figure 6), as well as on the sorts of locks we examined in Chapter 2. A mother would often sew a set of silver amulets depicting Shouxing and the Eight Immortals onto the hats of her male children.

Guanyin and Maitreya

Guanyin, the Goddess of Mercy who hears all prayers, often appeared either on the lid or inside a small silver shrine (Figure 7). Worshipped by the Chinese as the deity who brought sons, Guanyin also helped the sick, the lost, the senile, and even the dead in the Underworld. This goddess protected seafarers and farmers, brought money to businessmen, relieved pain, and made childbirth easy. Men and women alike adored her. Usually depicted in long flowing robes, sitting or standing on a lotus, Guanyin holds either a child, vase, lotus, or pearl. Occasionally, she folds her hands in prayer.

Destined to return to Earth and bring a great era of peace, Maitreya—Buddha's successor—usually appears with a bare chest, ample stomach, wide smile, bald pate, and either long hair or long ears. He is also known as the Laughing Buddha. In Figure 8, he embraces a huge fish. This artifact clearly represents peace and affluence. The collateral amulets give us simple babies on fish, conveying wishes for an abundance of high-ranking sons. Collectors sometimes mistake such infants for Maitreya.

On one of his trips to Earth, Maitreya stole several gold and silver ingots from the Buddha and used them to create numerous art objects, which he sold to keep himself alive. For this reason, goldsmiths and silversmiths regard Maitreya as their patron.

Ga'us

Worn as jewelry by both sexes, silver *ga'us*—also called amulet boxes or relic containers—served a religious as well as an

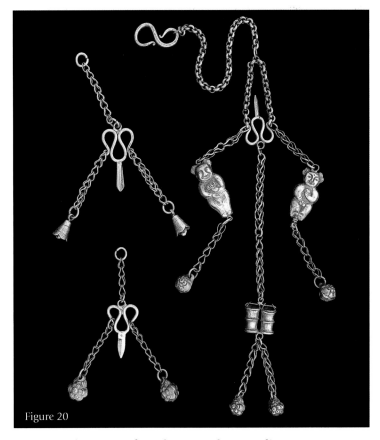

Figure 20

ornamental purpose for Tibetan and Mongolian men, women, and children. A *ga'u* protected its wearer from dangers encountered on a journey. When the owner was home, the amulet box rested on the family altar.

Whether the piece was made of silver or plain copper, the back pulled away to store one or more holy objects. Although a *ga'u* itself possessed no religious significance, it might have held a fragment of a monk's robe, a painted holy image, a clay ball which included a spiritual leader's ashes, a charm blessed by a lama, a peacock's feather to keep away moths, or a bit of a lama's meal molded into a disk and stamped with the image of a god. Naturally, it is rare to find a *ga'u* that still includes such a relic. When I opened the box shown in Figure 9, I was pleased to discover a piece of holy cloth, plus a *tsa tsa*, a clay ball which might include some of the ashes of a spiritual teacher.

Ga'us come in numerous shapes and sizes. Both men and women could wear the square, rectangular, and round varieties. The *ga'us* worn around the neck range in size from two to ten centimeters, while *ga'us* ranging up to thirty-five centimeters were worn across the chest with a leather strap or cloth band passing

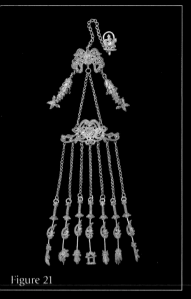

Figure 21

Figure 22

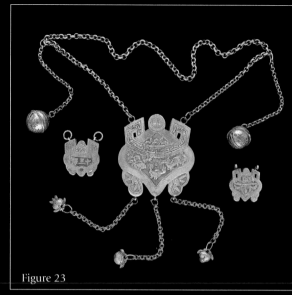

Figure 23

Figure 24

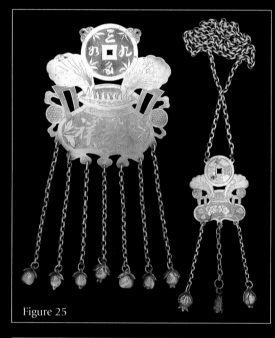

Figure 25

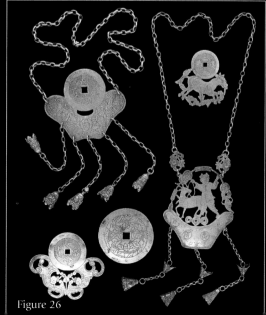

Figure 26

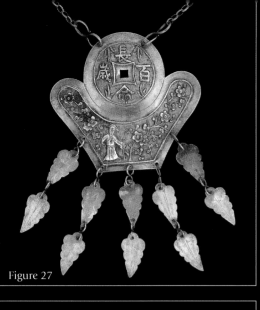

Figure 27

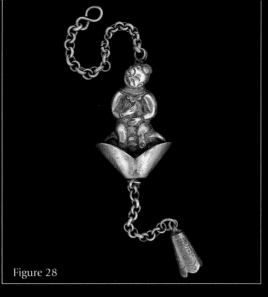

Figure 28

Figure 29

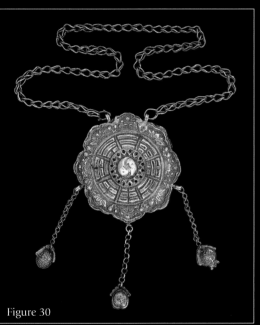

Figure 30

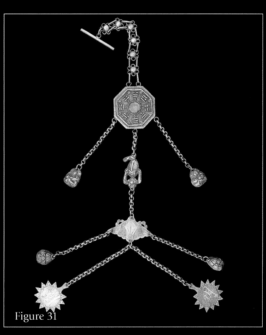

Figure 31

Figure 32

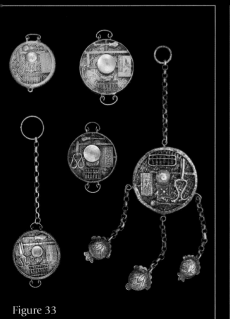

Figure 33

Figure 34

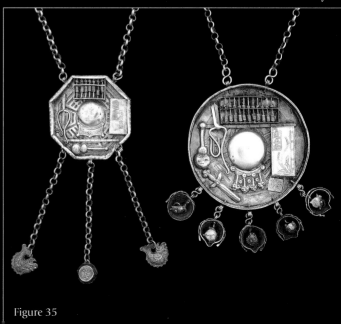

Figure 35

over the left shoulder and under the right arm. Many travelers wore four to twelve *ga'us* for protection on dangerous journeys.

Round *ga'us*, popular with monks as well as laymen, are usually covered with symbolic designs. Many have a center hole for a painted thangka. Every *ga'u* includes either a horizontal tube at the top or lugs on the side for a braided leather thong. In rare specimens—such as the one in Figure 10—a cord, complete with ornamental beads, still hangs from the wearable *ga'u*.

Rectangular *ga'us* with repoussé frames (Figure 11) held handpainted thangkas of guardian deities to ward off evil spirits.

An arched trefoil box shape, favored by Tibetan men, turned a *ga'u* into a shrine. The concavity would hold a tiny clay or metal god resting on cloth or a thangka. To create these *ga'us*, silversmiths scored the front, then turned the sheet of silver over and pounded repoussé designs into the back, and turned it back yet again to add decorative chasing. This process was repeated three to nine times. Men wore several of these flat-bottomed *ga'us* on long trips and set them up as an altar when resting. One shrine in Figure 12 is especially valuable because it includes an original hand-stitched protective leather casing.

In Figure 12, we also find an oval lozenge-shaped *ga'u*, probably worn by a woman, with a central chunk of coral and repoussé trefoil patterns. Figure 13 shows two *ga'us* featuring filigree work, stamped designs, and semi-precious stones. Women favored this style both as relic holders and jewelry. A girl's family gave her a *ga'u* as part of her dowry, but her husband added others if his status warranted it. The central stone represented the center of a lotus.

The face of a *ga'u* always features an elaborate design, and the sides are often decorated as well. In Figure 14, the Eight Buddhist Symbols—Wheel of Law, Conch Shell, Umbrella, Canopy, Lotus, Jar, Pair of Fish, and Endless Knot—appear in high relief on the top piece, while the lower item combines Tibetan foliate patterns with geometric schemes. Despite the loss of their relics and cords, the old Tibetan and Mongolian silver *ga'us* still fascinate with their unique beauty and intricate designs.

Protective Shrines, Scissors, and Hangings

In the Qing dynasty, a man going on a trip often hung a miniature shrine from his sash for protection. A shrine decorated a man's

Figure 36

everyday attire as well, but its importance increased on a long journey.

Each such replica featured either a single door that slid up and off (Figures 15 through 18) or two doors that spread open to reveal a tiny Buddha (Figure 19). Intricate enameling typically enhances the decorative images of the Eight Immortals, lotus leaves, magpies, plum blossoms, bamboo stalks, and bats. A miniature lion often posed protectively atop a shrine, safeguarding both the tiny temple and its owner. Sometimes the image of a goat-like creature reclined on the door. It might have represented either a sacrifice or a peace symbol. Bells to scare away evil spirits, charms of antique jade, or beads of carnelian or coral often dangled beneath a shrine.

Amulet chains typically held symbolic balls, babies, fruits, and—oddly enough—silver shears and water buckets. The tiny scissors in Figure 20 served to cut off contact with evil spirits. The buckets probably indicated prosperity, and so I imagine this amulet was a wedding gift, wishing the happy couple wealth, protection from harm, and the birth of many sons.

Figure 21 shows an elaborate hanging decoration with numerous redundant symbols. At the top, the mounted rider signifies a rise in rank. Following the chain, we find a large butterfly for longevity and two carp for abundance and marital bliss. The centerpiece might be either a stylized lotus for purity or a series of *ruyis* to give the owner anything he wishes. The plum blossoms promised longevity, while the symbols at the bottom—sword, lotus, umbrella, canopy, hand, and halberd—indicate a Buddhist owner. The hanging was probably presented to a young man for protection and good fortune, and might have been a wedding present.

Tripods

Thick-bodied bronze tripods assumed great importance during the Xia dynasty (2205-1766 B.C.), the Shang dynasty (1766-1121 B.C.), and the Zhou dynasty (1100-256 B.C.). The nine great tripods cast in the rule of Emperor Yu the Great (Xia dynasty) remain the most famous. Only a virtuous ruler could possess these treasures. If he became cruel or corrupt, the tripods would be transferred to a virtuous man, who would become the new monarch.

Craftsmen cast many tripods in addition to the famous nine. These three-legged bronzes, called *tings*, had both religious and practical significance. The simpler *tings* served as storage containers and—because the three legs fit easily over a fire—as cooking pots. The most elaborate ones were used in sacrifices to the gods. Beyond the visible, external ornamentation, the vessels contained writing on their inner walls. Some inscriptions included the name of the person who commissioned the *ting*, while others recorded history, Imperial orders, and contracts correcting boundaries.

In the Qing dynasty, silver tripod amulets represented a wish for wealth and protection from corruption. Typically given as presents to boys, young men, and bridegrooms, they came in many sizes. The usual fat-bodied tripod included two heavily ornamental handles and an inscription to the recipient. In Figure 22, the large tripod and the middle-sized one wished the owner five sons who would all achieve the highest grade on their civil service examinations. The smallest tripod offered a young boy protection, as well as the usual wish for wealth.

The large tripod in Figure 23 wishes the recipient a house full of jade and gold. Three animals adorn the front. In the center, we find what could be a pair of mandarin ducks (for conjugal bliss). Each side offers an image that looks like a deer (longevity). These double symbols and the inscription tell me the amulet was probably given to a young man about to be married.

The large urn in Figure 24 puzzles me because it contains the

Figure 37

"thirteen *tai-bao*" characters, indicating corrupt noblemen. Perhaps these characters had a different connotation in the Qing dynasty, or perhaps the amulet was meant to protect the wearer from such individuals.

Besides the three-dimensional amulets, boys received flat silver urns, such as those in Figure 25. The small one identifies the owner as a gift from Heaven and wishes him many successful sons. On the larger one, we find wishes for "abundant good fortune," for "everything the owner will ever want," and for the owner's eventual "rise like the sun."

Coin Amulets

Metal coins were first minted in China in the seventh century B.C., and later generations used them as talismans against disease-bearing demons, poverty, and other evils. The coins employed a square within a circle to symbolize the internal moral virtue of government officials. The rounded edge of the coin symbolized the official devotion to compromise and harmonious service: there were no sharp edges to menace the public.

A parent often hung a protective coin or string of coins around a young son's neck. The number of coins equaled the child's age up to fifteen years, by which time he'd supposedly passed the thirty dangerous barriers of life.

A silversmith often worked coin imagery into silver amulets for wealth, success, and safety. Figure 26 shows a boy's neck pendant consisting of a coin atop a moving horse. One side of the coin expresses a wish for the boy to make the highest grade on the civil service examinations, and the other side offers him a prayer for a hundred years of life. The swiftly running horse quite likely served to secure his rapid advancement and give him strength. The bats with the coin form a rebus for "blessings in front of your eyes." The most unusual specimen depicts Liu Hai with his three-legged toad, string of coins, and a deer for longevity.

A silversmith used repoussé to enhance the large coin sitting inside a silver ingot in Figure 27. Plum blossoms and the God of Longevity supplement the wish for prosperity. In Figure 28, we find a child sitting in an ingot, symbolizing fecundity and wealth. Singularly heavy, this amulet probably hung from a man's sash. In Figure 29, coins and ingots transform each sash hanging into an amulet for wealth. I purchased the two coral amulets, shaped like coins on the reverse—from an Inner Mongolian dealer.

The Eight Trigrams

Just as Western civilization employed sibyls, crystal-gazers, fortune-tellers, soothsayers, and augurs, the Chinese world used diviners to predict the future. A Qing dynasty diviner could help a person know the best time to open a business, choose a wife, bury a relative, or prepare for danger.

The Chinese art of divination centers on the Eight Trigrams, sometimes referred to as the Eight Diagrams. Their use was formalized in the Zhou dynasty by Wenwang, who wrote his famous *Book of Changes*—the *I Ching*—while a prisoner of the tyrant King Zhou Xin in 1144 B.C. Today, the *I Ching* enjoys tremendous popularity in both the East and the West.

According to legend, Emperor Fuxi, the first of the Three Divine Rulers who lived before 3000 B.C., devised the Eight Trigrams—combinations of broken and unbroken lines—while contemplating the shell of a tortoise. He thereby added a prophecy system to his list of inventions, which already included the cooking fire, hunting, fishing, marriage, and the domestication of animals.

The Eight Trigrams symbolize Heaven, Earth, Water, Fire, Lake, Wind, Thunder, and Mountains. The unbroken lines are male, the broken ones female. Often depicted with the yin-yang (male-female, Earth-Heaven, warm-cold, north-south) in the middle, the eight patterns may be configured to obtain the sixty-four hexagrams that constitute the text of Wenwang's oracle book. In Qing dynasty China, a man hung the silver Trigrams from his waist or around his neck, thus protecting himself from danger. Trigrams were also sewn to the garments of young boys.

The Eight Trigrams and the yin-yang embellish the large amulet in Figure 30. On the reverse side we find the symbols of the Daoist Eight Immortals—fan, sword, gourd, castanets, flute, flower basket, bamboo tube and rods, and the lotus. This amulet might have been worn by a wealthy nobleman, but a Daoist priest or a monk also used such an impressive piece for divination.

The amulet in Figure 31 shows the Trigrams on a waist hanging that also includes babies (fertility) and Liu Hai's three-legged toad with plum blossoms (longevity). The three emblems beneath the toad combine to form the diploma of a well-educated man. On the back of the amulet we find calligraphy predicting that the owner will have a great career, triumph in his civil service examinations, and enjoy a lasting, happy marriage.

The Trigrams also appear on divination amulets used for healing in Tibet. Usually made of heavy paktong, these amulets always include the twelve animals of the zodiac in a circle around the Trigrams (Figure 32). The "magic square" in the center contains nine numerals arranged so that every line (vertical, horizontal, or diagonal) adds up to fifteen. The outer rim incorporates symbols of the All Powerful Ten.

Occupation Amulets

The Chinese fascination with occupation imagery figured prominently in a boy's first birthday celebration. The big day usually began with the maternal grandmother presenting the baby with new clothes she had embroidered herself. Before the feasting began, the boy's relatives lit candles and incense before a statue of the Goddess of Mercy, and they placed a large woven bamboo sieve on a table, filling it with emblems representing various careers: a set of money-scales, a pair of shears, a foot-measure, a pen, an ink-slab, a book, toy weapons, an abacus, musical instrument, a silver or gold ornament, and an official jade seal. The parents set the baby, dressed in his new clothes, inside the sieve. The tension mounted as the guests anxiously watched his reaction. If the baby picked up the pen, ink slab, or book, he was destined to become a scholar. If he selected a weapon, he would become a soldier. If he chose the abacus, money scales, or ornament, great wealth awaited him. The shears foretold a tailor, and the foot-measure, a shoemaker.

The occupation amulets employed largely the same symbol system as the first-birthday emblems. They typically hung from a man's sash to bring good fortune in one's career and amity with fellow professionals. The amulets in Figures 33 and 35 include images of an abacus, a money-scale, a foot-measure, a round shiny mirror, a pair of shears, a sword, and a shape that looks like a musical instrument. The backs of some occupation amulets resemble a woven sieve, while others display the twelve animals of the zodiac encircling the Trigrams (Figure 34). Still other backs display the yin-yang and Trigrams (Figure 36). Most of the smaller amulets appear gilded. Many emerge in the Shanghai area, China's traditional center of commerce.

The beautiful enameled silver piece in Figure 37 shows a member of the Emperor's entourage with an inscription reading "First Rank Official in the Court." Presented to a wealthy young boy, this amulet wished him success on his civil service examinations. The images on such pieces were believed to influence the future: once the man passed his civil service examinations, and received his official post, he could continue to advance through the government—the amulets in Figure 38 depict such an official "stepping up" and achieving higher and higher rank.

Drums

In ancient China, drumbeats paced warriors marching into battle and gave them courage. In China today, drums are pounded on festive occasions. For example, the "Drum of Great Peace" is always struck on the New Year in Beijing.

In Figure 39, the flowers on the drum barrel symbolize the four seasons—peony (spring), lotus (summer), chrysanthemum (autumn), and plum (winter)—and wish the recipient wealth and distinction on a festive occasion. This piece might have been presented to a young man as a good luck charm before he took his civil service examinations, as an award for passing them, or as a wedding gift. The silver pomegranates dangling on the bottom wish him many sons.

Figure 38

Marital Happiness Amulets

The two silver amulets in Figure 40 were undoubtedly wedding presents. In the three-dimensional piece, the double happiness symbol is encased in silver about half a centimeter thick. The bell at the bottom tolls to frighten away demons before they can cause discord between the newlyweds. On the flat amulet, we find symbols for double happiness and longevity above an inscription wishing the couple one hundred years of wedded bliss. A row of suspended silver peaches offers a wish for immortality. The peaches clang together to frighten evil apparitions.

In Figure 41, we see two waist hangings that might have been wedding gifts. On the heavily-gilded piece, a double fish for conjugal bliss, is joined by three other symbols: a butterfly sipping nectar from a Buddhist endless knot, a musical stone for uprightness, and a dragonfish for passing the examinations with distinction. On the second example, also Buddhist, the two fish represent a balance of opposites, and surround a vase filled with a lotus, an endless knot, and a small canopy.

Hakka Women

Persecuted by several dynasties, the Hakka, a sub-group of the Han whose name means "guest people," were forced to emigrate from the province of Henan in the Yellow River plains of northern

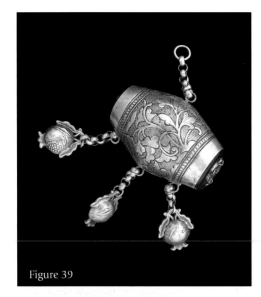

Figure 39

Figure 40

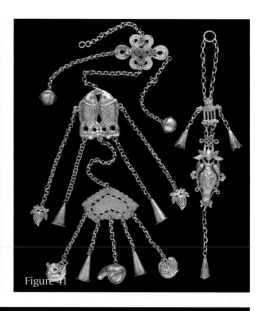

Figure 41

Figure 42

Figure 43

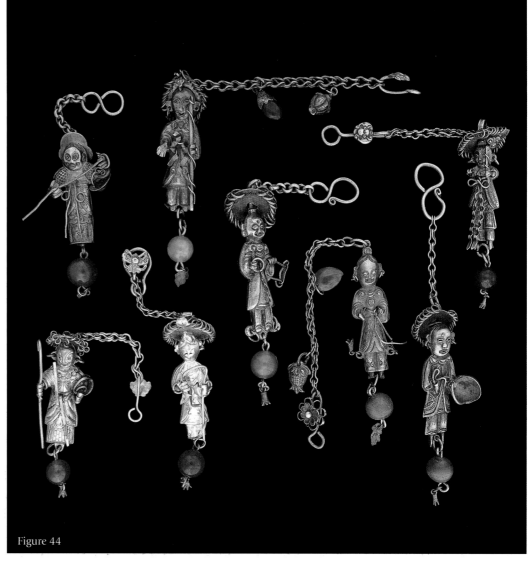

Figure 44

China to Guangdong, Szechwan, the new Territories, and other areas in southern China. By the Qing dynasty, many Hakka were reduced to being peddlers. Others labored as migrant farm workers until they could afford their own land. Many Chinese regarded the Hakka as clannish, thrifty, loyal to one another, and aggressive.

A Hakka man often ventured to another country for better wages, leaving his wife to run the farm and weave the fancy silk ribbons, which she sold along with her produce and livestock. Celebrated for their hard work and home remedies, Hakka women did not bind their feet or breasts, did not prostitute themselves, and they never hired wetnurses for their children. The Hakka women were also renowned as warriors. During the 1850 Taiping revolution, led by a Hakka man named Hong Xiuguan, Hong's sister fought by his side against the Manchus. She also unbound the feet of all the women who came under Taiping rule during the war.

Often called the "only feminist symbol in China," the Hakka women—rendered in silver—represented courage, perseverance, and industriousness. Such an amulet was probably worn to encourage diligence and insure success and wealth.

A silver Hakka woman typically carries a basket of fish or other produce on her arm, along with a fishing pole or a shepherd's staff (Figures 42 through 45). Strips of curled silver represent the silk ribbons a woman wove to earn extra money. Minuscule earrings, bracelets, and a fancy collar adorn the standard representation. Also typical is the fringed, circular "cool hat." In real life, the *leung mo* is a large woven straw hat with a black cloth fringe and a hole in the center. A silversmith used tiny silver circles to represent the fringe.

Whether simple or detailed, each Hakka woman wears a knee-length tunic coat over long trousers, or a long skirt. (The word for "trousers" in the Hakka language is *fu*, a homonym of the word for "good fortune.") Because Hakka women labored on a farm, they did not bind their feet. Major discrepancies exist in the feet of the silver miniatures in Figure 45. In some cases, the feet look relatively large. In other specimens, the feet seem bound and encased in tiny lotus slippers, thus betraying a gap in the silversmith's knowledge.

The facial expressions exhibit enormous variety. For certain figures, holes represent the eyes and mouth. In other cases, the smith used simple outlines. Some Hakka women appear to have their eyes closed. A few possess fat cheeks and happy expressions; occasionally one sees stoicism or even anger. Not every smith had the ability to depict lifelike features, and it must have been particularly difficult to render facial expressions on such a small scale.

Baskets

A basket filled with fruits or flowers is the symbol for Lan Caihe, one of the Eight Immortals. The patron saint of gardeners and florists, Lan Caihe wanders through the streets warning everyone that life is short. Eventually, the basket evolved into an emblem of abundance, and silver basket amulets were worn by Qing dynasty people to generate wealth, fertility, success, happiness, and longevity.

The baskets held not only fruits and flowers, but also symbolic bats, coins, or even children. As you can see, the amulets in Figure 46 strongly resemble the ones used as grooming kit centerpieces, and the two sorts of artifacts might have been interchangeable.

Did these silver amulets really bring their owners wealth, success, health, happiness, and longevity? In some cases, they surely did, given the known power of positive thinking and faith in charms. The modern aficionado of beautiful ornaments can be happy that the Chinese believed in the efficacy of amulets, for this belief engendered many wonderful examples of the silversmith's art.

Figure 45

Figure 46

The year is 1820. A wooden shanty in the poorest section of Beijing. Weiyuan huddles on the edge of the *k'ang*, wishing she had enough firewood to heat the surface. She clutches daughter against her breast to share her body's warmth and nourishment. Tears stream down her face and her black hair hangs loosely over the thin, worn blanket around her shoulders. The baby squirms and suckles noisily as Weiyuan rocks back and forth in distress.

"How could he, Lili?" she asks the baby. "How could your father take my silver hairpin? My parents, poor peasants that they were, saved for months to buy that for my dowry. So beautiful with its symbols for double happiness. Now it has gone to buy opium and I have nothing to pawn for food or wood."

Across town, in a two-story mansion near Liulichang Street, Kemei Wu watches her reflection in the stand-up mirror on her jewelry box as a servant waits beside her with a large bowl of towels soaked in warm water. Another servant, an old woman who was her personal *amah*—maidservant—when Kemei was a child, covers her face with the towels. When Kemei's cheeks tingle, the aged servant removes the towels and coats her mistress's face with a honey and perfume mixture before applying the fine rice-powder makeup. She outlines each eyebrow with the contours of a willow leaf, then smoothes rouge on her high cheekbones.

Kemei herself applies a touch of red to her lower lip. She smiles in satisfaction as the old *amah* twists and coils her long, thick hair into an elaborate chignon. She holds the hair in place with one hand as the other reaches into the drawer of the jewelry box. Silver hairpins tipped with carved jade or coral hung with beads, and gilded-silver hairpins decorated with real kingfisher feathers, eventually cover Kemai's head like a crown. She moves her head slightly to allow the pearls and coral strands to quiver seductively. The servants smile. Both are satisfied that Kemei will present the proper image of a court official's wife when her husband's cousin arrives for an afternoon visit.

Opposite: A Han woman is bedecked with various hair adornments.

Besides their obvious functions as adornments, a woman's hairpins in the Qing dynasty advertised her status and naturally represented a large portion of her dowry. To announce her passage into adulthood, the parents of a minority girl might give her a single hairpin, a *ji*, when she turned fifteen. Within other minority groups, parents presented their daughter with a hairpin for her dowry.

Noblewomen wore much of their wealth in their hair. Hairpins of every size and description have survived from the Qing dynasty. For weddings and special occasions, the wealthiest and highest in rank also wore tiaras and coronets covered with iridescent blue kingfisher feathers and metal ornaments containing semi-precious stones or Peking glass.

Hair adornment has a long history in China. In the Han dynasty (206 B.C. to A.D. 220), men wore either solid gold bar-type hairpins or "white brush" hairpins, which resembled the calligraphy brushes they would slip into their hair when thinking. Women in the Imperial household wore solid gold hairpins, including the *buyao*, a hair ornament that quivered when one walked. Not until the Tang dynasty (A.D. 618-907) did silver gain importance for adornment. During this era, Imperial household silver and gilded-silver hairpins were much longer than in the Han dynasty—twenty-five to thirty-five centimeters in many cases—and often included Buddhist symbols in repoussé. With the Song dynasty (A.D. 960-1279), we start to see shorter single-pronged and double-pronged gilded-silver hairpins, rounded diadems, and sets of as many as eleven hairpins, which formed a kind of crown when worn together.

By the Qing dynasty, the wives of officials, scholars, and successful merchants lavished fortunes on hair adornments. Distinct hairstyles, each necessitating a characteristic hairpin design, evolved among the different ethnic groups, and silversmiths gloried in the trend, fashioning some of the most elaborate bodily adornments in the history of China.

In Figures 1 and 7, solid silver repoussé pieces display emblems for fertility, happiness, wealth, and marital bliss. The single-pronged hairpins were called *zan*; the double-pronged were called *chai*. Many symbols combine to form even deeper meanings (Figure 1). The butterfly sipping nectar from a flower, for example, indicates pleasurable marital sex. The lotus, a symbol of purity amidst corruption (as well as fertility if shown with a seedpod), is ubiquitous, likewise the vase (indicating safety and peace) and the peony (wealth and distinction). The entwined lozenges represent a double victory; this piece would have made an

Figure 1

appropriate dowry or wedding present—as would the piece featuring a baby. Hopeful bridegrooms proffered pre-nuptial presents in pairs, and I suspect this illustration displays such an offering.

One of the most unusual single-pronged hairpins that I have ever seen is the gilded-silver artifact in the upper left-hand corner of Figure 7. Its owner probably ascribed medicinal powers to this piece. Sculpted creatures representing the Five Poisons—venom of frog, snake, centipede, spider, and scorpion—combine to counteract the often fatal bites and stings of their real-life counterparts.

Figure 2 illustrates a number of single-pronged silver hairpins tipped with carved carnelian. Some are enameled, others gilded. Blue remained the favored color for enameling in the Qing dynasty. I suspect that the carnelian carvings represent red flames. In Buddhist belief, red represents fire, and blue depicts the sky. Combining the two creates a fusion of natural energies.

The jade carvings on Qing dynasty silver hairpins boasts tremendous stylistic diversity (Figure 3). In earlier periods, only

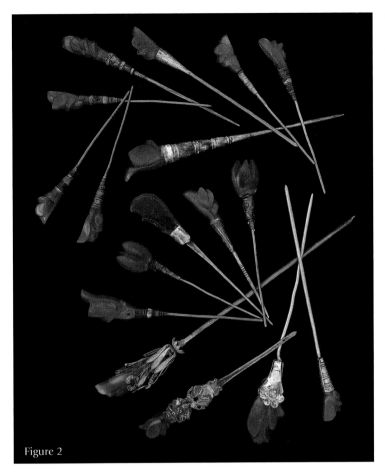

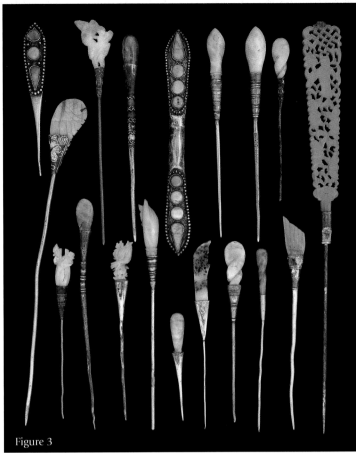

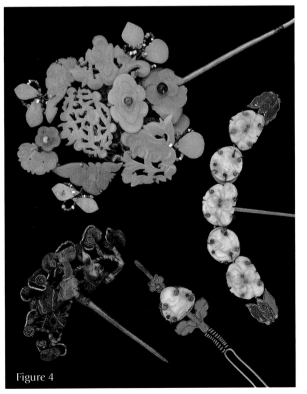

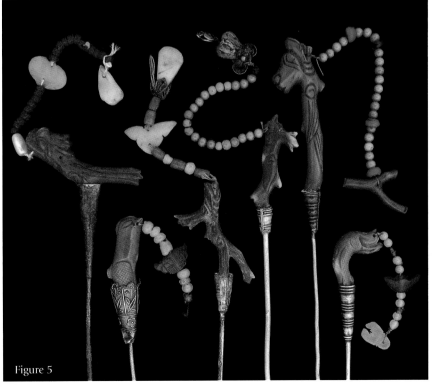

Figure 2

Figure 3

Figure 4

Figure 5

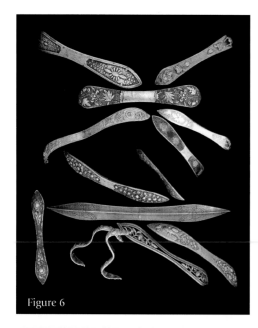

Figure 6

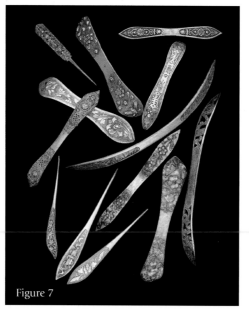

Figure 7

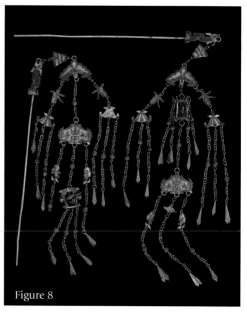

Figure 8

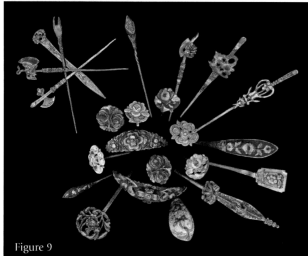

Figure 9

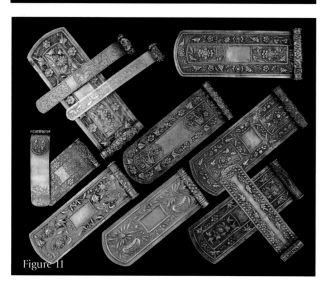

Figure 11

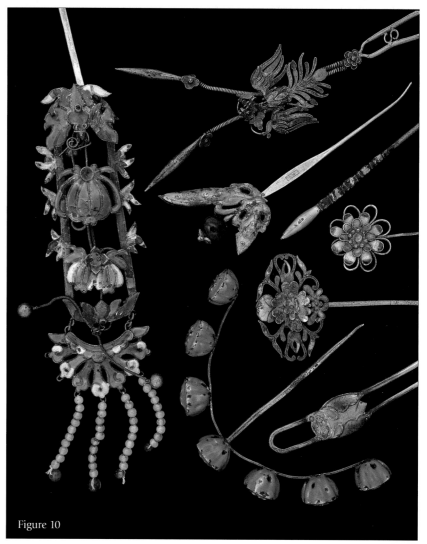

Figure 10

high-ranking officials received permission to wear jade, and it still denoted status in the Qing era. According to popular belief, jade protected the wearer from evil and secured good health. The color of the jade varied from piece to piece. Over a hundred different shades of green jade have allegedly appeared in China over the centuries.

By covering metal templates with jade and beads, artisans could create especially elaborate hair adornments. In Figure 4 intricately carved jade flowers, butterflies, and Buddhas are combined in ways thought to be auspicious and even sublime. Many such pieces also incorporate kingfisher feathers.

The Chinese believed that coral brought strength and good fortune and had a favorable effect on menstruation. Figure 5 illustrates how artisans could turn Italian coral into dragons and phoenixes. The artisan usually hung a single strand of coral beads, turquoise beads, or pearls from the creature's mouth. Since custom dictated that a true lady never lets her hairpins sway, a noblewoman learned to walk without moving her head.

In Figures 6 and 7 we find double-tipped hairpins, worn by the Han and certain minorities, which slid through the coiled center of the chignon (hair bun) to expose both carved ends. Longevity symbols, the endless knot, and the yin-yang often decorate these pieces, as do the plum blossom, pomegranate, and butterfly. The two ends usually mirror each other. Some designs include books and other emblems of scholarship, reminding us that wealthy young girls often received tutoring at home—although such a hairpin might also indicate the owner's status as the wife of a scholar.

Enameled silver hairpins enjoyed great popularity in the Qing dynasty. Early enameling employed crushed semi-precious stones, which added weight and stability to the pieces. The two similar pins in Figure 8 were probably sold as a pair. In one, the bird swings beneath an arch; in the other, the bird is caged. How enthralling it must have been to see the wearer walk gracefully across a room without letting the dangles sway. Other images in this group include dragons, musical stones, longevity symbols, and the double carp: I suspect these pieces were part of a dowry. If that was the case, the two birds might indicate the marital bond.

Slightly less elaborate enameled hairpins appear in Figures 9 and 10. Various shades of blue, green, and yellow predominate.

Figure 12

(Red quickly turned brown or maroon, and so it was rarely used.) The miniature weapons on the hairpins in Figure 9 represented protection from evil for Daoists, the piercing of ignorance for Buddhists. In Figure 10, the largest piece has retained its strands of pearls, as well as the coiled antennae of the butterfly. The solid diadem of lotus buds reminds us of the Song dynasty hairpin sets. Silversmiths loved creating enameled birds, flowers, and insects—especially the cicada—all of which offered opportunities for a splash of color. In time, most of the enameled hairpins chipped, but still offer hints of their former glory.

Flat pins added width to a Manchu woman's informal wing-tipped hairdo, while a smaller style adorned the coiffures of the Han. The intricate repoussé work in Figures 11 and 12 suggest a wealthy owner. The plain silver specimens usually exhibit detailed floral designs around a plain center. The gilded-silver ones display more refined designs. The images include Court officials, the Daoist Immortals, symbols for the Immortals, and the twin *Hehe*.

Many hairpins incorporated the traditional *ruyi* scepter, the symbol for fulfilling wishes. Most of the examples in Figure 13

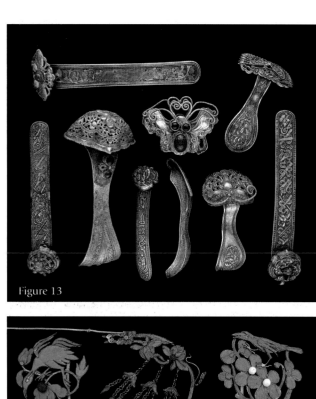

Figure 13

Figure 14

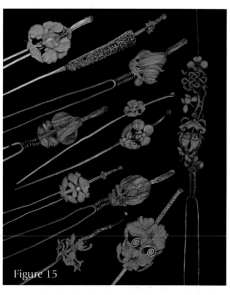

Figure 15

Figure 16

Figure 18

Figure 17

appear to have been dowry or wedding presents, as they typically exhibit the double happiness and longevity characters, the endless knot, the swastika, Liu Hai or the *Hehe*, the symbols of the Immortals, plus the butterfly or peaches. The large bulbous tops, which often include Peking glass or semi-precious stones, were usually soldered in place. In some cases, the tops actually unhooked. This detachability made the pieces easier to insert and also, simplified storage.

In Figure 14 we find elaborate gilded-silver hairpins. Double fish surround a vase filled with halberds and a musical stone for success and good fortune. Beneath the vase, we find a butterfly and double coins, bestowing conjugal bliss and wealth. The endless knot in the piece on the right curls in a *ruyi* shape. The pearls in the piece at the bottom might have lost their luster, but the gilded bat still protects the tourmaline stone. On the left, a small-carved monkey slides up and down a hairpin that also functioned as an earpick.

In Figures 15 through 19 we see silver or gilded-silver hairpins covered with actual feathers of the tiny kingfisher bird, indigenous to the mountainous regions of southern China. We know the Chinese used such feathers for decoration as far back as the Song dynasty, and fine examples of gold and kingfisher coronets have been recovered from tombs dating to the Ming dynasty. Over the years, the artisans found ways to incorporate kingfisher feathers into every form of jewelry—hairpins, earrings, bracelets, brooches, and even headdresses—as well as furniture, sedan chains, huge screens, panoramic pictures, and bedspreads. By the eighteenth and nineteenth centuries, the tiny feathers adorned hairpins worn by the aristocracy, the wealthier commoners, and even visitors from abroad.

When making a kingfisher hairpin, the silversmith first created the gilded-silver design, then edged each section with a thin frame. Next, the smith clipped the tiny feathers removed from the back and wings of the bird—the only iridescent blue ones—to fit the spaces within the metal frames. Finally, he fixed the feathers in place using the thinnest imaginable layer of adhesive. The completed pieces depicted flowers, birds, bats, fruits, insects, calligraphy, still life forms, and even tiny figures. Some were convex, others concave. On many artifacts, jade, carnelian, Peking glass, coral, or pearls enhanced the natural blue of the feathers. In

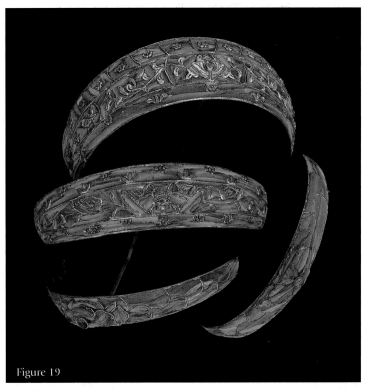
Figure 19

the headdresses, mirrors formed the calyx of flowers to frighten away evil spirits.

Some of the most remarkable kingfisher pieces featured minuscule springs to which the artisan attached silver insects, flowers, and even fish. These tiny hangings trembled as the wearer walked. In Figure 18 the older hairpins have lost many feathers, but the extraordinary efforts of the silversmiths—who spent hours, even days fashioning a single piece—lingers in the designs. As you can see, a few hairpins also include carved and painted bone.

A small diadem hairpin, representing royal dignity and authority, could slide into the top of an elaborate hairdo, where it became a tiara. In Figure 19 the smallest tiara (with a layered flower), measures just ten centimeters by one centimeter, while the largest—fourteen centimeters—contains gilded flowers and birds set against kingfisher feathers.

In Figure 20 we find a coronet of kingfisher feathers on gilded silver, probably worn by a noblewoman on her wedding day. Poorer women settled for tiaras with the feathers glued to cardboard frames, but the expensive coronets had gilded-silver or gold frames. On the back, huge double happiness symbols surround a lotus blossom and a stack of books: the books might indicate that the bride was literate, as many noblewomen were in

Figure 20

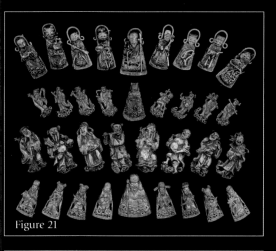

Figure 21

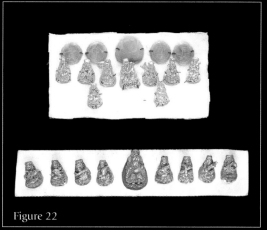

Figure 22

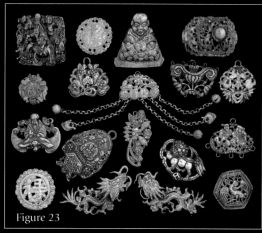

Figure 23

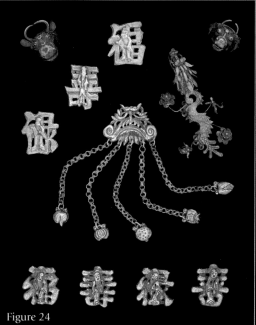

Figure 24

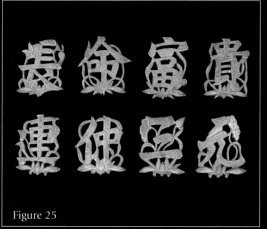

Figure 25

Figure 26

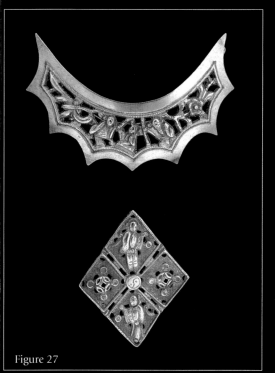

Figure 27

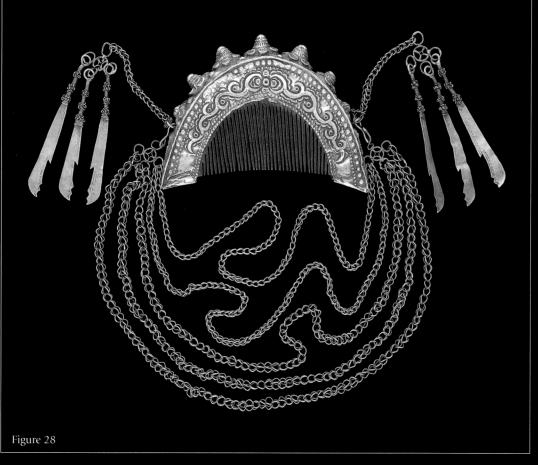

Figure 28

Figure 29

130

this period. On the sides, we find two butterflies for longevity, two carp for fertility, two dragons for royalty and fertility, mirrors to frighten away evil sprits, and swastikas for infinity and the resignation of the spirit that you find in the heart of Buddha. The top displays a plum blossom for longevity and sexual pleasure. The central front jewel is damaged, but I believe this is a *mani*, a wish-granting gem, symbol of the Buddhist trinity. Old carnelian, pearls, and coral beads highlight the blue of this extraordinary headpiece.

The last workshop to produce kingfisher pieces in Canton closed in the 1930's. By that time, the unfortunate species had been hunted to the brink of extinction in China. Happily, the government reintroduced the birds into China, and today they are reasonably plentiful. We can all hope this does not cause a resurgence in silver pieces adorned with real feathers.

Figure 30

With their elaborate hairstyles and hairpins, women wore few decorative hats in the Qing dynasty. A boy, however, was adorned in elaborately embroidered caps from infancy through his fifth year. The maternal grandmother made most of these caps, decorating them with silver amulets for both protection and status.

Figure 21 depicts four sets of silver baby hat amulets, which also decorated the hats and headbands of women in certain minorities. In each collection, we find the Eight Immortals, and occasionally, the God of Longevity (or a replacement—second row). Each Immortal represents a different quality; and each carries a characteristic emblem: a bamboo tube, a pair of Chinese castanets, a fan, a gourd, a sword, a flute, a flower basket, or a lotus blossom. Certain Immortals were associated with more than one artifact. For instance, He Xiangu, the patron saint of housewives, might be shown with either a lotus blossom or a flywhisk. This convention occasionally makes it difficult to determine whether a set is complete.

In today's antique silver market, the Eight Immortals, along with the God of Longevity, still appear as sets sewn to thick cardboard. In Figure 22, the gilded-silver set, accompanied by jade carvings, was surely made for a nobleman's son. The heavy silver sets, though more numerous, were often beyond the reach of the lower classes as well. Cheap, flimsy metal depictions of the Eight Immortals often adorn baby hats found in China today. These

pieces contain no silver, and often have an orange tint. The authentic antique silver pieces remain heavy and sturdy, and they do not bend easily.

Figure 23 illustrates artifacts that might have been sewn to the hats of either boys or women. In the upper left-hand corner, Zhang Guolao rides his donkey through a crowd. The multi-layered flower in the upper right undoubtedly adorned a woman's hat; the raised lip suggests that it was covered with kingfisher feathers. The God of Longevity, on the left, and the twin *Hehe* (on the far right) are skillful depictions of these popular characters. Such silver figures also graced the hats, aprons, and sashes of certain minorities, including the Yi in southwestern China.

The three-dimensional dragon in Figure 24 probably adorned a Han noblewoman's wedding coronet, as few commoners could have afforded such detailed pieces. The cows surely embellished a young boy's hat. In this illustration we also find the Fu Lu Shou (representing longevity, happiness, and good fortune) depicted on calligraphy characters.

Calligraphy wishing the wearer wealth, good fortune, longevity, and happiness often adorned hats for both women and children (Figure 25). In Figure 26, the Eight Immortals ride their designated steeds. The depictions of the elephant and tiger are particularly fascinating because the silversmith almost certainly never saw such animals. The artisan probably worked entirely from his imagination—as he surely did in the case of the qilin.

Figure 27 displays two repoussé barrettes with hand-twisted wire clasps. The first is convex and seems to fit under a bun. The second slips through the hair vertically. Both were probably decorative rather than utilitarian.

The minorities of southwestern China loved to groom and ornament their hair with silver combs. In Figure 28, a silver band covers a comb of bamboo. Rows of silver chains and six swords dangle from the comb. The scabbards might have functioned as hairpins, such as we see in Figure 29. The comb in the bottom specimen is solid silver, decorated with a repoussé top, and bent with age and use, as are the three in Figure 30.

During the Qing dynasty an official's coat often hid his Mandarin squares and belt plaque, so he needed something else to advertise his rank. Colorful hat spheres were the answer. Depending on the official's rank, the sphere might be coral, sapphire, lapis, moonstone, gilt, or Peking glass (this last often valued higher than semi-precious stones). Figure 31 shows a red glass sphere. Worn atop an official's informal hat, the sphere rested between a gilded base and a gilded top. Also called "Mandarin buttons", the spheres became mandatory for high officials in 1727.

The small silver finials in Figure 31 probably adorned the hats of young boys slated to become scholars. Scholar-officials wore finials several times this size. The example in the center depicts the treasures of the scholar, while the others feature an eagle, a tiger, and a person with a lotus blossom.

A full sized gilded-silver hat finial, worn on the crown of an official's hat for ceremonial occasions, appears in Figure 32. Designs in high relief cover the item's spherical base. A bulbous section, inlaid with a blue glass bead, surmounts the base, atop of which sits a section with a semi-precious stone. On the summit rests a tall gilt spike, replacing the usual jewel of rank. This hat finial was probably worn for official banquets and public ceremonies by a successful examination candidate who had not yet been given an official appointment.

Figure 33 shows an "eagle hat," its tips upturned like wings, which represented the lofty heights that the young male wearer could attain by study. The front displays eight silver Gods, an embroidered vase with three halberds, a musical stone, fish, flowers, and a longevity symbol.

Figure 31

Figure 32

The black silk hat in Figure 34 exemplifies the "open crown" design, characterized by a hole on the top. A mother preferred this style for her infant. Besides a wind flap to protect the back of the baby's neck, this example also features silver images of the Eight Immortals and Shouxing, the God of Longevity.

Figure 35 offers an unusual blue silk "eight segment" hat. The artisan fashioned the crown, with its center shaped like a lotus blossom, from eight segments, each embroidered with the

Figure 33

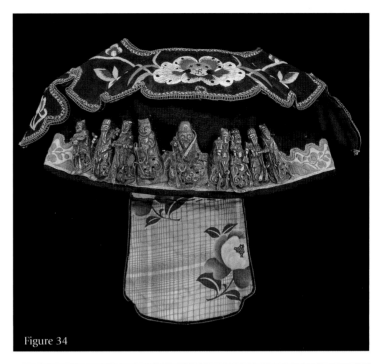

Figure 34

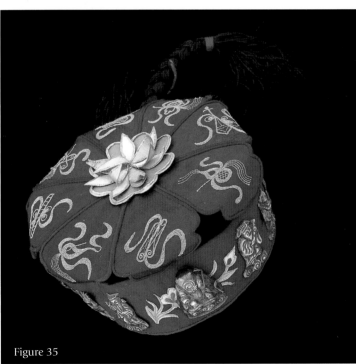

Figure 35

Figure 36

emblem of an Immortal. Silver figures of the Immortals with the God of Longevity decorate the brim.

Figures 36 and 37 depict a minority boy's hat from southwestern China. Amulets of low grade silver including bells, appear on the front, back, and tips of the wind flaps. Note the kingfisher feather ornaments. The central silver piece, a circular tiger, offered protection. The wearer probably needed less than usual, since the movements of any child wearing this noisy hat would have been easy to trace.

Figure 38 depicts the silversmith's art at its sparest. The three small silver lions on the front of this child's hat are elegant in their simplicity. The hat in Figures 39 and 40 features a tiger with teeth and eyes blazing. An imitation "official's sphere" surmounts this appealing article. An amulet with scissors (to cut through evil) and bells (to frighten evil away) hangs down the back.

Bai minority women's hats from Yunnan Province in southwestern China appear in Figures 41 and 42. Each back resembles the tail of a bird, which is why such hats are sometimes called "phoenix hats" or "bird hats." Silver amulets cover these artifacts in seemingly random fashion: semi-circles, dragons, qilin, dragonfish, calligraphy, Immortal figures, and multi-layered flowers. On Bai hats such as these, the artisan often left the paper backing beneath the sewn-on amulets, perhaps to keep the rough edges of the silver from tearing the cloth. Four cowry shells crown each hat in Figure 41; in both cases, an elaborate silver piece containing Peking glass or semi-precious stones adorns the front. It must have been amazing to see hundreds of Bai women wearing such hats at major festivals.

Figure 42 also includes a headband with silver representations of the Laughing Buddha and several lions. This decoration was worn by a minority woman, or possibly, a girl.

While a hat indicated a man's rank in the Qing dynasty, silver or gilded-silver hair adornments—decorated with jade, coral, carnelian, or kingfisher feathers—denoted the status of a Han, Manchu, Mongol, and minority woman. These artifacts brought prestige and security into their lives. Today, they bring beauty and aesthetic pleasure into ours.

Figure 37

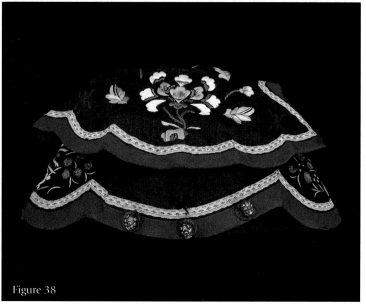

Figure 38

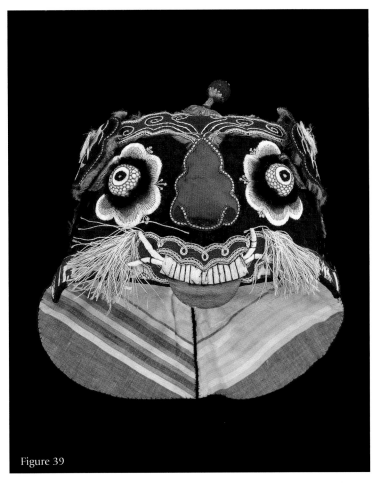

Figure 39

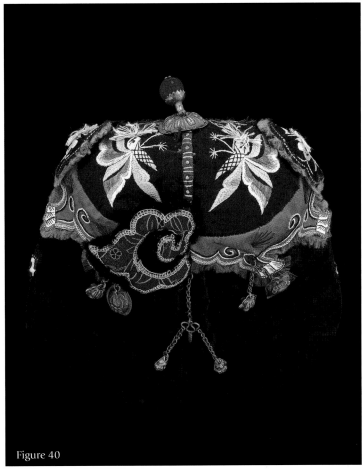

Figure 40

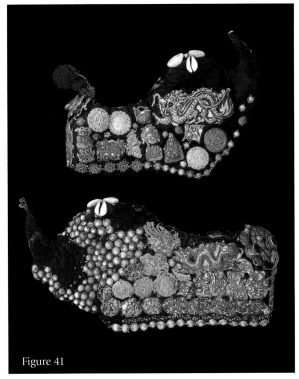

Figure 41

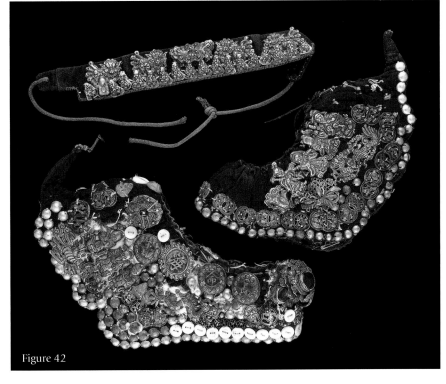

Figure 42

136

Try to imagine a suit without pockets, and you will appreciate a major challenge that a man faced in the Qing dynasty. His long flowing robe and short coat lacked any carrying compartments, even though this was an era when a man hauled around much more than a wallet and a set of keys. A typical set of male accessories included money, a fan, an eating kit, grooming tools, a personal seal, a pen, a fragrance carrier, a tobacco pipe, a snuff bottle, a medicine receptacle, a spectacles case, and a mustache comb.

Some of these accouterments had their own embroidered pouches; others hung from chains or cords. Both the pouches and the freely swinging items were attached to a sash of cloth, leather, and other flexible material. Connectors included metal rings, metal plaques, and silver and leather chatelaines. A pouch or artifact could also hang from a cord strung under and over a cloth sash and counterweighted by a toggle of metal or carved from wood, horn, bone, ivory, jade, or other semi-precious stones.

A particularly long sash of tightly woven silk, also called a *chaodai*, ("girdle") encircled the waist of the average Imperial Court member and scholar-official. The Emperor and his descendants preferred yellow, a nobleman wore red, and the Mandarin class blue or blue-black. Four elaborate plaques—gold or jade for the Imperial Court, silver for Mandarin officials—were strung to the sash. On two of the four plaques, silk ribbons or decorative kerchiefs hung from metal rings. The other two plaques held the accessories.

The commoner preferred especially strong material for his sash, such as woven hemp or horsehair covered with cloth. In an emergency, the sash could actually replace a broken bridle for the nomads. A Manchu, Mongol, and Tibetan nobleman favored a leather sash.

Eating Kits

The Chinese word for chopsticks, *kawaitsu,* literally means "quick ones," which translated to "Chop" in Pidgin English and later became the English term "chopsticks." Invented by the Chinese long before the Qing era, chopsticks were a fundamental utensil. *Kawaitsu* and a carving knife together constituted the basic eating ensemble. These implements lent themselves to storage in a cylindrical wooden sheath, and such an assemblage came to be called an eating kit.

A perforated metal template recessed near the top of the cylinder held the knife and chopsticks in place. The artisan might carve small compartments into the sheath for ivory toothpicks and earpicks.

A metal ring on the cylinder held a chain for securing the kit to the sash plaque (Figures 1 through 9). Many kits employed a second ring for a heavy tassel (Figures 3, 4, and 9).

The knife handle, which protruded from the template, often echoed the decoration on the sheath. Carved of bone, wood, ivory, horn, or jade, a handle usually terminated in a tip of silver.

Nomadic tribesmen in Manchuria, Mongolia, northern China, and Tibet wore utilitarian and beautiful eating kits as early as the Song dynasty. During the Qing era, their popularity increased until their heyday in the eighteenth and nineteenth centuries. The portraits in *Views of 18th Century China* include an infantry soldier, an Imperial purveyor, a tracker, a standard bearer, and a Mandarin's secretary, each wearing an eating kit on his sash.

As you can see in Figure 1 through 9, the wooden sheath was typically decorated with reinforcing bands of silver. In Figure 9, we find lighter, more delicate eating kits. The one on the left is tortoiseshell; the one on the right is sharkskin. Han or Manchu officials probably used these kits, as they seem too fragile for military or nomadic use.

After examining the repoussé on an eating kit, one may conjecture about the original owner. In Figure 3, the top silver overlay features a lotus blossom (symbol of purity amidst corruption) and an Indian *garuda* with wings and serpents coiling from his head (which for the Tibetan offered protection from disease). On either side of the *garuda* are symbols for the scholar. On the bottom overlay, we find the Chinese dragon protecting a home, a fish symbolizing abundance, and waves to represent the owner rising to an important official position. The owner of this eating kit evidently valued scholarly pursuits and high rank.

Certain motifs appear more frequently than others on the silver overlays. Geometric designs (Figures 1 and 5), dragons (Figures 2 and 4), the *garuda* (Figure 3), and two dragons fighting over the pearl of potentiality (Figure 6) were all popular. Chinese

Figure 1

art requires borders for completeness, and the basic border design, the "thunder pattern," embellished many sets. Small silver bats or butterflies with coins appear on the reverse of many eating kit sheaths.

Semi-precious stones embellish the silver on both Mongol and Tibetan kits. Green turquoise often indicates a Mongol set. The Tibetans preferred deep blue turquoise. The chunk of coral sometimes found on an eating kit might bear a hole through the middle, evidence of a past life as a trade bead.

The eating kit in Figure 7 includes a qilin for wisdom and success, a dragon for vigor and vitality, a fan for professional attainment, and a conch shell for victory. Quite possibly a high ranking military official owned this kit. The coral suggests either a Tibetan or Mongol owner.

An unusual ivory-and-silver eating kit appears in Figure 8. The repoussé overlay bears a stylized dragon and is studded with light coral and malachite cabochons. Ivory chopsticks and a rosewood-handled knife complete this elaborate set, which must have belonged to a member of the nobility.

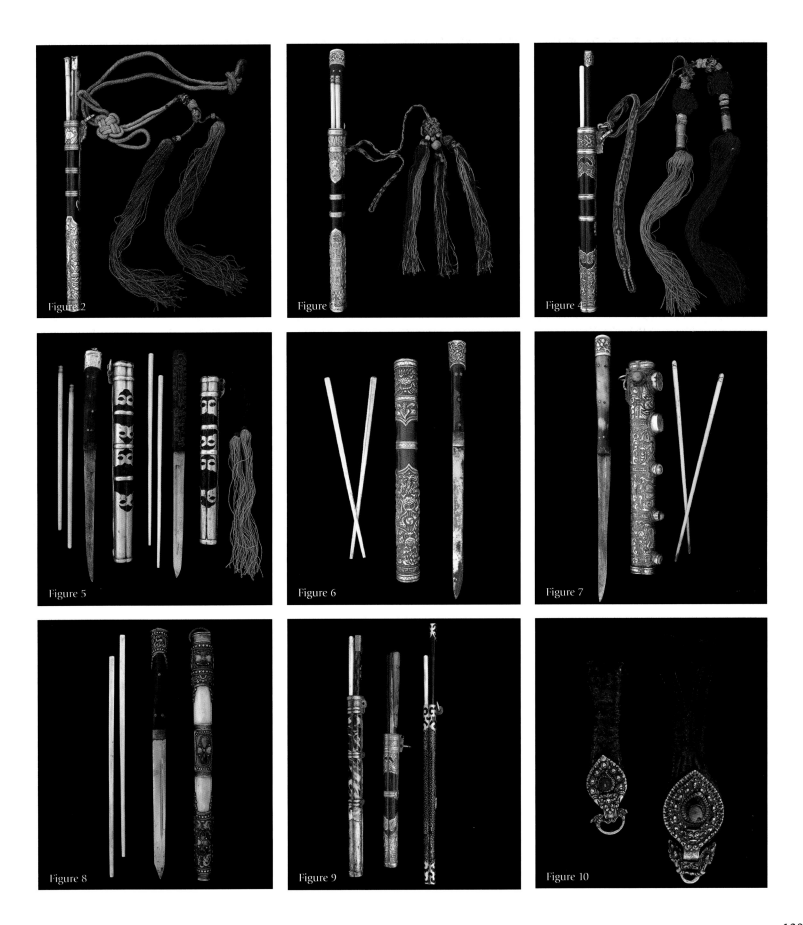

Figure 2

Figure 3

Figure 4

Figure 5

Figure 6

Figure 7

Figure 8

Figure 9

Figure 10

Chatelaines

In the context of Qing era personal adornment, a "chatelaine" is a large silver-and-leather clasp affixed to a belt or sash. A Tibetan eating kit often hung from a chatelaine. Such an accessory might also hold an eating kit, a tinder pouch, or a money purse.

Two chatelaines appear in Figure 10. A chunk of coral embellishes the center of each silver pendant. The smaller example depicts a guardian *kirtimukha*: the face of majesty, fame, and glory. Doorknockers, temple doorways, and weapons of war often feature the head and hands of this creature. The larger chatelaine features a *simhamukha*, or lion head, a variation of the *kirtimukha*.

Tinder Pouches

Among the most basic of all human technologies are the implements for starting a fire. Before the invention of lighters or even matches, the Mongols, Tibetans, and Manchus used tinder and strikers to light their campfires, cooking fires, and pipes, storing the tinder in leather pouches. Like an eating kit, a tinder pouch hung from a chatelaine, ring, or cord, on a sash. Its contents included chips of flint, dried bark, homespun, mugwort, and edelweiss. An elaborate tinder pouch was a sign of prestige.

Handmade of leather and ornamented with silver, the pouch included a bottom plate of thick steel, used as a striker. To start a fire or light his pipe, a man held a piece of flint against a clump of tinder. Grasping the pouch in the other hand, he struck the flint with the steel edge and created a spark, which flew into the tinder and ignited it.

Repoussé or engraved ornamental plates decorate the tinder pouches in my collection (Figures 11, 12 and 13). Curl-work patterns, flowers, and the double dragon and pearl motif are common. Coral and turquoise beads decorate some pieces. A simple clasp keeps each pouch closed. Some pieces, like the square one in the upper left of Figure 11, have a metal backing on the inside of the top flap for extra strength. The average pouch was first sewn together and then riveted. The edges of some pouches have been strengthened with sheet metal. In other cases, separate pieces of metal soldered to the framework reinforce the edges. The leather on my pieces is naturally scuffed and worn, and often smells of smoke.

Figure 11

An iron ring, attached to a brass or iron strip atop the pouch, secured it to a leather thong. Figure 11 shows how the thong slipped through two metal loops before joining a copper and brass counterweight. The pouch in Figure 13, which I collected with the thong still attached, might have hung from a sash or leather belt.

The Qing pouches often have incised geometrical designs on the upper metal strip. Sometimes the smith decorated the rings too. In Figure 11, one ring is covered with layers of old string, hiding (or perhaps protecting) its beautiful incised design. The strikers on these pieces were generally left plain, but occasionally one finds a compelling exception, as in Figure 12.

The pouch in the lower left of Figure 11, which a friend purchased in China for me, still contains a piece of flint. Other pouches in this illustration came with partially unraveled woolen homespun: tinder, no doubt. By looking closely, one can sometimes tell whether the pouch's owner was right-handed or left-handed. If the steel is worn down on the right side, as in Figure 13, the owner was probably left-handed, and vice-versa. Figure 13 reveals the difference between a money pouch and a tinder pouch. A tinder pouch *always* includes a steel plate on the bottom.

Pen Cases

A symbol of status for a Tibetan official or secretary, the silver-covered cast iron pen cases held wooden pens for writing letters and documents. In Figure 14 we find a case embellished with the

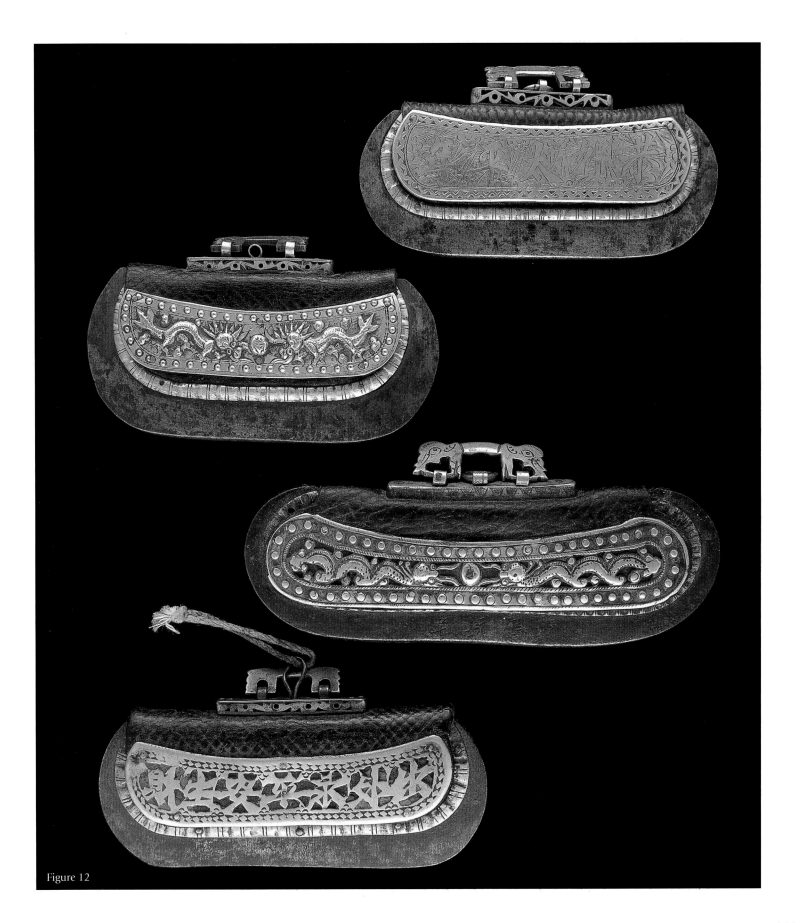

Figure 12

141

Eight Buddhist Symbols and engraved with a geometric design on the back. The owner could thread a cord through the two rings and thereby attach the pen case to his sash.

Tobacco Containers

The unusually shaped Tibetan tobacco container in Figure 15 is carved from an animal bone encased in silver. The lid, a plug of handcarved wood, fits snugly into the body. Chains, leather thongs, or heavy braids once slipped through the lugs. I'm not sure what hung from the bottom: perhaps an amulet, perhaps a pipe.

A silversmith used repoussé and chasing to create the stylized vines and leaves on the overlay. The lid includes what might be a representation of an eight-spoked Wheel of Law, representing Buddha's teachings and the spiritual path to nirvana.

All three of the tobacco boxes in Figure 16 appear to have been spring -loaded. You could push a designated button or knob and the top flew open. The mechanism is broken on two of them, but their design and craftsmanship still fascinate us. Calligraphy covers the top of one, while an elaborate enameled scene and a poem by eighth century poet Li Bai covers the top of another. The third features the shape of a man's shoe covered with a design of bats and dragons with longevity symbols. Two of the containers feature rings for hanging from chains or cords, while boxes of the enameled type had to be carried in dangling embroidered pouches during the Qing dynasty.

Spectacle Cases

In the Qing dynasty, spectacles enhanced both vision and self-esteem. Because eyeglasses symbolized scholarship, affluent gentlemen with perfect vision often wore clear crystal spectacles for appearance alone. Sadly, many people who really needed spectacles could not afford them.

Magnifying glasses had been put into wearable frames as early as the tenth century, but it wasn't until the nineteenth century that spectacles became "corrective." Artisans ground crystal, smoky quartz, and rose quartz to create the lenses.

Although spectacles were always prestigious attire, a supreme ruler never wore a pair until Reginald Johnson, the tutor of Puyi, the famous Last Emperor, insisted that the boy needed corrective lenses. After Puyi started wearing eyeglasses, others donned such

Figure 13

aids to show respect for the Emperor.

The most common form of spectacle case was evidently a two-piece wooden shell. Most were covered in shagreen sharkskin trimmed in copper or brass, but occasionally, we see a case trimmed with silver. An example appears in Figure 17. Beyond their decorative function, the silver bands keep the covering from chipping. Figure 18 shows a much rarer sort of case; neither the tan color nor the silver adornments are common. Both of these cases would have hung from the sash of a wealthy scholar…or a man pretending to be one.

Toggles

The Chinese have a very well developed sense of touch, and nowhere is this more evident than in their appreciation of toggles. Often used as counterweights in securing accessories to a sash, toggles in the Qing dynasty were fashioned out of everything from simple wood to precious metals. The sash toggles of China preceded the more familiar Japanese netsukes by several centuries.

While a nobleman owned several silver, ivory, or semi-precious stone toggles, a poor man probably treasured one of carved wood, antler, or bone, which often featured imaginative folk art. Whether peasants or nobles, Qing dynasty men loved to finger the smooth, broad, flat, or slightly rounded surfaces of their toggles as they talked.

Silver toggles in the shapes of gourds, babies, and animals were all common, but the simple disk form allowed the silversmith's artistry free rein. The round artifact in Figure 19 is evidently made of two halves soldered together. Judging by its weight, I would say the inside is hollow. On the back, a thick metal shank holds a silver ring for the cord. On the front, we observe aquatic animals—fantail goldfish, frog, crayfish, small minnows, clam, and water spider—in repoussé in high relief.

In the second example, a longevity symbol covers the torso of an enameled bat (happiness and good fortune). Hollow, but double-sided, the toggle incorporates the usual metal loop for a cord, chain, or thong on the reverse.

Silver Seals

In the Qing dynasty, a red ink impression of a man's jade seal represented his signature. With his seal-mark, a man entered into contracts, bought land, sold goods, and sanctioned transactions of all sorts. An artist signed his work with an ink impression, and a head of state gave a symbolic seal to every scholar he appointed to high office.

Qing dynasty jade seals always bore Chinese characters, never the owner's manual signature. The more skillful the engraver's calligraphy, the more valuable the seal. A man usually carried his jade seal in a small embroidered pouch, but a scholar or nobleman often wore a symbolic silver seal hanging from his waist sash.

Figure 20 shows a symbolic seal—and its many collateral hangings—that obviously belonged to an aristocrat. Atop the gilded silver adornment, we see a musical stone (good fortune), followed by a pair of carp (marital harmony). The seal itself appears in a metal box topped by a lotus for purity. Set on a tiny platform, beneath a descending spider for good luck, the box rests within a fence-like enclosure. Below the platform hangs a double bucket for the bond between husband and wife, followed by the lotus for purity and nirvana, and the swastika symbolizing 10,000 years of efficacies. On the three chains, we find an ax for power, a three-legged toad for longevity, and an unidentified object. Tiny gilded babies for fertility adorn the bottom. Given all of these marital and fertility symbols, it's safe to assume the owner received this adornment as a wedding gift.

In Figure 21, we find another symbolic silver seal, minus most of its amulets. Comparing the two pieces, we can appreciate how badly the second seal was violated when it was modified into a necklace.

Figure 22 shows two Tibetan seals of silver-plated iron. They still retain their old leather case and thongs. The seals were used by officials to sign letters and documents with lampblack ink. The Tibetans also used such seals to stamp boiled cowskin wax, thus closing a packet or marking a personal belonging.

Prayer Holders

The three silver tubes in Figure 23 represent one of the biggest mysteries of this book. I love their elaborate repoussé depictions of scenes from mythology and their emblems of the Eight Immortals, but despite my inquiries in China and America, I have failed to discover their purpose.

Each tube opens from the top and has a thin shaft running through the center connected to chains at either end. The shaft might tempt us to label each piece a fragrance carrier, but none have perforations to let the fragrance escape. Are we looking at needle cases? No. For each piece, the chain exits through a hole in the bottom of the tube. Obviously, needles would fall through these apertures.

So what are they? My latest such acquisition came with sheets of old paper rolled around the shaft, but the characters were too faded to read. I think it is possible, however, that these papers had appeals to the gods written on them. Hence, we may be looking at containers that held special prayers to help a person succeed or keep him from harm.

Mustache Combs

Although a Chinese man has less facial hair than a Westerner, mustaches achieved great popularity in the Qing dynasty. If a man owned a sash, its hangings almost surely included a small, oval, two-sided wooden mustache comb (Figures 24 through 27). Graced by a handle and a band of silver, the comb fit into a small embroidered purse or hung from a string of beads or chain.

Supplementing the vertical strip, two small silver bands stabilize the top and bottom. The carved bamboo teeth were about five centimeters high and approximately three centimeters wide. Considering their age, it is amazing that more of the delicate teeth aren't broken.

Geometric designs embellished the average silver mustache-comb handle. The smith occasionally decorated the silver band as well. In Figure 25, the band features a stylized swastika symbolizing 10,000 years of good fortune. In Figure 26, engraved plum blossoms swirl across the strip. One strip in Figure 27 is covered with enamel, the other with repoussé plum blossoms.

In Figure 26, we also find an unusual silver amulet representing a comb. I have seen such pieces used as amulets and grooming kit centerpieces, and I think they might relate to an old Hakka custom. When a Hakka woman died, a comb was broken in half to sever her remaining ties to the Earth. Smiths may have fashioned unbreakable silver comb amulets as wedding gifts symbolizing the young couple's perpetual bond.

Figure 28 offers examples of functional silver mustache combs. Note the dragon head handles and the hallmarks. When not in use, the comb in the center slips into a sheath covered in repoussé.

Medical Hangings

Figure 29 displays various sash hangings of medical utility. The vase probably held a powdered drug since the lid fits tightly. The object in the upper left-hand corner is a Tibetan *thogchak*, as well as a medicine spoon. A large chunk of coral embellishes the handle, and a suspension lug is soldered to the back: the spoon probably hung alone, but it may have functioned as a toggle.

If small gourds held enough medication for a week, the artifact in the lower left held enough for a month. Seven centimeters wide, this is the largest silver gourd adornment I have ever encountered. It also might have either hung by itself or served as a functional toggle. The double fish, lotus, and longevity symbols indicate a wedding or anniversary present. The vine tip unscrews, but instead of the typical opium spoon, we find a shaft with a long, deep furrow.

The illustration includes two makeshift acupuncture needles, handy for relieving pain in an emergency. The top one, which is Tibetan, employs a tiger claw encased in silver. The bottom one, probably Han, uses an animal tooth imbedded in the enameled head of a dragonfish.

Because they were pocketless, Qing dynasty robes offered silversmiths a wonderful opportunity to exercise their creativity. Unable to hide their accessories, men demanded eating kits, tinder pouches, spectacle cases, mustache combs, pen cases, toggles, seals, and medicinal supplies in ever more elaborate and beautiful designs.

Figure 14

Figure 15

144

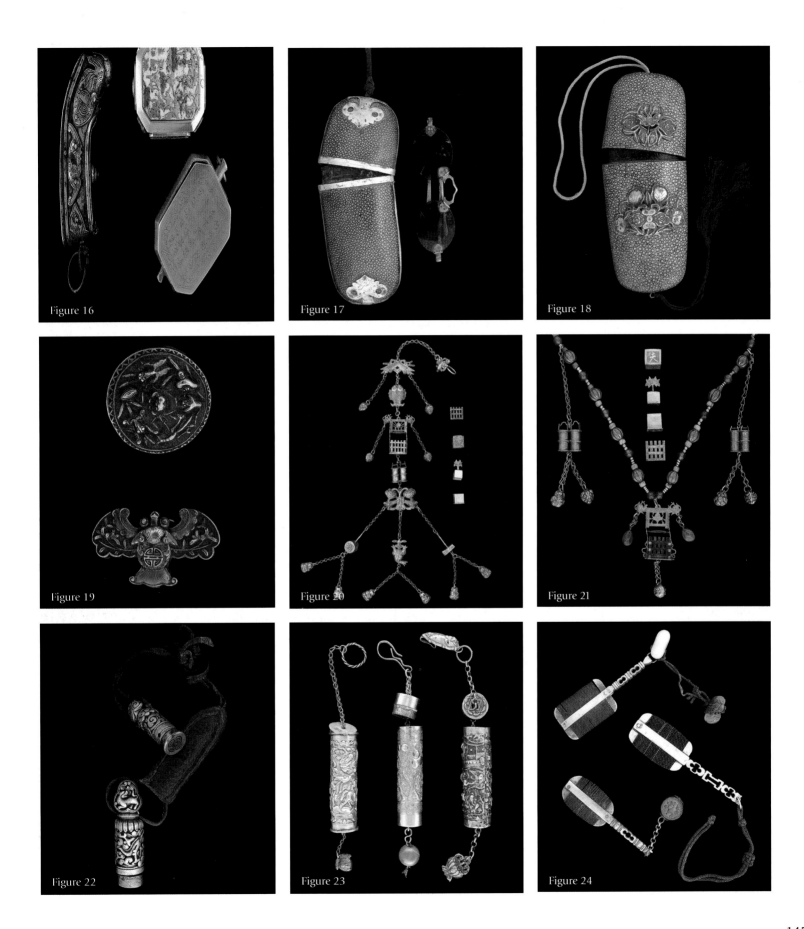

Figure 16

Figure 17

Figure 18

Figure 19

Figure 20

Figure 21

Figure 22

Figure 23

Figure 24

145

Figure 25

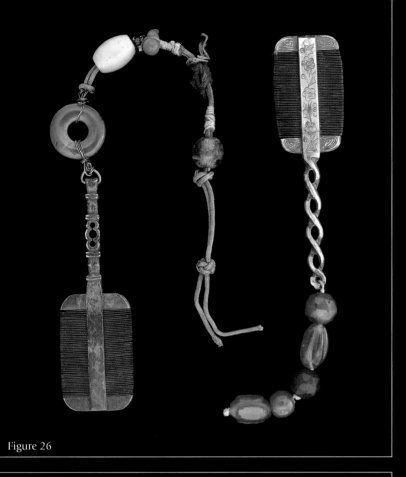

Figure 26

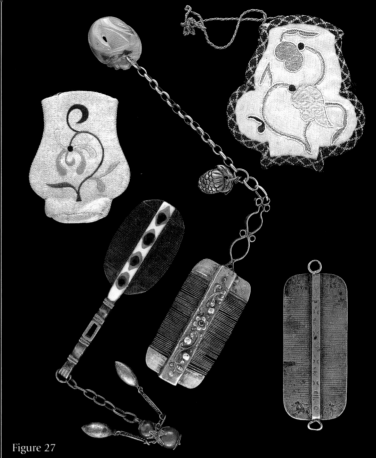

Figure 27

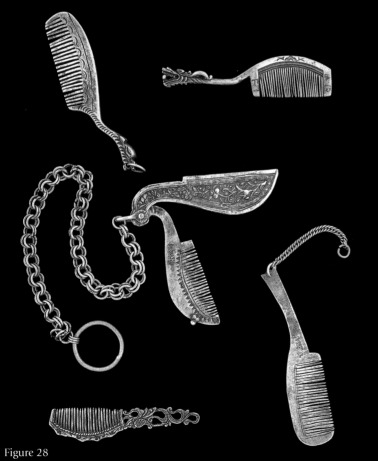

Figure 28

Figure 29

Mandarin and Minority Artifacts

Opposite: A Court necklace hangs round the neck of a Manchu official.

Ruyu trembles as her name is called and her two sisters lead her toward the inner room. She knows the foreign devil will be waiting with his apparatus, and she will have to hold still for the long procedure. It will be torture: she is sure of that. Ruyu takes tiny steps on her bound feet and fights the urge to bolt, but her sisters hold her fast. A scream threatens to escape from her throat, but custom will not allow it. Why, oh why, did her husband ever insist that she do this?

Following the Chinese assistant, the three women enter a room with a patterned rug and large windows, but even the bright sunlight cannot lift Ruyu's spirit. She spies the chair with the clamp and she freezes. Her sisters jerk her forward. Ruyu notices the large black box on a thick wooden pedestal with rollers. That monster will strip away her soul.

The foreigner enters the room. Tall like most men from England, he wears a cheap tan suit and a dark mustache. In perfect Mandarin, but with a British accent, he asks Ruyu to take a seat. As she does so, her sisters straighten the hem of her new silk robe decorated with embroidered irises. They also make sure the counting beads on her Court necklace are even and the kingfisher crown on her head is straight.

The photographer explains that Ruyu must set her neck in the clamp to keep her head still. She cautiously leans backward as the assistant adjusts the clamp. Next, the photographer instructs her to place her hands in her lap so that the long gilded fingernail guards on her ring fingers and little fingers will show to best advantage.

Satisfied, the photographer rolls the camera into position. Ruyu clenches her teeth. The photographer tells her to relax. Her sisters chatter to distract her as the photographer vanishes beneath the black cloth behind the box.

The photographer's assistant hands him a thin, flat black square. He drops it into the top of the camera, creating a loud thud, and Ruyu shudders, despite the clamp.

The photographer emerges from beneath the cloth. He pulls a black metal sheet from the camera and stands beside it. He tells Ruyu to hold completely still as he counts to twenty.

With a fluid motion, the photographer removes a black disk from the front of the camera, revealing a round piece of glass. Ruyu stares at the glass as he counts—1, 2, 3. She thinks of how her husband will soon depart on his two-month mission for the Emperor—8,9,10. She imagines all the beautiful women he might encounter on his journey—13,14,15. Perhaps it will be best if he carries her picture to keep him from temptation—18,19,20. The photographer replaces the black disk. He asks Ruyu if she would mind if he makes a second exposure to make sure they get a good one. Ruyu finally smiles.

Hushan follows Linlin, as she likes to be called, up the long, winding staircase rising from the foyer of the brothel. As he watches her young, firm buttocks, he realizes he doesn't even know her real name. No matter. She understands him in a way that his wife never can. Their relationship is beyond names.

They enter the room that Hushan always reserves, the one with the ornately carved door. Bas-relief scenes from mythology decorate the bed frame. Linlin removes his opium box from the embroidered pouch on his sash and places it on the tray. Slowly, Linlin removes his clothing, caressing him and speaking to him softly as he stares at a carving of a dragon. Naked at last, he climbs into the bed and adjusts his cylindrical pillow as he watches her methodically undress for him. He craves her, but he waits, knowing that the opium will increase his pleasure.

As Linlin enters the bed, she lights the small lamp on the tray. Grasping Hushan's opium box, she removes the silver sleeve, disclosing a pornographic scene on one side, his favorite poem on the other. She slowly reads him the verses in her sensual voice, then opens the opium box and uses the long slender spoon to remove a pea-sized ball of the drug. She hands Hushan the spoon, caresses the long stem of his opium pipe and finally, offers it to him as well.

Holding the long spoon over the flame, Hushan watches the opium bubble and turn viscous. The air sweetens. Hushan pours the heated opium into the small hole atop the pipe bowl, then passes the pipe back and forth over the flame.

The instant the opium combusts in a gray cloud, Hushan sucks on the stem, and draws the heady smoke into his lungs. His body relaxes. He will have to fill his pipe at least five more times before he reaches the desired state of euphoria, whereupon he will draw Linlin to his side. At the moment of ecstasy he will feel as if he could climb the highest mountain, slay the fiercest dragon. He

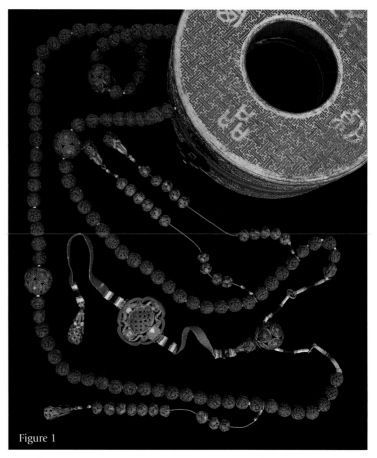

Figure 1

will forget that he is a second son. He will forget that he has a barren wife who is a shrew. He might even forget that he failed his civil service examinations. As Hushan watches Linlin close her long-lashed eyes and slowly inhale her own pipe, he feels all of his problems vanish through the ornately carved door.

Yunnan Province. Southwest China. Midaw, the old Yi grandmother, anxiously watches the overcast sky as she sits on a tattered blanket alongside her vegetables. Midaw's husband, now crippled, relies upon her to support them with the vegetables she grows. Thunder ripples through the thick clouds on the horizon. Midaw nervously fingers the silver chain—a dowry gift she received fifty years ago from her mother—holding her embroidered apron.

A young Han woman with a baby squats down and picks up one of Midaw's cabbages.

"The best quality," Midaw says. "How much will you pay?"

The young woman offers a ridiculous price. Midaw counters with a higher one. The young woman raises her offer slightly.

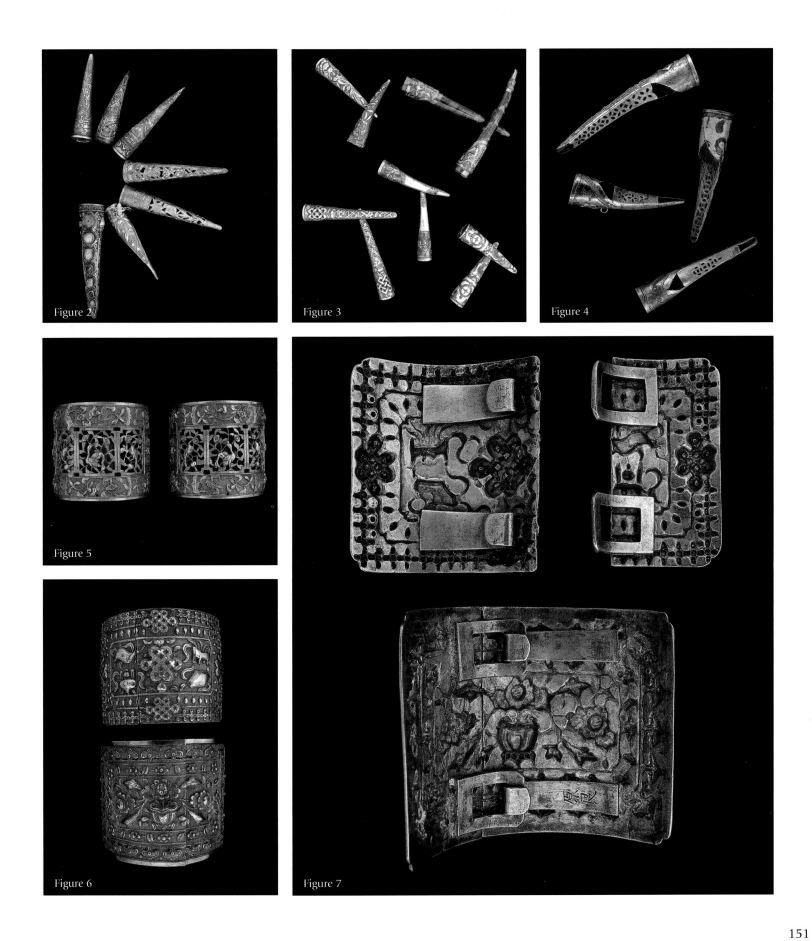

Figure 2

Figure 3

Figure 4

Figure 5

Figure 6

Figure 7

151

Midaw lowers her price. And so it goes until they reach an impasse. Midaw shakes her head. As the young woman throws down the cabbage, Midaw says, "Okay, okay," and shoves the cabbage toward her. The sky darkens. The thunder bellows.

"Very fresh, best price," the grandmother tells the passers-by. She sells several more items before feeling the droplets on her head. She unfastens her apron, pivots it on the silver chain, and reties it with the embroidery on the inside so that the dyes will not run. She slings her shawl around her shoulders to protect her chain. Soon the rain pours down, and the shoppers hurry home. With a long sigh, Midaw gathers her unsold produce in the old blanket, hoping it won't rot before tomorrow, and throws it over her shoulder with a groan. She makes sure she still has the few coins she earned, and hobbles down the street on her swollen feet, thinking of the medicinal herbs her husband needs, and wondering how much she could get if she sold her apron chain.

The Mandarin nobility and the ethnic minorities used many beautiful silver ornaments in their daily life and also for special occasions. Intriguing mysteries surround many of the artifacts discussed in this chapter. I hope that the examples offered here will encourage other collectors to seek out more such items and attempt to learn their origins and uses.

Court Necklaces

In the Qing dynasty, the Emperor, a member of the royal family, a civil official above the fifth rank, a military official above the fourth rank, and any high-ranking woman wore a distinctive necklace with his or her Court attire. Inspired by a set of Buddhist prayer beads given to a Chinese Emperor by the Dalai Lama, the Manchus added several features to transform the original Tibetan artifact into a unique adornment.

The primal necklace consisted of one-hundred-and-eight beads—four sections of twenty-seven beads—divided by three large "Buddha head" beads and one anchor bead in a contrasting color. The Manchus added three rosary-like "counting strands," each comprising two five-bead segments plus a drop bead. A man wore two counting strands hanging down his left shoulder, and one counting strand on the right. For women, by contrast, the pair dangled on the right side. As a counterbalance, a long cloth tape hung from the anchor bead down the wearer's back, decorated with a large ornamental pendant and another bead.

Depending on his or her rank, a person might own a Court necklace with beads of jade, Peking glass, amber, cloisonné, ivory, lapis, tourmaline, turquoise, crystal, amethyst, coral, carved wood, porcelain, linden seeds, or fruit pits. Status even dictated the stringing material. Since the Imperial family reserved the right to wear yellow, their beads were always strung on yellow silk.

For formal Court occasions, a man wore one Court necklace (also called a Mandarin necklace), but a woman could wear three— one over each shoulder (draped under the opposite arm), and one down the middle.

Most Court necklaces contain only precious or semi-precious stones, but occasionally you find one with silver beads. Carved fruit pits display elaborate openwork on the example in Figure 1. Separating the pits are three head beads, a gourd-shaped anchor bead, an ornamental pendant, and thirty counting beads fashioned from enameled silver. Various shades of blue enameling cover each silver bead. The cloth tape also employs different shades of blue. The donut-shaped enameled storage box is contemporary with the necklace itself.

Fingernail Guards

Shaped like hollow claws, fingernail guards—metal sheaths that protected the long fingernails of the aristocratic women who wore them—remain perhaps the most famous symbol of the Qing dynasty. Whether gold, gilded, enameled, tortoiseshell, jade, or silver, a fingernail guard proclaimed the wearer's social status, and the fact that she did no manual labor.

Such ornaments predate the Qing dynasty. In 1979, a pair of compressed and curled gold fingernail guards surfaced in a tomb from the Warring States Period (475-221 B.C.)—the time of Buddha, Aristotle, and Alexander the Great. A pair of gold fingernail guards from the Han dynasty (206 B.C. to A.D. 220) is on exhibit at the Jilin Provincial Museum in China, and ten matching cast-silver guards were discovered in a Xian tomb from the Sui Dynasty (A.D. 581-618).

For at least 2000 years the Chinese aristocracy accorded its fingernails an almost fetishistic attention. Nails could be cut only on certain auspicious days. An accidentally broken nail was a mishap verging on a tragedy. A member of the nobility would save his fingernail clippings throughout his life so that he could be interred with them. According to one reference, when a warlord pillaged the tomb of the Dowager Empress Cixi in 1928, he found, among other items, a bag of her fingernails.

Given these attitudes toward fingernails, it's not surprising that the Qing nobility greatly prized fingernail guards. Measuring anywhere from three centimeters to almost fifteen centimeters in length, the guards came in pairs crafted to fit over the little finger and the ring finger. The right-hand pair usually differed from the left-hand pair. Portraits of the Dowager Empress Cixi often show her wearing a jade pair on one hand and a gold pair on the other.

Most silver or gilded-silver fingernail guards feature repoussé or engraved designs. Favorite subjects included bats, lotus blossoms, the endless knot, coins, and the Eight Symbols of the Daoist Immortals (Figures 2 and 3).

If you study a Qing silver fingernail guard closely, you'll see that the lower flaps are folded over one another to form a strong but adjustable band that fits over the finger. The smith soldered a second piece—a reinforcing plate with holes for ventilation—to the back of the guard. By contrast, the jade and tortoiseshell pieces from the Qing era have fixed bands. If you find a metal guard without the overlapping flaps, it is probably an export piece made after the fall of the Qing dynasty (Figure 4, bottom).

Sleeve Buckles

A Mandarin scholar typically used a pair of silver buckles to keep the long sleeves of his gown from interfering as he worked on a painting or calligraphy (Figures 5 through 10). Each buckle consisted of two rectilinear halves, curved to follow the contours of the arm. One half was sewn to the top of the outside of the scholar's sleeve. The other half was sewn near the bottom of the sleeve, right above the cuff. By gathering up the sleeve, and then clipping the two pieces together around the folds, the scholar could prevent the material from smearing ink or paint over the rice paper as he worked.

Figure 5 shows a matching pair of two complete gilded-silver buckles, one buckle for each sleeve. I purchased these from Glenn Vessa, a reputable dealer in Hong Kong, who actually saw such artifacts in place on Mandarin gowns in a Tianjin warehouse in the mid-1970's. The cranes on this pair oppose one another, and the flowers swirl in opposite directions.

In Figure 6 the top buckle offers books, a painting, and sacrificial urns surrounding the endless knot of Buddhism. On the lower example, a bowl of peonies represents wealth and distinction. Figure 7 reveals how the two halves of a buckle fasten together.

The flowers adorning the upper buckle in Figure 8 bring a multitude of good wishes for purity amidst adverse surroundings, wealth, distinction, longevity, and a life of ease. In the lower example, the buckle displays yet another bowl of peonies, this time with the addition of the crane and deer for longevity.

Groups of figures were popular motifs for sleeve buckles. Figure 9 shows two specimens that, though not a pair, are nearly identical. If you look closely, you'll see that the plum blossoms in the top example have inverted centers, while the centers protrude on the lower item. There are also differences in the details on the three mythological characters and their surrounding foliage.

Some scholars preferred depictions of lions for courage, energy, and wisdom on their sleeve buckles. Figure 10 shows two examples of markedly different sizes. I suspect that the smaller artifact was made for a wealthy young boy studying to pass his examinations.

Opium Boxes

The Arabs introduced the Chinese to opium during the seventh century Tang dynasty. Initially, the drug's purpose was medicinal. Taken as a pill, or dissolved in soup, opium purportedly cured dysentery. People also believed that opium was an aphrodisiac. Eventually it became known that opium held its own intrinsic—though dangerous—pleasures.

Then someone discovered that smoking opium allowed the drug to reach the blood stream more rapidly than eating it. The new pastime gained immense popularity, and addiction quickly became a major social problem. By 1729, Emperor Yongzheng prohibited both opium dens and the sale of opium. His edict had little effect.

Although China cultivated its own poppies, connoisseurs preferred the Indian and Turkish varieties, thus insuring a thriving opium trade. By 1780, the British East India Company had established

Figure 8

Figure 9

Figure 10

Figure 11

Figure 12

Figure 13

Figure 14

155

a monopoly on Indian opium. The basic unit of sale was a three-pound (less than one-and-a-half kilo) sphere of opium wrapped in opium petals held together with liquid opium. Once it dried, an opium sphere could be stored for years without losing its potency.

Members of all classes and ethnic groups in China enslaved themselves to the drug. Aristocrats lost fortunes. Lower class families became utterly destitute. Thwarted by laws against opium importation, companies resorted to bribery and smuggling to keep the trade alive in the port of Canton. Sometimes the traffic was temporarily curtailed. In 1839, Commissioner Lin Zexu managed to confiscate tons of opium from the drug merchants. He mixed it with lime and dumped it into the bay. He also destroyed opium paraphernalia and the year's opium crop.

Despite Lin's efforts, Britain refused to stop shipping opium to China. War broke out in 1839 and lasted until China's defeat in 1842, when a treaty was signed in Nanking. China lost Hong Kong and almost twenty million dollars in reparations. The opium trade continued to thrive.

A regular user carried his own long-stemmed opium pipe and stored his supply in a personal container, usually a simple paktong box covered with calligraphy. Figure 11 offers six examples. The inscriptions reveal the owner's feelings about the drug. One reads: "If you use this, you can live longer. The outside quality is very good, but inside it is beautiful." Another inscription insists: "This is what my heart needs," and declares that the opium is beneficial and gives one energy, so that "everything is finally within one's power." Another states: "When you inhale this, all the waters of the Yangtze are within your control." The largest box chronicles an entire poem: "He came to the house of ill repute to purchase a prostitute and enjoy the rain outside. Inside, he found gentlemen enjoying life. Around the building were beautiful bamboo trees, and the sky was covered with light clouds. The rain finally stopped, and the rare birds pursued one another." The backs of some boxes bear engraved scenes of lounging Chinese. Other backs feature additional calligraphy. Obviously, the larger the box, the more complicated the message—and the richer the owner.

When placed in an embroidered pouch hung from a man's sash, an opium box proved very portable. Many users liked to carry the drug to brothels, using it to increase their sexual pleasure. The

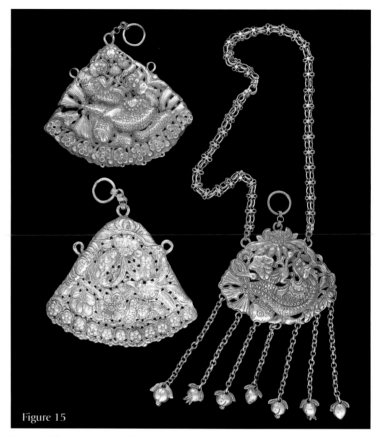

Figure 15

inevitable connection between opium and sex is apparent from the boxes in Figure 12. In each case a silver sleeve, engraved with the image of a proper woman, covers an erotic scene on the box itself.

Different styles of silversmithing adorn the silver opium boxes in Figure 13. Such repoussé images were evidently a source of pride among the smiths, because these boxes typically include a signature stamped on the bottom. Other examples in this photograph, such as the peony box, are engraved. Cloisonné designs cover still others.

Members of the ethnic minorities often suspended small six-sided opium boxes from their grooming kits, belts, or buttons. In Figure 14 a different floral design covers each container. The large cylindrical box still holds some opium, now hard-caked. The tall specimen on the left resembles an opium box, but is actually a container for lime, as the shaker top reveals.

Apron Holders

Each Chinese ethnic minority has a distinctive mode of dress. Different groups favor different types of aprons. Some groups wear the low bodices, others the high. Some favor a square top; others

Figure 16

Figure 17

Figure 18

Figure 19

prefer the rounded. Some embroider the whole apron, others use stitchery only on the bodice. But no matter the style, every bodice is held up with a silver ornament.

Each of the three triangular apron holders in Figure 15 has a loop at the top that fits over a button on a blouse or vest. The smaller loops hold a neck chain, as we see in the example. Created by the Bai minority of Yunnan Province, two holders depict both a conventional fish and a dragonfish. In Chinese lore, the sturgeon of the Yellow River is fated to swim against the current, but if it passes through the Dragon Gate and the Rapids of the Longmen, it will turn into a dragonfish. The Chinese dragonfish therefore symbolizes perseverance (always connected to success in the civil service examinations, which every mother wished for her son). In the piece with the chain, we find a fish, a dragonfish, a pair of birds for marital happiness, and a lotus for incorruptibility.

Figure 16 illustrates a Yi minority apron with a round holder sewn to the top of the bodice. The loop on the holder hooks onto the button of a blouse. Figure 17 offers variations of one of the most common apron-holder scenes: a temple gate with dragons (fertility) twisting around the posts, a pair of phoenix birds (female element), fish in water (marital bliss), and either flowers or a baby (fertility). Why a gate? I believe it might represent the famed Dragon Gate of Longmen.

The Yi apron holders in Figure 18 each feature a scene from the novel, *Journey to the West*. Set in the 600's, this classic novel tells of Xuanzang, a monk sent to India to bring Buddhism to China. The author presents Buddhism as the supreme religion, but, interestingly, is revealed as equally strong. On each apron holder, the priest (human frailty) leads Xuanzhang's horse, while the monkey (symbolizing human failings) and the pig (symbolizing baser nature which may be suppressed), accompany and protect Xuanzang.

The smaller triangular apron holders in Figure 19 are from the Bai, Dong, and Miao minorities. Butterflies, flowers, fish, and the phoenix decorate these pieces, some of which are enameled.

Chains

In the Qing dynasty, silver chains served various functions: utilitarian, decorative, and symbolic. The Yi, Zhuang, Yao, Shui, Bouyei, and Hui minorities used chains to hold up their aprons.

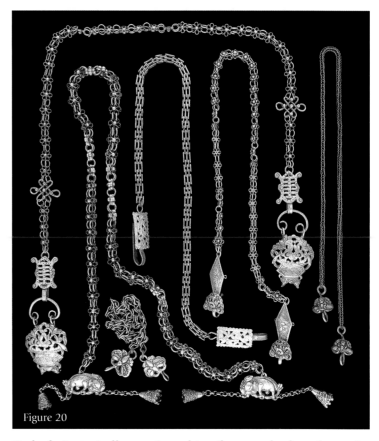
Figure 20

Each chain typically terminated in silver two baskets, longevity symbols, lions, *ruyi*, butterflies, or engraved plaques (Figure 20). The styles and weights of the chains varied as much as the groups who wore them.

The long chain in Figure 21 weighs an impressive 220 grams. It looped over the wearer's neck and might have secured an apron, but the size and weight lead me to believe it held silver adornments. Many ethnic groups, notably the Tibetans, wore such heavy chains and accompanying dangles at festivals as a display of wealth.

Many old silver chains defy easy identification. In Figure 22 an ornate silver chain weighing an incredible 320 grams, is topped by butterfly hooks. Beneath these we find small baskets with Maitreya, the Laughing Buddha, inside. Judging from Maitreya's orientation, I would guess that the chain hung down the front of the wearer's costume, but I cannot say whether it was suspended from a collar, an apron, a neckpiece, or headgear.

Collar Buttons

A Qing dynasty silversmith brought pride and skill to all his

Figure 21

creations—even the simplest collar buttons. In Figure 23 we see gilded-silver collar buttons of the type worn by wealthier women of the Dai minority. The phoenixes are intended to hang by their tales from the ends of a woman's collar. The phoenix represented the Empress, and phoenix collar buttons on a woman's wedding dress made her "empress for a day."

The Dai and the Yi minorities both used round, square, and oblong collar buttons, which were sewn to the high collared neck of a blouse, shirt, or vest (Figure 24). A hole in one side of the button fitted over a protrusion on the other. Designs such as the double fish (connubial bliss), plum blossom (longevity), the double dragons, and the double bats tell us that collar buttons often adorned wedding costumes.

Minority Necklaces

Some minorities used beads, as well as enameled pieces, to form elaborate necklaces. In Figure 25, a large butterfly symbolizing joy, marital happiness, and longevity, hangs from double strands of silver beads interspersed with small enameled symbols such as the gourd, books, and the rhinoceros horn. This piece came from the Kunming area and might be either Hani, Yao, or Bai. Large, but not burdensome, it could have been worn by either a man or a woman.

The common type of Chinese neckpiece is simply an amulet on a chain, whether the hanging is a qilin, lock, rider, or god. But occasionally one encounters a piece that was evidently conceived as a full necklace. A good example is the Miao artifact in Figure 26. The large one-hundred centimeter bat for happiness and good fortune has a longevity symbol as its torso. From the bottom hang Buddhist swords to cut away ignorance.

Hangings

One of my most unusual finds is the large hanging in Figure 27. Reputed to be from the Yao minority, this artifact measures an amazing eighty-nine centimeters long and weighs 681 grams. At the top we find a huge silver butterfly, followed by balls within balls, a fish, and a bottle gourd. During special festivals, certain minorities today suspend pieces of this length from the shoulder or waist as a show of wealth.

In Figure 28, two officials guard an altar, behind which stands

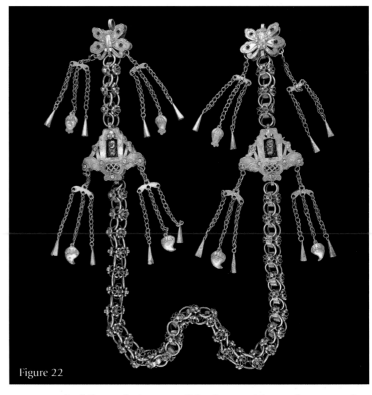

Figure 22

a woman holding a baby, possibly the Goddess of Mercy, who was a bringer of children. Two phoenixes, a lotus, a butterfly, and numerous dangles complete the ensemble, probably worn on special occasions.

A profound difference existed between the ornamentation of the Mandarins and that of the minorities. The Mandarin officials and their wives, along with members of the Imperial family, wore very traditional accouterments suited to their positions. However unusual its particular details, a Mandarin necklace or a fingernail guard is always of the same basic type.

The ornamentation of the minorities displays much more diversity. Variations in shapes, sizes, and style abound. In many instances, we know which minority produced an item, but we do not know how or why it was worn.

The silver pieces favored by the Chinese minorities today little resemble those items worn by their ancestors in the Qing dynasty. The new artifacts are machine pressed, lightweight, and feature simple designs. The older pieces, with their deep repoussé and heavy, hand-soldered chains, remind us of a time when the minorities displayed their wealth and provided their families with treasures that we are only now beginning to appreciate.

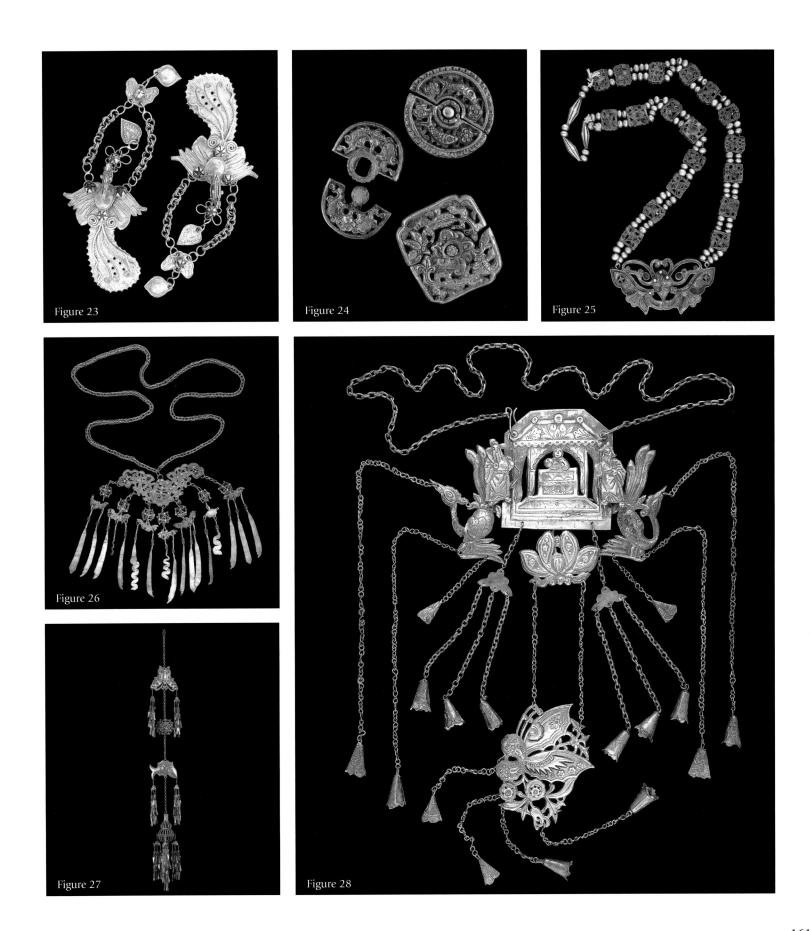

Figure 23

Figure 24

Figure 25

Figure 26

Figure 27

Figure 28

161

Opposite: A woman from the Xiling minority in Guangxi province wearing numerous silver adornments with beads.

Something was missing. As I wandered through the tiny shop in the heart of Beijing, no larger than a walk-in closet, with barely enough room for two browsers in the aisle, I marveled at the abundance. On the shelves, tarnished paktong water pipes huddled close to bronze deities, cloisonné vases, and chipped ceramic tea jars, while dusty wooden jewelry boxes, carved brushpots, ceramic vases, and bronze incense burners littered the floor. But as I examined the silver pieces—the grooming kits, qilins, and baby locks dangling from nails on long chains, barely recognizable under layers of oxidation—I could not escape my feeling that something was missing. Suddenly the answer came to me. The Chinese silver adornments sold in America invariably featured beads. And yet, except for certain Mongol and Tibetan pieces encrusted with chunks of coral or turquoise, none of the silver artifacts in this shop included any beads. Where were the beads?

This stark contrast held true for every shop I patronized. In the American antique-jewelry malls, even a small Chinese amulet would feature an old bead—usually carnelian or turquoise—swinging from a lug, while many necklaces displayed several old beads strung between the pendant and the chain. In the Beijing stalls, meanwhile, I never found even one silver pendant augmented by beads. I knew that the Chinese valued beads. They'd been making glass beads for over 3,000 years, and collections of Qing era carved stone invariably included carved beads of jade, tourmaline, ivory, turquoise, and coral. So what was going on here?

Five years and seven trips to China later, I finally found my answer—in the United States. According to the co-proprietor of a very reputable Chinese antiques and import establishment in New York, a government-owned Beijing company hired Chinese workers in the 1970's and 1980's to transform antique silver pieces—collected during the Cultural Revolution and stored in the warehouses—into wearable jewelry for Western women. They added old Mongol, Tibetan, and Chinese beads to the qilins, locks, fragrance carriers, needle cases, grooming kit centerpieces, hat adornments, animal amulets, large bells, and personal shrines. Unfortunately, this procedure violated the original aesthetic of the silver artifact, and often destroyed their function as well.

As supplies dwindled in the 80's, the Beijing company terminated its enterprise and sold the remaining beaded and un-beaded pieces to buyers from the West. Today, antique Qing silver pieces keep surfacing in Beijing shops and on Internet auction sites as Chinese families sell off heirlooms hidden during the collections. Predictably, most contain no beads.

To understand the lack of beads on the original Qing artifacts, we must look to the Chinese religious heritage. Daoism rejected worldly goods; Buddhism sanctioned beads mainly on ritual objects; and Confucianism did not encourage personal adornment. Economics also explains the bead scarcity. Only the wealthy could afford the beaded items, such as the Court necklaces and gilded-silver kingfisher pieces. Other classes wore silver adornments, but without the luxury of beads.

Even though it was imposed from above, the "beaded period"—when old beads and chains were added to pieces for sale in the West—still figures in the history of Qing dynasty silver. In this chapter we'll inspect the coral rope-chains and kingfisher pieces of the elite, Tibetan and Mongol silver pieces that initially included embedded cabochons or chunks of stone, and silver pieces that had beads imposed upon them for sale to the West.

Coral

The most highly prized coral in Qing dynasty China came from the Mediterranean waters off the coast of Italy. Deep red, softer than glass, it entered China from trade routes through India, Russia, and Tibet.

In China only the wealthiest could afford the lush crimson coral. Royal and aristocratic women coveted this material, believing it brought them good fortune, strength, and freedom from menstrual problems.

Women of the Imperial Court wore rope-chain necklaces made of tiny coral beads. The example in Figure 1 features a basket covered with kingfisher feathers and filled with beads representing fruit. Beneath the basket, another kingfisher dangle holds a bead cluster. Such a necklace cost a small fortune, as a worker had to spend hours stringing the hundreds of little beads together. Every necklace of this type I've seen terminates in two large Peking glass beads and a gilded silver pendant.

Larger coral beads occasionally enhanced a silver bangle, similar to the bamboo and jade examples in Chapter 7. Irregular and obviously handcarved, deep red beads strung on a wire beautify the bangle—possibly Mongol—in Figure 2. Today, the

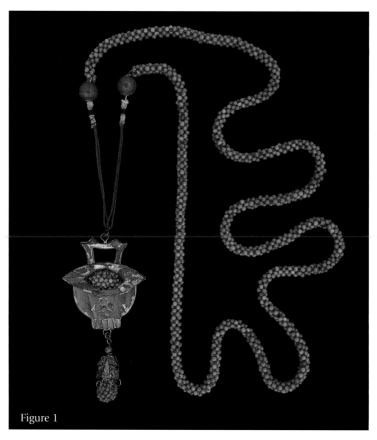

Figure 1

antique coral is more valuable than the silver.

Coral branches, pearls, carved jade, carnelian, and kingfisher feathers on gilded silver embellish the old wedding crown in Figure 3. We can only imagine its original majesty. Figure 4 shows various gilded-silver kingfisher hairpins for noblewomen, each decorated with coral and other beads. I enjoy picturing these pins adorning the hairdo of a royal consort in the Qing court.

In the chapter on hair adornments, we examined carved coral and silver hairpins similar to the ones in Figure 5. In these examples, dangling beads have replaced the original pearls and jade, but the carved heads still deserve attention.

An ancient chunk of coral, considered a precious stone in Tibet, adds it amuletic value to the silver top of a needle case in Figure 6. This silver plate fits over a handsewn leather needle case. Before sewing the leather pieces together, the smith secured the plate by passing metal prongs on the back through holes in the leather, then spreading the prongs apart. On one artifact, a repoussé silver *garuda*, the "Lord of Birds," protects a Tibetan owner from such afflictions as kidney failure, plague, and cancer. On the other, we discover a divinatory tortoise and what I believe is a

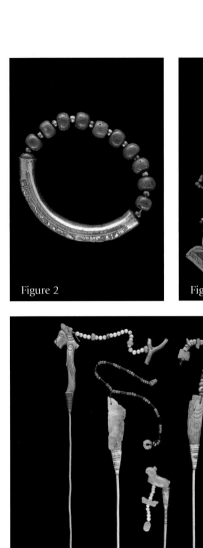

Figure 2

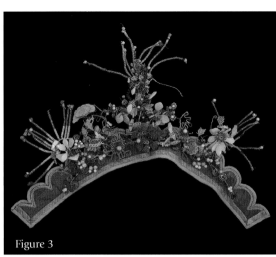

Figure 3

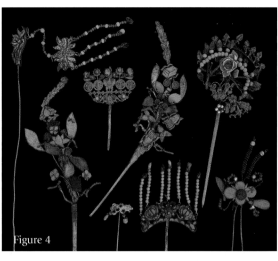

Figure 4

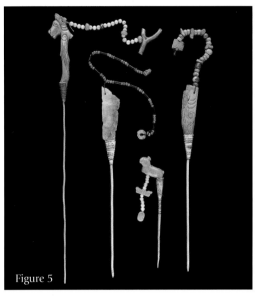

Figure 5

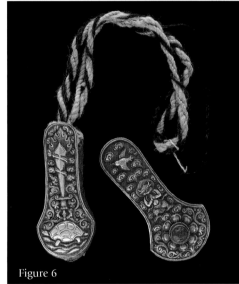

Figure 6

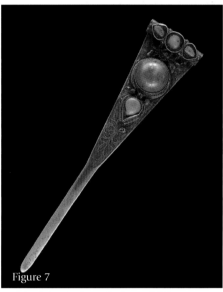

Figure 7

Figure 8

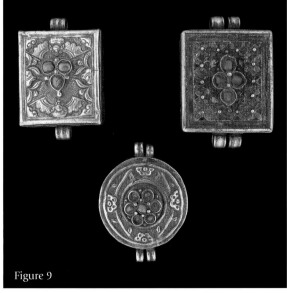

Figure 9

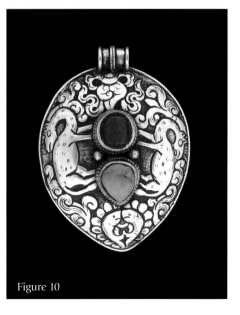

Figure 10

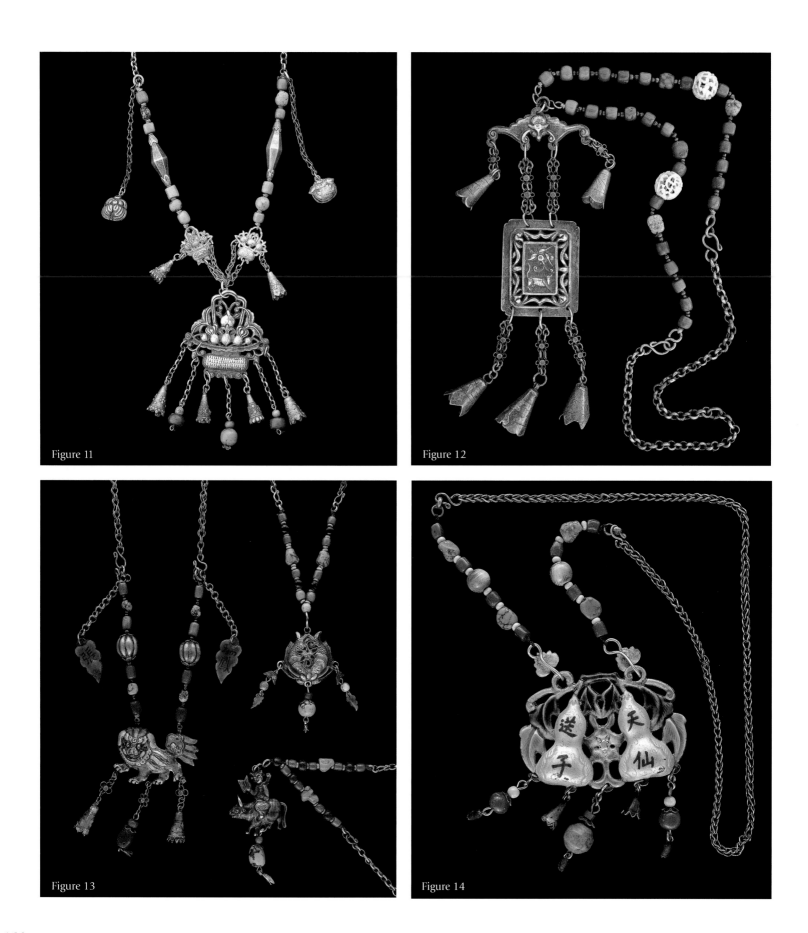

Figure 11

Figure 12

Figure 13

Figure 14

flaming wisdom sword.

A huge coral cabochon, two small coral beads, and chunks of turquoise decorate a Mongol hairpin in Figure 7. These stones often appear together on Tibetan and Mongol silver because Buddhists believed that combining the blue of the sky with the red of fire caused a fusion of natural energies, creating harmony in the universe. They also felt the two had power to prevent disease and protect one from evil forces.

Mongol craftsmen sometimes complemented silver artifacts with drum-shaped coral and native green turquoise. In Figure 8 we see this technique realized in a Mongol grooming kit centerpiece (missing two tools), an amulet box, and an ornament that was almost certainly sewn to clothing (note the thread holes). Each soldered and sealed amulet in Figure 9 probably hung from a Mongol headdress.

The large, heavy pendant in Figure 10, purchased in Tibet, depicts a conch shell for authority, two horses for endurance, and the double fish for conjugal bliss. On the reverse, the silversmith engraved an elaborate lotus.

Artifacts modified with coral and turquoise beads after the Cultural Revolution appear in Figures 11 through 16. By adding just a few beads on a string, a worker in a government shop could quickly transform any silver piece, no matter what its historical or cultural significance, into a woman's necklace. I purchased these items in the United States from dealers who bought them in Beijing during the 1980's.

In its pristine state, the basket in Figure 11 either functioned as an amulet (with dangles), or as the centerpiece on a grooming kit. The two different styles of chain betray the tampering.

In Figure 12, we can see how coral, turquoise, and carved-bone beads were used to turn a Qing dynasty grooming kit centerpiece into a neckpiece. Strangely, this anonymous bead stringer left the original silver bat and some of the chains. Since grooming tools probably hung from the bottom of this item, I suspect that the stringer also added the bells.

The government workers logically attached smaller beads and chains to the smaller amulets, such as the three enameled pieces in Figure 13. A beautifully enameled blue lion, which once guarded a young boy, now hangs from coral and turquoise beads. Two of the bells, still enameled, match the lion and are in all probability

Figure 15

original to the piece. Tiny coral, turquoise, bone, and glass beads adorn the double-fish amulet for marital bliss or a balance of opposites. Similar beads supplement the enameled silver boy carrying a lotus and reading a book astride his ox.

To create the mongrel in Figure 14, the stringer added drum-shaped coral beads, chunks of turquoise, and carved-bone beads to the double-gourd pendant with its wish for the birth of many sons. Notice that the stones on the necklace differ in shape and color from those on the amulet. Because all of these stones detract from the gorgeous enameling on the silver, I don't believe any are original.

Figure 15 depicts two unusual needle cases that resurfaced as pendants on necklaces. The silver baby (for fertility) standing in the ingot (for wealth) clasps a second ingot in his hands. On the second example, a character in a lotus position holds a *mani*, or Buddhist wish-granting stone. When the stringer added the neck chain and beads, both of these expensive dowry pieces became useless as needle cases.

The old fragrance carrier in Figure 16 still boasts its original chain just above the lid. But the neck chain is obviously new, and

Figure 16

the coral and turquoise beads clash with the carnelian dangles (which are themselves probably replacements).

Turquoise

Tibetans have always treasured imported deep blue turquoise, "the stone that stole its color from the sky," for its talismatic power against evil spirits and disease. According to Tibetan belief, turquoise purified the blood, protected one from the evil eye, cleansed one from any diseases affecting the liver, and prevented bad dreams. They incorporated deep blue turquoise into their adornments and their ritual artifacts, and they even used it as currency. Their native green turquoise, meanwhile, was unappreciated since they also felt that blue turquoise turned green when an individual harbored an illness.

The pieces in Figure 17, made for a woman's headdress, each features a valuable deep blue chunk of turquoise. The artisan obviously crafted the silver to fit over the irregularly shaped stone. Similar turquoise chunks adorn Tibetan rings, earrings, bracelets, *ga'us*, and eating kits.

Although Marco Polo mentions Szechwan turquoise-mining operations in his notes, this mineral rarely appears on Han or Manchu silver pieces from the Qing dynasty. The Chinese believed that turquoise, which they called "the green fir-stone," came from conifer trees, and so they regarded it as rather mundane. Occasionally, we find a silver piece inlaid with turquoise or a bit of turquoise carved into a representational image, such as the dragon's head on the hairpin in Figure 5. In Figure 18 a turquoise cabochon enhances an enameled amulet. The center of such a piece usually contains either a semi-precious stone or a compass.

Carnelian

Native to India, the semi-precious stone called carnelian probably found its way to China over the Silk Road. Once they appreciated its properties, Chinese craftsmen turned this mineral into pieces of every imaginable size and shape. Carnelian often occurs in a deep orange hue similar to that of red coral, and I suspect the Chinese therefore credited it with semi-magical powers.

The large silver plaque in Figure 19, which has a carnelian in the center, adorned the front of a Tibetan woman's dress. It's a wholly authentic piece, as opposed to the amulets in Figure 20.

Figure 17

I believe all the carnelian in these items was added to the silver for sale to the West.

The government workshops were also responsible for the neckrings in Figures 21, 22, and 23. Every piece of this type I have seen contains a qilin or a lock with a qilin on it on the bottom, two dragons fighting over a pearl in the center, and a wire ring with carnelian and blue-enameled silver beads. The diameters of Qing carnelian neckrings vary greatly. The stones are sometimes oval, (Figures 21 and 23), and sometimes circular (Figure 22). We find both orange and white carnelian in Figure 24. The turquoise and carnelian beads on the bottoms of Figures 21 and 22 probably replaced bells, similar to the ones dangling from the qilin in Figure 23. Despite their many differences, I feel these pieces all bear the imprint of a single workshop.

Figure 24 shows how a government worker could use carved carnelian beads, turquoise, and silver dangles to transform a simple qilin into a necklace for a woman. Another unknown artisan employed a similar technique to create the piece in Figure 25, converting a beautiful enameled shrine into wearable jewelry.

Jade

The Qing dynasty Chinese valued jade above even gold or diamonds, and they attributed special properties to it. In Chinese belief, jade was considered the "link between Heaven and Earth." This mineral preserved the body and guaranteed resurrection. When a person died, relatives set a jade cicada on his tongue to secure his soul's passage to its new life. As extra insurance, the relatives sometimes filled all nine of the body orifices with pieces of jade. They would also place over the corpse's heart a round jade *pi* disc, which has represented Heaven in Chinese rituals as far back as the Neolithic era.

Some people believed that, mixed with dew water and rice, powdered jade insured longevity. Others felt that a man could live a thousand years if he swallowed a piece of jade under certain auspicious circumstances.

The sound of jade tinkling on a robe announced that the wearer was a gentleman. Qing dynasty males wore jade discs, grooming tools with jade centerpieces, and jade amulets combined with silver, suspended from their sashes.

Beyond conferring immortality and status, jade also protected the wearer from disease and misadventure. Women wore jade rings, earrings, bracelets, pendants, and even sewed jade pieces to their skirts.

Chinese jade pieces are actually shaped by grinding, not carving. In ancient times, craftsmen used water, hollow bamboo rods, and abrasive sand to work the stones into a pleasing form. Authenticity has always mattered. The artisans knew that real jade cannot be scratched with steel, has an oily appearance, and causes a drop of water to bead (not spread) on the surface.

In Chapter 3 we examined some Qing dynasty grooming tool sets with jade centerpieces. Craftsmen preparing kits for the nobility tended to enclose the jade in a silver or gilded-silver frame to protect it, but smiths fashioning grooming kits for the minorities did not bother with this flourish. Lotus blossom centerpieces of carved jade and beads of jade, amber, and glass embellish the grooming kit in Figure 26. Some of the chains and beads on this piece, purchased from the family that owned it, are obviously replacements. The supplements destroyed the symmetry, but they give the kit a certain character.

In Figure 27 the carnelian Monkey King (for protection), the

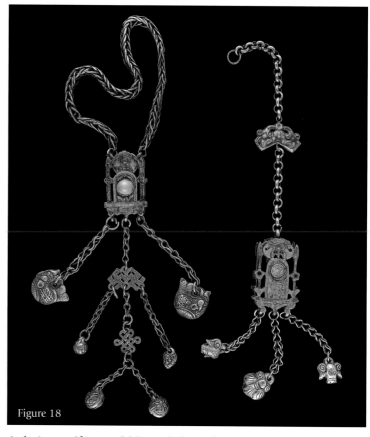

Figure 18

jade ingot (for wealth), and the jade musical stone (for good fortune) add meaning to a grooming kit probably worn by a wealthy minority official. The minorities also favored large carvings of old jade suspended from silver chains. The fine example in Figure 28 comes from the Bai. Most dealers today would appraise the jade at a higher value than the silver. In Figure 29 a man's waist hanging includes the double fish for conjugal bliss, coral for strength and good fortune, a jade *pi* symbolizing Heaven, and silver bells to frighten away evil spirits.

Small jade carvings, some with moving parts, enhance many of the silver artifacts purchased in China in the 1970's and 1980's. Each silver amulet in Figure 30 was probably originally a centerpiece on a small grooming kit. Young boys or women originally wore the qilins in Figure 31. The jade dangles on all these pieces, while appealing in their own right, undoubtedly represent missing silver parts and now detract from the qilins.

By adding tassels and silver beadcaps, an artisan could transform an old carved jade bead into a toggle. Figure 32 shows such pieces, probably of Tibetan or Mongol heritage. The silver bead caps are studded with turquoise and coral.

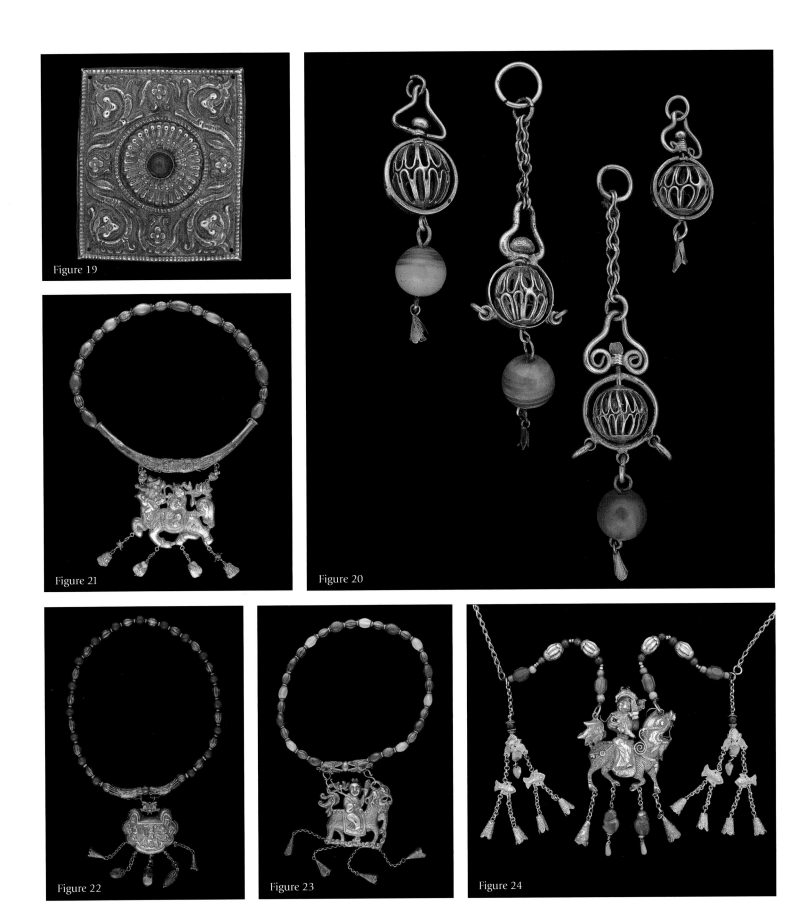

Figure 19

Figure 20

Figure 21

Figure 22

Figure 23

Figure 24

A Plea for Preservation and Purity

I would like to use my final beaded pieces—the odd collections of amulets enhancing the artifacts in Figures 33, 34, and 35—to argue that we collectors of Chinese silver should follow a particular ethic. Our obligation, I feel, is to preserve these works in their original form.

The mustache combs, in Figure 33, found in antique shops in the United States, appear to be genuine cultural artifacts. Their owners added the various beads and amulets primarily as security talismans, but also to make the combs more visually appealing.

By contrast, the hangings in Figures 34 and 35, which I purchased in Beijing in 1999, are probably recent assemblages made for the tourists. The string looks brand new, and I believe the hangings represent an attempt to sell the pieces with random beads to Westerners. This time around, however, it isn't the government that's creating the mongrels. These pieces issue from individual entrepreneurs.

Some of the timeworn beads are valuable in their own right, but neither they nor the silver talismans were ever worn this way in the Qing dynasty. Strangely enough, such hangings—as well as the beaded necklaces—are becoming collector's items and the money that dealers ask for these amulets often exceeds the prices of genuine Qing era artifacts.

Other hybrids surface closer to home. In the United States, and in Europe, jewelry designers are still using Qing dynasty locks, fragrance carriers, needle cases, qilins, and centerpieces of grooming kits, in their contemporary creations. To do this, they often remove original chains and dangles, and destroy the intrinsic function of the silver relic. Unfortunately, the new constructions sell well in museum gift shops and in small boutiques.

We purists can only shake our heads at the damage still being done—as it was in the 1970's and 1980's—and try to counter the crisis by collecting the remaining artifacts in their original styles and configurations. Each authentic item we rescue becomes a piece in the fascinating and valuable puzzle known as Chinese social history, so much of which was lost or distorted during the Cultural Revolution.

The Qing dynasty peoples—Han, Manchu, Mongol, Tibetan, and the various minorities—preserved many beautiful customs, beliefs, and myths in their silver adornments. For a time, these

Figure 25

artifacts and the heritage they bespoke lay buried in the warehouses of Beijing. Now, by good fortune of the sort in which the Qing peoples so obviously believed, the silver adornments have surfaced again. We must seize this opportunity to protect these pieces from the ravages of time and exploitation, and thereby safeguard their significance for future generations.

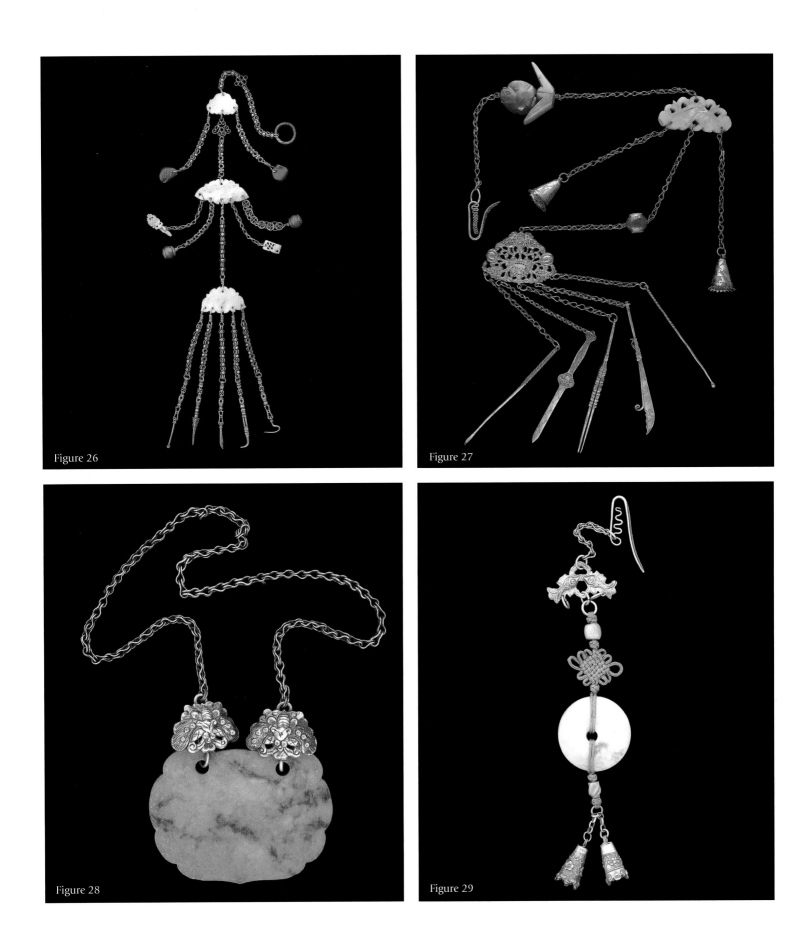

Figure 26

Figure 27

Figure 28

Figure 29

Figure 30

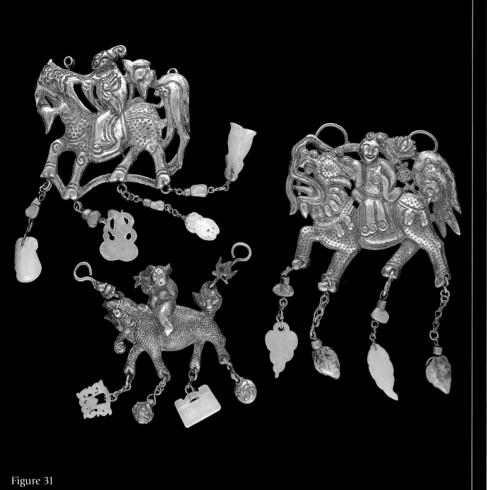

Figure 31

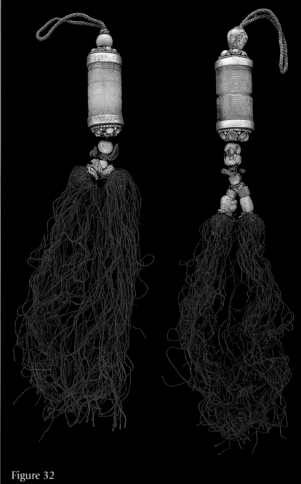

Figure 32

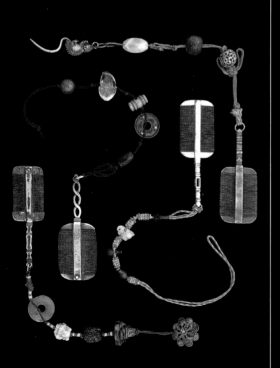

Figure 33

Figure 34

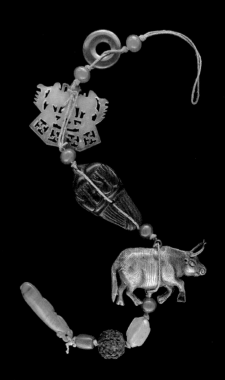

Figure 35

Eight Buddhist Symbols

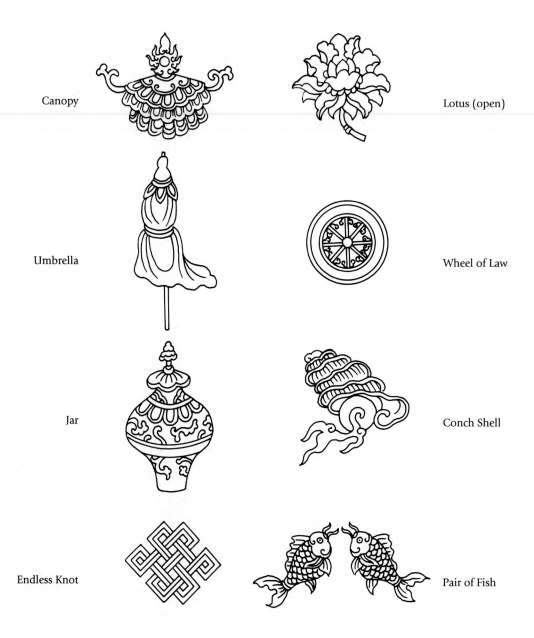

Canopy

Lotus (open)

Umbrella

Wheel of Law

Jar

Conch Shell

Endless Knot

Pair of Fish

Glossary of Chinese Symbolism and Rebuses

In Chinese art, certain objects and mythological characters denote happiness, fertility, longevity, wealth, mutual devotion, and protection. These symbols are easily recognizable to most Chinese. When they are combined in certain ways, they form new meanings through the use of rebuses or puns on words that sound the same.

For instance, the word for bat, *fu*, sounds like the word for blessings or happiness. A bat hovering over an antique Chinese coin—with a square center known as an eye—forms a rebus for "happiness in front of your eyes."

Deciphering the meanings of the symbols or rebuses often indicates the purpose—birth, betrothal, wedding, birthday, retirement, etc.—for the original presentation. In this glossary, I have attempted to present the symbolic meanings of the items and characters most often found on silver, as well as some of the rebuses that may be formed by combining them.

AMBER A symbol of courage, amber is considered to be the "soul of the tiger" in China. It also denotes longevity because it is derived from ancient pine tree resin. Amber is found in Yunnan Province and also imported from Burma.

ANIMALS OF THE ZODIAC According to legend, Buddha called all the animals to him, but only twelve answered his summons. The twelve yearly cycles of the Chinese calendar were named after the twelve: the Rat, the Ox, the Tiger, the Rabbit, the Dragon, the Snake, the Horse, the Sheep, the Monkey, the Rooster, the Dog, and the Pig.

APPLE The word for apple forms a rebus for "peace," and also symbolizes female beauty.

BABY A symbol for fertility and potency, a baby is often shown holding a lotus blossom, which forms a rebus for "successive sons." A baby sitting or standing in an ingot denotes a wish for both wealth and male progeny.

BADGER Phonetically similar to the word for enjoying oneself, the badger and magpie together express a wish for the experience of great happiness. Two badgers form a rebus for "double happiness" or marital bliss.

BAMBOO A popular symbol for honest officials, the bamboo represents longevity (because it is an evergreen), courage in the midst of adversity (since it explodes in a fire and frightens away demons), modesty (since it has an empty interior), fidelity, and integrity. The bamboo and plum represent man and wife in a scene, and if a couple is also present, marital bliss.

BASKET A decorated basket, symbol of Daoist Immortal Lan Caihe, represents abundance. It is often the contents of the basket that are important, however. A basket with a baby depicts a wish for abundant sons, whereas a basket with a bat denotes a profusion of happiness. The flowers and fruits found in baskets all have individual meanings and give the piece added significance.

BAT The word for bat, *fu*, is a homonym for good fortune, blessings, happiness, and prosperity. An upside down bat forms a rebus on the word "arrived" and proclaims the arrival of happiness. A bat descending from clouds brings blessings from heaven, a bat carrying a swastika on a ribbon in its mouth denotes 10,000 efficacies, and 5 bats broadcast the Five Blessings—old age, wealth, a love of virtue, health, and a peaceful death. A bat poised over the top of a coin with a square center forms a rebus for "blessings in front of your eyes."

BELLS The sound of bells terrifies evil spirits and offer protection. The Chinese word for bell, *zhong*, also stands for "hitting the mark" so bells also represent success.

BOOK A book symbolizes the wisdom of a scholar.

BOTTLE GOURD The bottle gourd, symbol of Daoist Immortal Li Tieguai, held a magic potion, which allowed him to raise the dead or trap evil spirits. Because of this, it is associated with longevity and healing. The bottle gourd also symbolizes fertility because of its many seeds and swelling contour, wealth since it is a homonym for *hulu* meaning good fortune, and longevity. Numerous gourds on vines form a rebus for "ceaseless generations."

BUDDHA'S HAND The citron fruit, *fushou*, resembles a Buddha's hand with fingers outstretched. The name is homophonous with the words for happiness and longevity, which it symbolizes. Since the plant is also very aromatic, it is thought to dispel demons and the dried peel has medicinal value. Together with the peach and

Eight Symbols of the Daoist Immortals

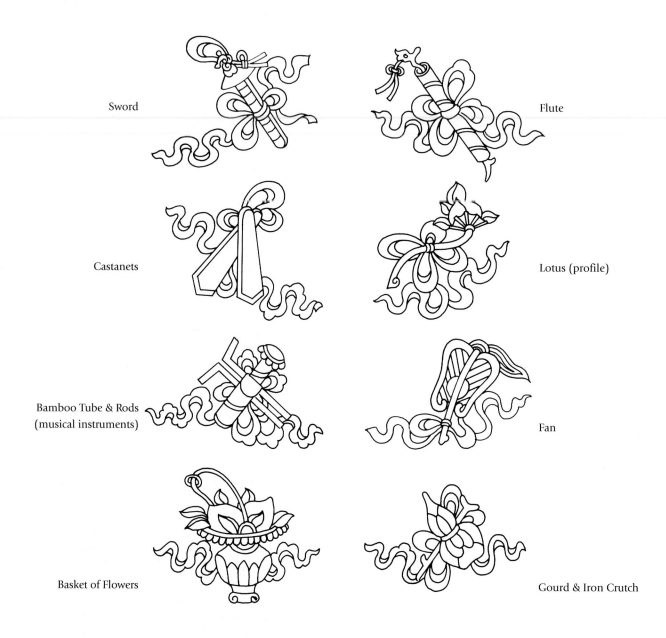

Sword

Flute

Castanets

Lotus (profile)

Bamboo Tube & Rods
(musical instruments)

Fan

Basket of Flowers

Gourd & Iron Crutch

pomegranate, the trio form the "Three Plenties"—happiness (citron), longevity (peach), and fertility (pomegranate).

BUTTERFLY Often called the "Chinese Cupid," the butterfly brings longevity, summer, joy, and marital happiness. The Chinese word for butterfly also sounds like the word for "eighty."

CAT The word for cat, *mao*, is a homonym for seventy so it represents longevity. With its ability to see in the dark, the cat dispels evil spirits and symbolizes protection. The cat (70) is often shown with a butterfly (80), forming the rebus *maodie*, which is an auspicious expression for longevity.

CHRYSANTHEMUM A symbol of autumn and contented middle age, the chrysanthemum denotes a life of ease and a peaceful retirement. It blooms when most flowers shrivel in the early frost, giving it a positive meaning for an elderly person. The word for the flower is also similar to words meaning "to remain" and "long time," forming an association with longevity.

CICADA The cicada, with a life span of 17 years, indicates longevity, but it also signifies immortality, rebirth, and eternal youth.

CLOUDS Often used to unify a design, clouds symbolize good fortune and happiness, and in connection with rain, fertility. The "thunder pattern" evolved from archaic pictographs of meandering spirals representing clouds and thunder.

COIN A round Chinese coin encircling a square center symbolizes abundance and the desire for wealth. Coins or a coin shape hung around a child's neck protected him and helped him overcome adversity. Many families threw coins and coin amulets onto a marriage bed to insure the birth of numerous successful sons. Interlocking coins are a popular motif on both Chinese fine art and folk art.

CORAL The deep red stone brings good fortune and strength, and prevents hemorrhages.

CRAB The crab dispels evil spirits, and also engenders harmony when found with a stalk of grain in its mouth.

CRANE Legend gave the crane, often shown with a pine tree or a stone, a life span of 2,000 years so it symbolizes longevity. The White Crane transports Xiwangmu, the Queen Mother of the West, and other Immortals. Since the crane rules over all the birds, a crane standing on a rock denotes an official. Two cranes flying toward the sun represent a wish for the recipient to rise in position. A crane shown with a pine tree carries a wish for a bride and groom to live together for many years.

DEER The word for deer, *lu*, is a homonym for "official's salary" so a deer represents wealth and achievement. Since the Chinese believe that the deer lives a long time and is the only animal who can find the sacred fungus of immortality, it also denotes longevity. Shouxing, the God of Longevity, is occasionally shown on or beside a deer. In the novel entitled *The Metamorphoses of the Gods*, Jaing Ziya rides a deer. A scene depicting an official with a deer on a piece of silver symbolizes a wish for the recipient to achieve fame and acquire wealth.

DOG Since it is believed that a dog can bite evil spirits, a silver dog is worn for protection. In southwestern China, people also believe that a dog brought rice to mankind.

DONGFANG SHUO An official in the Court of Emperor Wu (140-87 B.C.), Dongfang symbolizes longevity and cleverness. One legend claims that he drank some of the elixir of immortality that belonged to the Emperor. When threatened with death, Dongfang insisted that he could not be killed since he was now immortal and he was believed. Another legend insists that he stole peaches of immortality from the garden of the Queen Mother of the West and lived for thousands of years. He is often depicted as a bearded old man carrying a heavy branch laden with peaches.

DONKEY The donkey, emblem of Daoist Immortal Zhang Guolao, could carry him 1,000 miles a day, making him a symbol for endurance. Usually depicted upside down with his feet tied in the air, he was kept in a container by Guolao until he needed him.

DOUBLE HAPPINESS Two linked joy characters, *shuangxi*, form this wish for marital bliss, which we often find adorning wedding presents.

DRAGON A symbol for male vigor, bravery, power, nobility, and fertility, the good-natured Chinese dragon often appears on silver wedding gifts. The emblem for Imperial authority, it also represents a bridegroom, who is "emperor for a day." The *lung* dragon, which inhabits the sky, is often depicted with the antlers of a deer, the head of a camel, the ears of a cow, the neck of a snake, the stomach of a frog, the scales of a carp, and the claws of an eagle. A beard dangles beneath its chin and whiskers hang from the sides of its mouth. Legend tells us that it could bring rain and protect one from demons. The five-clawed and the four-clawed dragons could only be used in the adornments of high officials, but the commoner could incorporate the lesser, scaleless, forked-tail *ch'ih* dragon or the dragonfish into a design. The word *ch'ih* is a pun on the word "cure," increasing its protective value. Two dragons chasing a pearl denote thunder and fertility.

Eight Treasures

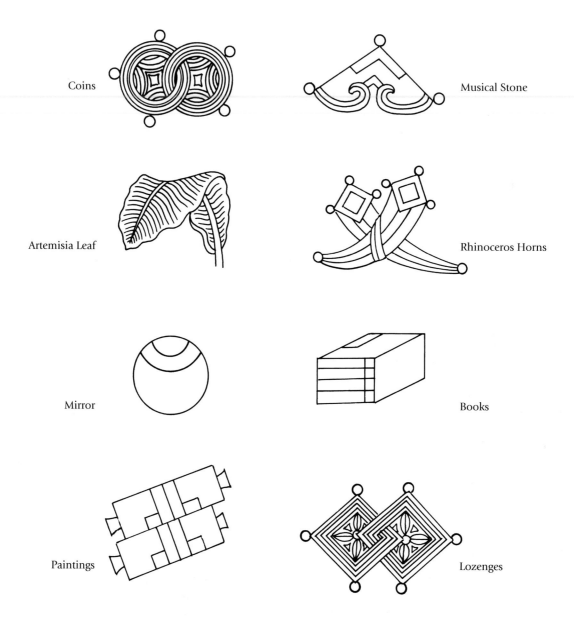

Coins

Musical Stone

Artemisia Leaf

Rhinoceros Horns

Mirror

Books

Paintings

Lozenges

DRAGONFISH When the sturgeon of the Yellow River fight through the rapids and pass through the Longmen Gate, they become dragonfish. Because of its struggle and eventual success, the dragonfish symbolizes success on the civil service examinations.

DUCK Two mandarin ducks bring marital bliss and fidelity, while the Buddhists believe that a single duck suppresses evil.

EAGLE A symbol of courage and bravery, the eagle offers protection from demons.

EIGHT BUDDHIST SYMBOLS These eight auspicious symbols came to China by way of India in the Middle Ages and were originally associated with Buddha.
Canopy—Buddha's victorious enlightenment, as well as protection from evil.
Lotus—purity, divinity, and renunciation of desires.
Umbrella (also called a parasol)—nobility, as well as protection
Wheel of the Law—Buddha's teachings and the transformation they bring. The hub stands for moral discipline, the 8 spokes represent Buddha's Noble Eightfold Path, and the rim denotes meditation.
Jar (also called Treasure Vase)—inexhaustible treasures topped by the wish-granting tree, whose roots contain the elixir of immortality.
Conch Shell—used to call the faithful to prayer, it represents the voice of Buddha preaching. A symbol of authority, its blast also frightens away evil spirits and illness.
Endless Knot—happiness, longevity, and Buddha's endless wisdom and compassion.
Pair of Fish—complete freedom from all restraints and a balance of opposites in nature.

EIGHT DAOIST IMMORTALS (AND THEIR SYMBOLS) The Eight Immortals are deified human beings who have no temples, but are nevertheless worshipped as symbols of longevity and immortality. They reached their positions through meditation, good deeds, and sacrifices. They have the power to raise the dead, become visible or invisible on demand, and can turn anything into gold by using the Philosopher's Stone. Also called the *Baxian*, each one carries an identifying symbol. Along with the God of Longevity, silver depictions of the Eight Immortals often adorn baby hats.

Lu Dongbin, who was a scholar, is the patron saint of barbers and scholars, but the sick also pray to him since he owns a sword of supernatural power to slay dragons and drive away evil spirits and illnesses. He often slings the sword over his shoulder and carries a flywhisk.

Han Xiangzi, the patron saint of musicians, is always shown with a flute. He could force flowers to blossom instantaneously,

but did not know the value of money. If he ever received any, he scattered it over the ground.

Cao Guojiu, the patron saint of actors, always wears the Imperial robes of a Court official since he belonged to the royal family during the Sung dynasty. He carries a pair of castanets, originally Court tablets which allowed a person free access to the palace.

He Xiangu is recognized by either her long-stemmed lotus seen in profile, or her flywhisk. According to legend, she wandered the hills and lived on powdered mother-of-pearl and moonbeams, which made her immortal. She is the patron saint of housewives.

Zhang Guolao may be recognized by the *Yu Ku*, a musical instrument consisting of a bamboo tube and rods with hooks on the end, but he might be better known for the donkey he rides. When he doesn't need the donkey, which can carry him 1,000 miles a day, he folds it up and stores it in a gourd. Zhang Guolao is the patron saint of artists and calligraphers.

Zhongli Quan, the head of the Eight and patron saint of military personnel, may be recognized by the fan he uses to raise the dead. He knows the formula for the elixir of life and invented transmutation. An obese man with a bare stomach, he supposedly has the power to turn mercury and lead into silver.

Lan Caihe, the patron saint of florists, is depicted as a young man carrying a basket of flowers through the streets warning everyone that life is fleeting.

Li Tieguai, the patron saint of both the sick and herbal healers, is always depicted with a gourd and an iron crutch. According to legend, his spirit was summoned by Laozi, who appreciated his expertise in magic, and when he returned late, he found that his assistant had burned his body. Looking for a body to enter, he could only find a crippled beggar. He was the first to attain immortality after Xiwangmu cured his leg ulcer and tutored him. Worshippers pray to him for both good fortune and longevity.

EIGHT TREASURES The Eight Treasures, also known as the Eight Precious Things, were originally associated with Buddhism, but today, they possess the efficacy of a charm.
Coin—represents wealth, abundance, and success in one's career.
Musical Stone—denotes good fortune and prosperity.
Artemisia Leaf (also known as yarrow or mugwort)—frightens away evil spirits.
Rhinoceros Horns—used in identifying poison in a liquid.
Mirror—protects the owner from evil spirits by reflecting their image and also embodies marital happiness.
Books—symbolize the wisdom of a scholar.
Paintings—represent the culture of a scholar.
Lozenges—denote victory.

EIGHT TRIGRAMS Eight groups of three broken (female) and unbroken (male) lines arranged in a circle around the yin-yang is called the *Ba Gua*, or Eight Trigrams. It was, and still is, used in divination and also protects the owner from evil. Emperor Fuxi devised the symbol from the markings on the back of a tortoise in 2852 B.C. Seventeen hundred years later, Wenwang wrote the *Book of Changes* explaining their meaning.

EIGHTEEN LUOHAN The Eighteen Luohan are the main disciples of Buddha and guardians of the scripture. Each has his own emblem and pose. They are the Buddhist equivalent of the Eight Immortals of Daoism.

ENDLESS KNOT The endless knot symbolizes happiness and a long life without any setbacks. One of the Eight Buddhist Emblems, it also represents Buddha's endless wisdom and compassion.

FAN The fan, emblem of Daoist Immortal Zhongli Quan, raises the dead, and symbolizes both goodness and the rank of an official. Many gods also use it to dispel evil spirits.

FISH The word for fish, *yu*, is phonetically the same as the word for affluence so the fish symbolizes abundance and wealth. Two carp or goldfish represent marital bliss, fertility, prosperity, or in Buddhist belief, a balance of opposites. A small boy with a fish represents a wish for an abundance of high-ranking sons. Fish swimming in water form a pun for "agreeing like fish and water." A school of fish swimming in water denotes a houseful of wealth, as well as marital happiness. A goldfish wrapped in a lotus leaf forms a rebus for "a purse filled with gold." If a fish is combined with a chime, a combination often found on silver grooming kits, it represents an abundance of joy. The word for catfish sounds like the word for "year" so two catfish, a *ruyi*, and fungus form a pun for wishes coming true year after year.

FIVE POISONOUS CREATURES The Five Poisonous Creatures include the snake, scorpion, centipede, spider, and toad. Occasionally, a lizard will replace one of them. On the fifth of May, pictures of the group are attached to the beams of houses to protect the residents from their venom and from evil spirits. Silver adornment showing the creatures are worn for the same purpose.

FLOWERS OF THE FOUR SEASONS Certain flowers typify the different seasons—the peony or lotus for summer, the chrysanthemum for autumn, the plum blossom for winter, and the magnolia or orchid for spring.

FLYWHISK The flywhisk is usually the sign of an official, but in Daoism, it denotes an instrument of magic, and for Buddhists, it represents the prohibition against killing.

FOUR MYTHICAL CREATURES This quadrangle is represented by the dragon who rules over the East and controls spring by determining rainfall, the tortoise who controls the North and the harsh winter, the phoenix who is an emblem of the South and brings the joys of summer, and the qilin who indicates the West and the maturity and fulfillment of fall.

FOUR SCHOLAR SYMBOLS In the Qing dynasty, books, paintings, a chessboard, and the lute represented the leisure pursuits of a scholar.

FOUR TREASURES OF THE SCHOLAR'S STUDY Four items— the ink stone, inkstick, paper, and writing brush—symbolize the scholar.

FOX The fox, worshipped as a harbinger of good fortune, also lives a long time and can represent longevity.

FROG Because of its great reproductive powers, the frog is a fertility symbol and some even believe that the frog's seed falls with the dew from heaven. In ancient times, the frog was considered a god and amulets were worn for protection from evil spirits.

FU LU SHOU These three mythological celestial figures, also known as the Three Star Gods or the Three Stellar Gods, bring happiness, good fortune, and longevity. Fuxing, the God of Blessings or Happiness, was a retired scholar-official and often cradles a ruyi or a child and has the symbol for happiness on his robe. Luxing, the God of Rank, wears an official's hat with winged flaps and carries an official ceremonial tablet or a *ruyi* and has the deer symbol on his robe. Shouxing, the God of Longevity, may be recognized by his elongated forehead, bald head, long white beard, a peach in one hand, and a staff of knotted wood with a gourd tied to the end in the other. The symbol for longevity often adorns his robe and a young acolyte, a deer, or a crane might also accompany him. Shouxing, the God of Longevity, riding a deer (a rebus for *lu* and Luxing) with a bat (a rebus for *fu* and Fuxing) behind or above him forms a rebus for the trio.

FUNGUS The *lingzhi*, or fungus of immortality and longevity, grows around the roots of trees. It frequently appears in illustrations with Daoist Immortals since it thrives on the islands where they live. It may also be found in the mouth of a deer or the beak of a crane. It represents all that is good, and is also a wish-fulfilling symbol like the *ruyi*, which resembles the shape of the plant.

GA'U The *ga'u* was an amulet box worn by Tibetans and Mongols for protection on a journey. They often wore several at once, and when they were not traveling, the *ga'u* sat on the family altar.

GOAT (and SHEEP) The goat represents peace in retirement. In China, little distinction is made between goats and sheep, but a lamb denotes filial piety. One of the six sacrificial animals, the goat was known in China long before the sheep, which was imported and called the "Hun-goat." The fat-tailed ram of the Mongols symbolized wealth, security, fertility, and endurance since it could survive the brutal Mongol winters on the fat stored in its tail.

GOOSE Since geese mate for life and always fly in pairs until one dies, they represent marital bliss and fidelity.

GRAPES Introduced into China in 126 B.C. from the Indo-Scythians, grapes represent the birth of many sons.

GUANYIN Guanyin, the Goddess of Mercy, often appears with a child in her arms, but can also be found carrying a vase, lotus, or pearl. Sometimes she simply folds her hands in prayer. Both men and women worship her and invoke her benevolence to give them sons, and heal or protect them in this world and the next.

HALBERD This ancient Chinese weapon brings good fortune and happiness. Three halberds in a vase with a musical stone and fish wish the recipient success in the three parts of the civil service examinations.

HEHE The Heavenly Twins, or *Hehe erhxian*, are usually shown as two young boys. They bring harmony, blessings, and wealth to a marriage or a business partnership. One always carries a lotus blossom, while the other totes a box filled with riches. They are a late manifestation of two poet monks, Hanshan and Shide, who lived in the Tang Dynasty and were the patron saints of marriages. In early representations, they are older and carry a broom and a fan, but in the Ming and Qing dynasty, they were usually represented as boys with the lotus and box. The lotus and box may also represent them and when these two items are combined with a *ruyi*, they form the rebus "may you enjoy a harmonious marriage in which all your dreams come true." Many still believe the pair also bring fertility to wedded couples.

HORSE Only officials could ride horses so the horse represents a wish for high office, as well as speed and perseverance. In addition to riderless horses, a popular figure on Chinese silver is the horse carrying a *Chuang-yuan*, a successful civil service candidate returning in triumph.

INGOT The saddle-shaped sycee indicates wealth. A child sitting in, standing in, or carrying an ingot represents a wish for riches, as does an official holding a sycee.

JADE According to Qing dynasty belief, jade granted status, longevity, and immortality, and protected the wearer from disease and harm.

LAOZI Laozi, a philosopher depicted as an old man riding an ox, supposedly wrote the *Tao Te Ching*, the basic text of Daoism. According to legend, he tired of the corruption in the Tang dynasty and headed West toward Central Asia. At the Hangu Pass, he gave his book to the official and was never seen again.

LICHEE The lichee fruit, usually represented with a rough skin, represents fertility and is often put under a wedding bed to bring an early arrival of sons. Together with the water chestnut, it forms a rebus for intelligence or cleverness.

LILY A symbol of harmony and friendship, the lily also forms a pun for "one hundred." When combined with a *ruyi*, it becomes a rebus for "a hundred wishes." Shown next to a box on a wedding gift, it wishes the bride and groom a hundred years of harmony. The day-lily, on the other hand, symbolizes fertility and also helps you to forget your problems.

LION The lion symbolizes courage, energy, and wisdom. For Buddhists, it also protects the law and official buildings.

LIU HAI As a benevolent money-giving deity, Liu Hai is usually pictured as a young boy or a man dancing around with a string of coins and his three-legged toad. The toad, which transports him wherever he wants to go, often escapes down the nearest well and Liu Hai uses the string of coins as bait to lure him out again.

LOTUS Rife with meaning, the lotus grows in mire but is not sullied by it, symbolizing purity in the midst of corruption, social advancement, and success on the civil service examinations. The lotus and an egret signal an honest official. Since it may be known as either *hehua* or *lianhua*, which form rebuses with "harmony" (*he*) or "continuous" (*lien*), the lotus also denotes marital bliss. Two lotus flowers on the same stalk are said to symbolize longevity and eternal love. The lotus, shown with a box and *ruyi*, forms a rebus for "a harmonious marriage where all wishes come true." Since the seedpod is already present when the lotus blooms, it predicts the early arrival of sons. A baby with a lotus is a rebus for the birth of successive sons. For Daoists, the lotus is usually shown with a long stem in profile. For Buddhists, who believe that the eight-petaled lotus represents the Eightfold path, the flower is usually shown with open petals. The lotus leaf denotes Buddha himself.

MAGNOLIA In ancient times, only the Emperor could own a magnolia, and occasionally, he presented a root to someone who had earned his favor. The white magnolia symbolizes feminine beauty, purity, and marital happiness. It may also be used as a pun for the word "jade," and combined with a crab apple, represents Hanlin Academy, also known as the Jade Hall.

MAGPIE The word for magpie, *xi*, is a pun for "happiness" so the bird is a harbinger of good news and joy. Regarded as a sacred bird by the Manchus, two magpies indicate marital bliss. A single magpie perched on the tip of a prunus branch forms a rebus for "happiness up to your eyebrows."

MANDARIN DUCKS Mandarin ducks mate for life and symbolize marital fidelity and bliss. If the ducks carry the lotus blossom and fruit in their beaks, this adds a wish for the blessing of sons.

MANI The *mani* is a Tibetan wish-ganting jewel, which fulfills the desires of anyone it shines upon.

MAITREYA Maitreya, previously known as Mi Lo Fu, is Buddha's successor and destined to return to earth to bring a new era of peace. Also called the "Laughing Buddha" or the "Fat-Bellied Buddha," he is depicted with an ample stomach, bare chest, bald pate, either long hair or ears, and a wide smile. The name Maitreya means "kindness" or "gentleness."

MEANDER The repeated border design of the key pattern symbolizes rebirth and abundance. Originally drawn as pairs of spiral figures, they were eventually joined and formed variations such as the cloud and thunder pattern, the swastika pattern, and the fish scale pattern.

MELON With its many seeds, the melon is an obvious fertility symbol. A melon and a butterfly form a rebus for numerous descendants.

MONKEY In China, the monkey is associated with high rank (marquis) and fertility. A monkey with a baby on its back forms a rebus for one's descendants to become high officials. A monkey on a horse embodies a wish for the recipient or his descendants to rise to the rank of an official. Often pictured with the peach of immortality, the monkey also represents the power to bestow longevity and is worshipped by Buddhists who seek health, protection, and success. The monkey and peach also form the rebus for "nobility and longevity" for the recipient and his descendants. An adult monkey with smaller monkeys around him or on his back is a pun wishing the person's descendants to have descendants of high rank.

MOUNTAINS Cloud-capped mountains symbolize earth in Chinese art. They insure cosmic order, permanence, and longevity. The most famous mountain, Kunlun, was the home of many deities including Xiwangmu. The tall, slender Shou Shan Mountain often pictured in Chinese scenes, is the Mountain of Longevity. Pine and bamboo trees, as well as rocky crags, often adorn its surface.

MOUTH ORGAN A mouth organ consisting of numerous bamboo pipes, the Chinese mouth organ, or *sheng*, is homophonous with the word meaning "to give birth." A baby or child with a *sheng* in its hand symbolizes the birth of sons who will attain high rank. Many of the riders on qilins are carrying a lotus and a *sheng*.

MUSICAL STONE One of the oldest instruments in Chinese history, the *qing* is phonetically the same as the word for blessings and good luck, so the instrument represents good fortune and prosperity.

MUSHROOMS Since mushrooms suddenly appear in profusion in barren soil, they represent fertility among the poor. For the rich, they denote a sudden rise in one's career "like mushrooms in the morning."

NARCISSUS Since it blooms around the Lunar New Year, the narcissus symbolizes good fortune in the coming year, career advancement, and marital bliss. Since it is thought to be able to recognize hidden talents, the narcissus brings recognition and rewards for diligence. Shown with a bamboo tree and stones, it denotes longevity and prosperity. Combined with the lingzhi fungus, nandina flower, and rocks, the group forms a rebus for the longevity fairy bestowing birthday greetings.

ORCHID The orchid embodies many meanings in Chinese art. It represents love, beauty, numerous progeny, and the couple itself, making it popular at weddings. Since Confucius praised its characteristics, it also symbolizes the superior man. Orchids in a vase represent compatibility and concord in a relationship since the *Book of Changes* refers to words of harmony resembling fragrant orchids.

OX In China, the word for ox and cow are interchangeable and typify abundance, strength, fertility, and marital bliss. Men and boys wore a silver ox to enhance their fertility and a merchant wore one to insure prosperity. A male child playing a flute on the back of an ox is a Buddhist metaphor for attaining nirvana.

PAVILION If a round or multi-cornered pavilion sits on a rock surrounded by clouds and cranes, it represents the Daoist Paradise, the Island in the Eastern Sea, where the Immortals live. Pavilions outside villages offer safety from the elements so it could also symbolize protection.

PEACH The peach has many meanings in Chinese art, but the most common is that of longevity and immortality. The peaches of immortality grow in the Heavenly Peach Orchard next to the Golden Palace of Xiwangmu. When they ripen every 3,000 years, she invites the Immortals and the Gods for a feast. In the novel *Journey to the West*, the monkey breaks into the orchard and eats the peaches, making him immortal as well. The peach also drives away evil spirits and has wondrous medical properties. The fruit cures lung diseases, the flower works as a laxative, the sap is a sedative, and an elixir made from the bark cures jaundice, dropsy, and asthma. No wonder the God of Longevity often holds a peach in his hand. The peach also symbolizes springtime and marriage, and many couples wed during February, when the peach tree blooms. A peach tree on a mountain with bats flying overhead and waves splashing at the base forms the following rebus for a birthday "May you live to be as old as the Southern Mountain with happiness as deep as the Eastern Sea."

PEARL The Chinese feel that a pearl captures the essence of the moon and symbolizes feminine beauty and purity. In Chinese mythology, pearl and jade trees covered Kunlun Mountain. Two dragons fighting over the pearl of potentiality adorned the Chinese Imperial coat of arms from the Han to the Qing dynasties.

PEONY A peony, the "King of Flowers," represents wealth and advancement, as well as spring, love, affection, and feminine beauty. It is frequently depicted with a phoenix. When shown with the pine tree, it symbolizes wealth, distinction, and longevity. The peony, combined with the crab apple and white magnolia, forms a rebus for "wealth and rank in the Jade Hall." The Jade Hall was Hanlin Academy, the official offices of China's brightest scholars. Thus, the rebus represents both wealth and the attainment of high official rank.

PHOENIX In mythology, the phoenix, or *feng huang*, only appears during the peaceful and prosperous reign of a just Emperor. It symbolizes happiness, warmth, the Empress, and the harvest. It can also influence fertility and when combined with a dragon at a wedding celebration, depicts the couple and marital bliss. The phoenix has been described as having the beak of a chicken, the crown of a mandarin duck, the neck of a snake, the front of a swan, the hinder parts of a qilin, the arched and vaulted back of a tortoise, the stripes of a dragon, and feathers of five colors. It is supposedly six feet in length and like the qilin, a vegetarian. The phoenix eats the seeds of the bamboo, lives in the dryandera trees, and wherever it flies, it is followed by a train of small birds.

PIG As a symbol of prosperity, fertility, and virility, pork is always served at wedding feasts and consumed before taking the civil service examinations. The most famous pig in Chinese literature is Chu Pachiai, who accompanied the monkey and the Buddhist monk Xuanzang to India to gather the sutras of Buddhism in the novel *Journey to the West*.

PINE TREE As an evergreen, the pine tree is one of the numerous longevity symbols, but it also represents nobility, strength, and vitality as it stands tall and strong in the harshest winter. Since the needles of a pine tree grow in pairs, the tree also symbolizes

wedded bliss. A pine tree and a crane, an important wedding motif, generate a wish for the new couple to live together into old age.

PLUM The five-petal plum blossom (prunus) denotes longevity, perseverance, and endurance because it blooms on a leafless branch in early spring. The delicate flower also represents beauty and virginity, as well as marital bliss when it is combined with a magpie, so it is a particularly popular motif for dowry gifts such as needle cases. On a gift for an elderly person, the magpie and plum may be interpreted as "happiness and longevity."

POMEGRANATE The pomegranate, with its many seeds, is a natural symbol for fertility, abundance, and posterity. It is usually depicted with part of the skin removed or else cut in half to show all of the seeds since the word *zi* can mean both "seed" or "son." A picture of a pomegranate, cap of office, and a jade belt sends a wish for the descendants of the recipient to hold the same high office. When Liu Hai's three-legged toad carries a branch of the pomegranate in its mouth, it symbolizes an abundance of both children and wealth.

QILIN The mythological qilin, like the phoenix, only appears during the reign of a benevolent ruler. He represents wisdom and cosmic harmony and is also thought to bring sons with the ability to become high officials. Composed of a dragon's head, one to three fleshy horns, a scaly body shaped like a deer, the hooves of a horse, and the tail and mane of a lion, the qilin also symbolizes longevity since it was thought to live for 2,000 years.

RABBIT In Chinese mythology, the rabbit (often called hare) resides on the moon and either singly, or as a pair, pounds out the elixir of immortality.

RAT Known for his ability to hoard, the rat symbolizes wealth, making him a favorite of the merchant class. Since rats are so hard to eliminate, some also consider them symbols of longevity.

RAVEN The red three-legged raven resides in the sun and is associated with fire and piety. In the beginning, there were ten sun-ravens, but their heat threatened to burn up the earth. Hou Yi, a famous archer in the Imperial guard, was called in to shoot down nine of them, leaving only one sun (sun-raven) in the sky.

ROOSTER The crowing of a rooster petrifies evil spirits so a rooster represents protection, as well as reliability and courage. The crowing also symbolizes achievement, male vigor, and fame so silver roosters were worn by boys and men for both protection and success in their endeavors. A rooster with a cockscomb flower above it forms a rebus for "one cockscomb above another" or "a rise in rank."

RUYI The curved *ruyi* scepter, a symbol of rank, is a wish-granting symbol. The *ruyi* also represents longevity and was originally used for defense. In the Qing dynasty, the *ruyi* was given as a wish for prosperity and longevity.

SHELL A shell, because of its shape, represents fertility, but in Southwest China, it was used for money and still denotes wealth and status. A conch shell represents authority and frightens demons.

SHOE Shoes symbolize harmony, but in the southern part of China, they also represent a wish for a son. Lotus shoes denote a wish for the woman to bear one son after another, while a shoe within a shoe is a wish for one's children to have children.

SHOU This symbol for long life may be depicted in 100 different ways. Combined with the swastika, it represents "10,000 years of long life." If it joins the symbol for happiness, we have "great happiness without limit." When seen with the endless knot, it forms "a long life without end."

SHOUXING Shouxing, the God of Longevity, is a stellar god who resides in a palace at the South Pole, the region of life. He is easily recognizable by his elongated bald skull, his long white beard and eyebrows, and the peach of immortality and knotty wood staff he holds in his hands. Often shown riding or standing next to a deer, Shouxing might also be accompanied by the crane who bears him through the clouds. Occasionally, a boy-servant appears at his side. This small figure might denote either renewed youth or posterity.

STREAMS The rippling sound of mountain streams represents the music of the flute.

SQUIRREL In a Sung dynasty painting, artist Ming Yuan Chuang first depicted the squirrel scampering amidst bunches of grapes. The grapevine spreads over everything, symbolizing ceaseless generations. The squirrel, capable of producing several litters a year, and the clusters of fruit containing numerous seeds, all symbolize fertility and the desire for sons. The squirrel is also considered industrious and persistent, adding encouragement to the need for male descendants.

SUN WUKONG In a humorous novel by Wu Chengen entitled *Journey to the West*, Sun Wukong is the monkey king who accompanies a Buddhist monk named Xuanzang on his pilgrimage to India to bring back the doctrines of Buddhism. In this sixteenth century novel, the mischievous monkey breaks into the orchard of Xiwangmu and eats the peaches of immortality slated for the banquet of the Immortals. As a result, he becomes immortal himself.

SUN The sun represents heaven and the Emperor, as well as intellectual enlightenment. It is masculine and the source of all brightness on earth.

SWASTIKA The swastika, one of the oldest symbols in China, sounds like *wan* in Chinese and forms a rebus for 10,000 efficacies. It is also associated with immortality, infinity, and the resignation of the spirit since it also represents Buddha's heart and is found in the footprints of Buddha.

SWORD The demon-slaying sword is the emblem of Immortal Lu Dongbin, but in Buddhism, the sword is a symbol of wisdom, cutting through all doubts on the path to knowledge.

THREE FRIENDS OF WINTER The pine, bamboo, and prunus trees are the three evergreens which symbolize friends who remain constant in the midst of adversity.

THREE-LEGGED TOAD Since a toad can live for thirty or forty years, it symbolizes longevity, but the three-legged toad also symbolizes wealth and the unattainable. Liu Hai owns a three-legged toad, which carries him anywhere he wants to go. When it escapes down a well, he lures it out again with a string of coins.

TIGER The tiger symbolizes courage and bravery since it drives away evil spirits. Chinese children's hats often have a silver tiger sewn to the front, and a painted tiger head decorated the shields of soldiers. The "King of the Wild Beasts" also represents magisterial dignity. Potolo, one of the Eighteen Luohan, is often seen riding a tiger, as are other deities. If a boy rides one, it becomes a symbol for filial piety.

TORTOISE One of the Four Mythical Animals of China, the tortoise symbolizes longevity and winter since it lives for such a long time. It also typifies strength, endurance, and steadfastness. Since the vaulted back of the tortoise signifies heaven, and the underside denotes the flat disc of earth, the whole animal represents the universe. Its shell was often used in divination.

TOWER A Chinese tower simply means the second story of a building, often a watchtower in a village, so it symbolizes protection.

TURQUOISE The stone that "stole its color from the sky" symbolizes protection from disease and evil spirits.

VASE The Chinese word for vase, *ping*, is a homonym for peace, but the vase also represents safety and harmony. The vase shape is often used for silver needle cases. Three halberds in a vase, a musical stone, and fish represents success in the three parts of the civil service examinations.

WAVES In Chinese ornamentation, waves represent water, the sea, and the tide. The word for tide, *chao*, is a homonym for "audience," which refers to an audience in the Imperial Court. In this case, a piece of silver with waves represents a wish for the recipient to rise to the position of a high official.

XUANZANG In the novel, *Journey to the West*, this monk travels to India with a monkey, pig, and a friar to bring back the sutras of Buddhism. He represents man's finer nature, which can attain immortality.

XIWANGMU Xiwangmu, the beautiful Queen Mother of the West, lives in a solid gold palace decorated with precious stones on Kunlun Mountain near the Lake of Jewels. When the peaches of immortality ripen every 3,000 years in the Heavenly Peach Orchard next to her palace, she invites the Gods and the Immortals to a feast to celebrate her birthday. It was on one of these momentous occasions that the monkey Sun Wukong broke into the orchard and ate the peaches himself. She is the only divinity who receives visitors in her home. She travels on a white crane (longevity), and bluebirds are her messengers. Two handmaidens attend her—one fans her, while the other holds a basket of her peaches. According to one legend, she has a consort named Dun Wang Gun, the Royal Lord of the East, with whom she had nine sons and twenty-four daughters. In other legends, she met with great emperors such as Fuxi and Muwang, but she is better known for giving the pill of immortality to Hou Yi, the archer who shot down nine of the ten sun-ravens before they could burn up the earth. She also tutored the Immortal Li Teiguai when she cured an ulcer on his leg and made him the patron deity of herbal healers.

YIN AND YANG Yin and Yang represent the dualistic natural principles in ancient Chinese cosmology. The Yin is the female, associated with the negative, the earth, the cold, even numbers, and the North. The Yang, or male principle, represents the positive and is related to heaven, warmth, odd numbers, the South, and the Emperor. The Great Ultimate created first the Yang, then the Yin. From them came the five elements, which generated the ten thousand things (everything). There is no Yang without Yin, and nature constantly strives to maintain a balance between the two. In the *Book of Changes*, the broken lines are Yin, while the unbroken lines are Yang.

Works Consulted

Alexander, William, and Mason, George Henry. *Views of 18th Century China: Costumes, History, Customs.* London: Studio Editions, 1988.

Alexeiev, Basil M. *Chinese Gods of Wealth.* Singapore: Graham Brash Pte Ltd, 1989.

Apfel, Iris Barrel. *Dragon Threads.* Newark: The Newark Museum, 1992.

Ayscough, Florence. *Chinese Women Yesterday and Today.* Boston: Houghton Mifflin Co., 1937.

Ball, Katherine M. *Decorative Motives in Oriental Art.* New York: Dodd, Mead & Co., 1927.

Barondes, R. de Rohan. *China: Lore, Legend and Lyrics.* New York: Philosophical Library, 1960.

Bartholomew, Terese Tse. *Myths & Rebuses in Chinese Art.* San Francisco: Asian Art Museum of San Francisco, 1988.

Beauty, Wealth and Power: Jewels and Ornaments of Asia. San Francisco: Asian Art Museum of San Francisco, 1992.

Beer, Robert. *The Encyclopedia of Tibetan Symbols and Motifs.* Boston, Shambhata, 1999.

Berger, Patricia, and Bartholomew, Terese Tse. *Mongolia: The Legacy of Chinggis Khan.* San Francisco: Asian Art Museum of San Francisco, 1993.

Berliner, Nancy Zeng. *Chinese Folk Art.* Boston: Little, Brown & Co., 1986.

Borel, France. *The Splendor of Ethnic Jewelry.* New York: Harry N. Abrams, Inc. 1994.

Boyer, Martha. *Mongol Jewelry.* London: Thames and Hudson, 1995.

Bredon, Juliet, and Mitrophonow, Igor. *The Moon Year: A Record of Chinese Customs and Festivals.* New York: Paragon Book Reprint Corp., 1966.

Burkhardt, V.R. *Chinese Creeds and Customs.* Taiwan: Book World Co., 1953.

Byron, John. *Portrait of a Chinese Paradise: Erotica and Sexual Customs of the Late Qing Period.* London, Quartet Books, 1987.

Catalogue of the Exhibition of Ch'ing Dynasty Costume Accessories, Taipei: National Palace Museum, 1986.

Christie, Anthony. *Chinese Mythology.* Middlesex: Paul Hamlyn, 1968.

Cooper, Elizabeth. *The Love Letters of a Chinese Lady.* Edinburgh and London: T. N. Foulis, 1919.

Cormack, Mr. J. G. *Chinese Birthday, Wedding, Funeral, and Other Customs.* Peking: The Commercial Press, 1923.

Cummins, Genevieve, and Taunton Nerylla. *Chatelaines.* Woodbridge, Antique Collectors' Club, Ltd, 1994.

Dawson, Jessica. *Chinese Ornament: The Lotus and the Dragon.* London: British Museum Publications, 1984.

Dickinson, Gary, and Wrigglesworth, Linda. *Imperial Wardrobe.* London: Bamboo Publishing, Ltd., 1990.

Doolittle, Rev. Justus. *Social Life of the Chinese.* New York: Harper and Brothers, Publishers, 1865.

Dursum, Brian A. *Birds, Beasts, Blossoms, and Bugs in East Asian Art.* Miami: The Lowe Art Museum, 1993.

Eberhard, Wolfram. *A Dictionary of Chinese Symbols.* London: Routledge and Kagan Paul Ltd., 1986.

Ecke, Tseng Yu-ho. *Chinese Folk Art 11: In American Collections, from Early 15th Century to Early 20th Century.* Honolulu, Tseng Yu-ho Ecke, 1977.

Fang, Jessica. *Chinese Silvers.* Taipei: Monet Designs Co., 1985.

Fang, Jing Pei. *Treasures of the Chinese Scholar.* New York, Weatherhill, 1997.

Fawdry, Marguerite. *Chinese Childhood.* New York, Barron's, 1977.

Garrett, Valery M. *A Collector's Guide to Chinese Dress Accessories.* Singapore: Times Editions, 1997.

Garrett, Valery M. *Traditional Chinese Clothing.* Oxford: Oxford University Press, 1987.

Gyllensvard, Bo. *Chinese Gold, Silver, and Porcelain: The Kempe Collection.* New York: The Asia Society, Inc. 1971.

Giles, Herbert. *China and the Manchus.* Cambridge: The University Press, 1912.

Hawley, W. M. *Chinese Art Symbols.* Hollywood: Hawley Publications, 1993.

Hoobler, Dorothy and Thomas. *The Chinese American Family Album.* Oxford: Oxford University Press, 1994.

Jackson, Beverley. *Splendid Slippers: A Thousand Years of an Erotic Tradition.* Berkeley: Ten Speed Press, 1997.

Jones, Schuyler. *Tibetan Nomads.* New York, Thames and Hudson, 1996.

Kennedy, Sylvia S. J. "Some Aspects of Children's Amulets," *Ornament,* 9(4), 1986.

Kuang Shizhao (editor). *Cothings and Ornaments of China's Miao People.* Beijing: The Nationality Press, 1985.

Lee, Lily Xiao Hong, and Stefanowska, A. D. *Biographical Dictionary of Chinese Women: The Qing Period, 1644-1911.* New York: M. E. Sharpe, Inc., 1998.

Lefebvre d'Argence, Rene-Yvon. *Treasures from the Shanghai Museum 6,000 Years of Chinese Art.* Shanghai and San Francisco: Shanghai Museum and Asian Art Museum of San Francisco, 1983.

Little, Mrs. Archibald. *The Land of the Blue Gown.* London: T. Fisher Unwin, 1908.

Li, Raymond. *A Glossary of Chinese Snuff Bottle Rebus.* Hong Kong: Nine Dragons Press, 1976.

Li, Raymond. *The Miniature Arts in China: Toggles, Pendants, and Other Accessories.* Hong Kong: Nine Dragons Press, 1988.

Li Yihua (editor). *Jewelry and Accessories of the Royal Consorts of Ch'ing Dynasty.* Beijing: Forbidden City Publishing House and Parco Publishing Co., 1992.

Liu, Robert K. *Collectible Beads: A Universal Aesthetic.* Vista: Ornament, Inc., 1995.

Liu, Robert K. "Imported Chinese Jewelry," *Ornament* 7(4), 1984.

Mack, John. *Ethnic Jewelry.* New York: Harry N. Abrams, Inc., 1988.

Masterpieces of Chinese Miniature Crafts in the National Palace Museum. Taipei: The National Palace Museum, 1971.

Meng, Ho Wing. *Straits Chinese Silver: A Collector's Guide.* Singapore: Times Editions Pte Ltd, 1984.

Minick, Scott and Ping, Jiao. *Arts and Crafts in China.* New York: Thames and Hudson, 1996.

Pal Pratpaditya. *Art of Tibet.* Los Angeles: Los Angeles County Museum of Art, 1990.

Palmer Martin, and Zhao, Ziaomin. *Essential Chinese Mythology.* San Francisco: Thorsons, 1997.

Paludan, Ann. *Chronicles of the Chinese Emperors.* London, Thames and Hudson Ltd., 1998.

Perkins, Dorothy. *Encyclopedia of China.* New York, Checkmark Books, 2000.

Pruitt, Ida. *A Daughter of Han.* Stanford, Stanford University Press, 1945.

Ren, Shan. *Cream of Yunling.* Yunnan: Yunnan Publishing House, 1998.

Reynolds, Valrae. *Tibet A Lost World.* New York: The American Federation of Arts, 1978.

Rossi, Gail. *A Hidden Civilization: The Dong People of China.* Singapore: Hagley & Hoyle Pte Ltd.

Roth, H. Ling. *Oriental Silverwork: Malay and Chinese.* Oxford: Oxford University Press, 1993.

Sanders, Tao Liu. *Dragons, Gods, and Spirits from Chinese Mythology.* New York: Shockton Books, 1983.

Shi, Shongshan (editor). *The Costumes and Adornments of Chinese Yi Nationality Picture Album.* Beijing: Beijing Arts and Crafts Publishing House, 1990.

Silver Ornaments of Miao Nationality. Beijing: Cultural Relics Publishing House, 2000.

Sinclair, Kevin. *The Forgotten Tribes of China.* Ontario: Cupress (Canada) Ltd., 1987.

Stalberg, Roberta Helmer, and Nesi, Ruth. *China's Crafts: the Story of How They're Made and What They Mean.* New York: Eurasia Press, 1980.

Stevens, Keith. *Chinese Gods.* London: Collins & Brown Limited, 1997.

Suyin, Han. *The Crippled Tree.* New York: G. P. Putnam's Sons, 1965.

Szeto, Naomi Yin-Yin and Garrett, Valery M. *Children of the Gods.* Hong Kong: Hong Kong Museum of History, 1990.

Tait, Hugh. *Jewelry: 7,000 Years.* New York: Harry N. Abrams Inc., 1986.

The Arts of the Ch'ing Dynasty. London: Charles F. Ince & Sons, Ltd., 1963.

The Forbidden City. Rotterdam: Museum Boymans-van Beunigen, 1990.

Tsi, Lee King, and Chang, Hu Shih. *Dragon and Phoenix: Chinese Lacquer Ware.* Cologne: The Museum of East Asian Art, 1990.

Vollmer, John E. *In The Presence of the Dragon Throne: Ch'ing Dynasty Costume (1644-1911) in the Royal Ontario Museum.* Toronto: Royal Ontario Museum, 1977.

Walters, Derek. *Chinese Mythology: An Encyclopedia of Myth and Legend.* London, Aquarian/Thorsons, 1992.

Wan Yi, Wang Shuqing, and Lu Yanzheng. *Daily Life in the Forbidden City: The Qing Dynasty 1644-1912.* New York: Viking, 1988.

Wang, Fushi (and other compilers). *Ethnic Costumes and Clothing Decorations from China.* Sichuan: Hai Feng Publishing Co., 1989.

Wang, Loretta H. *The Chinese Purse: Embroidered Purses of the Ch'ing Dynasty.* Union City: Heian International, Inc., 1986.

White, Julia M. and Bunker, Emma C. *Adornment for Eternity: Status and Rank in Chinese Adornment.* Denver: Denver Art Museum and the Woods Publishing Co., 1994.

Williams, C.A.S. *Outlines of Chinese Symbolism and Art Motives.* New York: Dover Publications, 1976.

Wilson, Verity. *Chinese Dress.* New York, Weatherhill, and the Victoria and Albert Museum, 1986.

Wimsatt. Genevieve. *A Griffin in China.* New York: Funk Wagnalls Co., 1927.

Wrigglesworth, Linda. *The Accessory.* London: Rustin Clark, 1991.

Wong, Grace, and Kheng, Gosh Eck. *Imperial Life in the Qing Dynasty: Treasures from the Shenyang Palace Museum.* Singapore: Historical and Cultural Exhibitions, Pte. Ltd.

Yang, Xin, and Zhu, Chengru. *Secret World of the Forbidden City.* Santa Ana, The Bowers Museum of Cultural Art, 2000.

Yutang, Lin. *My Country and My People.* New York, Reynal and Hitchcock, 1935.

Zhou, Xun, and Gao, Chunming. *5000 Years of Chinese Costumes.* Hong Kong, China Books and Periodicals, Inc. 1987.

Captions to Illustrations

CHAPTER ONE: NEEDLE CASES

1.   Regardless of style, most Chinese silver needle cases included a sheath that slid along a chain to seal the inner compartment.

2.   For the wealthier client, the silversmith created repoussé and enameled needle cases. He often added numerous dangles to enhance both design and symbolic meaning.

3.   This expensive needle case contains most of the original enameling. Blue was the favored color in the Qing dynasty. Note the dragon handles on the vase, the silver musical stone and upside-down bat for the arrival of good fortune, the lion handles for protection, and the baby dangles for fertility.

4.   Han women enjoyed costly repoussé needle cases. The four-sided vase with lion handles is highly unusual.

5.   Each side of an expensive vase-shaped needle case typically featured a different design. The silversmith took great care to achieve visual and mythic harmony among the symbols. Fish, birds, flowers, and emblems of the Eight Daoist Immortals adorn their examples.

6.   Engraved needle cases, rarer than their repoussé counterparts, were often hallmarked with the silversmith's signature. Many originated with the minorities of southwest China. The example with the two flags hails from the Republic period.

7.   Pierced needle cases, with their three-dimensional effects, took a long time to create and were probably expensive. Most featured twisted wire handles.

8.   This pierced tube-style pendant no longer functions as a needle case, for the sheath is now soldered in place. However, the elaborate plum blossom design still offers us its beauty and wishes for longevity.

9.   Note the piercing on these flat needle cases. The ensemble on the left includes a cicada-shaped fragrance carrier. These both feature the squirrel and grape theme.

10.   Enameling often covers the flat-topped needle cases. The silversmiths expressed their creativity by varying shapes and decorations.

11. Notice how skillfully each silversmith meshed the top and bottom designs on these unique needle cases, which incorporate a lid that lifts from the center.

12.   Needle cases varied dramatically in size. In general, the larger the case, the more elaborate the design. The plum blossoms on the small case are lovely, but cannot compare in intricacy with the squirrel and grape motif on the larger one.

13.   When it came to creating lifelike baby-shaped needle cases, some silversmiths were obviously very adept. Compare the expressions and clothing.

14.   The backs of these babies offer further evidence of the craftsman's skill. The small indentation on the back of each baby's head remains a mystery.

15.   Baby-shaped needle cases varied tremendously in size, shape, and complexity.

16.   These primitive babies, dressed only in simple *doudous*, appear older and less expensive than the examples in Figure 13. Auspicious red yarn replaces a broken or lost chain on one case. A gourd shape enhances the back of two of the figures, and the one on the left wears separate tiny bracelets. These babies also bear small indentations on the backs of their heads.

17.   Note the difference in the wings, torso, and head of each cicada in this fascinating collection. (Compliments of Robert Liu)

18.   A needle case in the shape of a scaled fish often surfaces in southern China, where many minorities earn their living by fishing. As the archetypal symbol for abundance, however, it is a popular motif for any region.

19.   A silver Hakka woman needle case symbolizes industriousness. Note the differences in the facial expressions, as well as the tiny jewelry, and staffs, and the ribbons that these women wove to sell.

20.   This rare blue and green enameled Hakka woman needle case with jewelry, ribbons, cool hat, and basket of fish obviously hung from a button on a wealthy woman's dress.

21.   A bell-shaped needle case often depicted the yin-yang or traditional Tibetan scrollwork. It could also portray typical Han figures such as the one on the right: Liu Hai with his string of cash and three-legged toad.

22.   The God of Wealth, in full military regalia and carrying an ingot, was probably a popular needle case design among the wives of wealthy merchants.

23.   Some needle cases possess unusual shapes, such as the antique coin on the right. Other cases depict unique designs on rectangular sheaths. A small opium box hangs from the needle case in the center.

24.   Fine examples of repoussé designs enhance these cylinder-shaped needle cases. The silversmith hammered the design into the back of a flat sheet of silver, then bent it into shape. Most of these cases feature typical floral patterns, but the one on the right contains all eight symbols of the Daoist Immortals.

25.   Minority needle cases often incorporated holes on the side for hanging. Round and hexagonal cases often surface with their old string or yarn cords still attached. Birds, flowers, and scenes from myths and folk tales adorn such cases.

26.   Leaf and floral designs embellish the surface of these needle cases from southwest China. Note the tapered ends on some.

27.   Six-sided needle cases may exhibit alternating designs, identical designs, or different designs on each panel.

28.   The engraved hexagonal case appears more primitive, and older than the others.

29.   Trees, mountains, horses, people, geometric designs, and monkeys decorate the old paktong needle cases.

30.   The four-sided paktong cases often employed pairs of figures on each side.

31.   Occasionally an old paktong needle case comes with an added bonus—an engraved design on the inside shaft. A Liu Hai figure for wealth or a bat for happiness may have charmed the original owner.

32.   Blue, green, or yellow enameling often adorned needle cases in the Qing dynasty. Red

enameling is rare since it tended to turn brown or maroon in firing. Different scenes enhance each panel of the six-sided case in the center, which sits on an unusual round base.

33. Muted green and yellow colors and leaf shapes emanating from the mouth of the vase enhance the old needle case on the far right. The cicada, with its orange enameling, probably hails from a later period.

34. The double needle cases of the southwest minorities appear nearly identical at first glance. Upon closer inspection, one finds subtle differences in the designs.

35. Beads of carved jade, glass, and silver heighten the intricacy of this needle case.

36. A tiger claw acupuncture tool, a revolving ball, various animals, fruit-shaped bells, and a silver fish hang from these complex assemblages.

37. The outer sheath of a double or triple tube needle case can feature repoussé or engraving.

38. These light, delicate cases employed lugs on the side to hold the chain. Older examples usually surface without chains. A figure often embellishes the top; flowers adorn the bottom.

39. These larger needle cases, which also utilize lugs on their side, weigh a great deal for their size. The chains either terminate at the bottom of the case or continue into dangles. Opium boxes and fish shapes frequently dangle from this style.

40. The engraved needle case hanging on a leather cord is a traditional Tibetan piece. The one on the left is reputed to be Mongol. The case in the center comes from the minorities, and employs unusual copper tips.

41. Tibetan cases, with their typical yak-hide interiors, often incorporate stones in the designs. The example on the right boasts a turquoise chunk on one side and coral on the other.

42. This Mongolian needle case—more delicate than most Tibetan and Han examples—includes a centerpeice of coral.

43. The baby "stepping up" on this needle case represents a wish for a son who will advance rapidly. The conversion to a pendant prevents us from raising the sheath to use the receptacle.

44. The needle case on this recent assemblage proves that such Qing dynasty artifacts were also gilded. Unfortunately, the necklace designer has removed the upper chain.

45. Similarities among certain cases indicate that they may have been created by the same shop or silversmith.

46. The silversmith's hallmark can often be found on the inner shaft of a needle case. This signature may be engraved—or stamped, as it is on all of these cases.

CHAPTER TWO: SYMBOLIC LOCKS

1. A silver lock symbolically secured a child to earth. Scenes and symbols typically adorned one side and a message in calligraphy enhanced the other. A scene from the historical moral drama "*The Romance of the Three Kingdoms*" appears in the upper left. In the upper right, Liu Hai joins the God of Longevity, the God of Rank, and a deer. Dongfang Shuo appears in the lower left, carrying his branch of immortality. In the lower right, Liu Hai plays with his string of cash and three-legged toad.

2. On these scallop-edged locks, Liu Hai tempts his toad, the God of the South plays chess with the God of the North to determine the length of a man's life, and the three Fu Lu Shou appear in a primitive rendering. The lock on the lower left contains metal balls to frighten away evil spirits (and help keep track of the toddler wearing it).

3. The designs on some scalloped locks do not extend to the edges. A plain, wide border often surrounds the decoration. The first lock features the Daoist Immortal Lan Caihe, while the others include a couple (the man wears the hat and fan of an official), a crane for longevity, and a figure who might be Luohan.

4. Locks, originally worn on plain chains, now frequently serve as centerpieces on beaded necklaces for women.

5. Double dragons with intertwining tails often frame a scene on the flat locks. In the upper left, Laozi gives his book, the *Tao Te Ching*, to the gatekeeper at the Hangu Pass. The other locks include an official riding a qilin, and the twin *Hehe*.

6. Silversmiths gilded both Han and minority locks for wealthy clients. A thin panel of silver separates the front from the back on the heavy, thick minority locks. The Han artifacts appear more traditional in both size and design.

7. Small scallop-shaped locks often surface with their enameling intact, despite layers of dark patina on the silver. Books for a scholar, peaches,

plum blossoms for longevity, and a lotus blossom for purity adorn these examples.

8. Patrons preferred the color blue on their enameled locks. The peony, crane and deer, and plum blossoms on these examples offer a scenic complement to the calligraphy.

9. A horse with an official, a dragon, a qilin, and a deer on these plain silver locks offer good examples of minority workmanship.

10. These locks number among the oldest in this book. The two on the left are paktong, while the one on the upper right bears old enameling. The qilin on the lower right represents the primitive style of earlier craftsmen.

11. Dragons and dragonfish adorn the edges of each of these puffy locks. The God of Longevity, cranes, and an official on a qilin sprawl across the surfaces. Most locks of this type bear the "longevity and prosperity" greeting on the back, but the unusual lock on the lower right carries a wish for the recipient to live as long as the evergreen.

12. Two fish for marital bliss and abundance, a lotus blossom with seeds for fertility, and a musical stone for good fortune (in addition to the message) indicate that this lock was associated with a wedding.

13. Neither of these locks has a plate on the back. Their outer edges are smooth, however; indicating that it was intentional. Without a back, a piece weighed less, making it more affordable for poorer clients.

14. The backless style allows one to examine the underside of a piece of repoussé. In this illustration, we see what the silversmith saw as he created his design by pounding shapes onto the back of a sheet of silver.

15. Flat locks cost even less than locks without backs, but the designs could still be incredibly intricate. The puffy lock without a back offers a slight variation.

16. The flat locks depicting the scholar on horseback and Liu Hai riding his toad display a high level of craftsmanship. The silversmith added an extra ridge to the lock with Liu Hai for strength and distinctiveness.

17. The top lock is another example of the backless variety. The example on the bottom illustrates the way the dangles hung on the flat variety.

18. Engraving enhanced most of the flat locks. The top one still has its original chains and dangles.

19. This flat lock includes dangles with common last names engraved on the leaves. The names may belong to the people who contributed to the lock, or they may represent the Chinese people as a whole.

20. Silver leaves engraved with names hang from two "longevity and prosperity" locks in this illustration. Some of the leaves are missing from the smaller one. Oddly, it originally had more leaves than the larger one.

21. The lock on the left, with a peony, wished the recipient wealth and advancement; the one on the right encouraged purity amidst corruption and success on the civil service examinations.

22. The enameled lock depicting a lion's head was obviously meant to protect a male heir. On the other, we find the three Fu Lu Shou with an unusual depiction of Fuxing.

23. A pair of dragonfish and the Shou symbol wished this recipient longevity and success on the civil service examinations.

24. Symbols for scholars and Daoist Immortals fill the space around the bearded official on horseback, who might be Wen Ch'ang, the God of Literature. Plum blossoms curl around the edge of this enormous lock, which measures 27 cm wide.

25. Small kidney-shaped locks featured either repoussé or engraving, Most bore floral designs.

26. Artisans favored flowers, birds, or calligraphy on the round locks with circular shanks. A wish for longevity accompanies most of these locks.

27. All of the shanks are soldered in place on these locks, as are the straight shafts on the bottom. Curiously, each has a small hole on its bottom edge.

28. People and flowers wind around these drum-shaped locks; many feature flowers for longevity and fertility, and couples carrying fans. The largest depicts the Fu Lu Shou.

29. Elaborate repoussé enhances many rectangular locks, although their sizes vary greatly. Intricate scenes, flowers, and fruits adorn the fronts. Wishes for longevity and prosperity, or a houseful of wealth, appear on the back.

30. Many rectangular locks bear the signature of the silversmith.

31. This unusual engraved lock hangs from beads and a chain added after the Cultural Revolution. On this hundred-family protection lock, originally presented to a young boy, we find symbols for some of the Daoist Immortals.

32. This huge lock, wishing the recipient double good fortune and prosperity, might have been worn at a wedding. Symbols for four of the Immortals hover over a couple beside a temple and an official with a fan in a scene from *"The Western Chamber."*

33. Small, rectangular hundred family protection locks usually display Chinese calligraphy on each side. The example with the engraved floral design is rare.

34. These large, multi-edged locks refer to the birth of an emperor, probably a polite reference to a new son. Such locks appear with or without dangles.

35. Undoubtedly the most elaborate lock described in this chapter, this heavy lock exhibits the fine workmanship of a true artist. It was probably fashioned for a teenage boy to wear at the New Year celebration, and carries a wish for longevity, wealth, and nobility. In addition to the three Fu Lu Shou, we find a deer for longevity, a baby with a lotus blossom for the birth of continuous noble sons, a bee sipping nectar from a flower, and a magpie heralding good news.

36. These small square locks wished a newborn longevity, prosperity, or protection.

37. The swinging leaf on the front of the padlock-shaped lock hides the keyhole, while the six-sided lock includes a jade disk to protect the wearer from disease and harm. (Top lock compliments of Robert Liu)

38. The silver butterfly shape, symbolizing happiness, quickly earned popularity as a wedding adornment. An allegorical or ritual scene usually embellishes the front, as shown in this illustration. The other side of this one (see Figure 42) depicts the whole butterfly. Rarely do these locks contain any calligraphy, but they often open by pulling out the shank.

39. The style of the calligraphy characters can help date a piece. Simpler characters and messages appear after the Cultural Revolution.

40. Gilded calligraphy is featured in the center of what seems to be the front of this silver lock. A plain silver qilin enhances the other side. The front of the chain, which hung from an article of clothing, is soldered to the side with the calligraphy.

41. Locks from the Republic era frequently display two flags. The curled ends of the old cloth neckring were sewn together.

42. Some locks—such as the examples in this illustration—actually functioned. Note their unusual keys.

43. Keyholes appear in different shapes and sizes on almost every lock. Few have keys, and most seem non-functional as a regular lock.

44. Many locks surface on cloth neckrings. This hundred-family protection lock features a magpie as the bringer of good news. The three-legged toad for longevity, the baby for fertility, the double fish for marital bliss, and the musical stone for good fortune indicate that it might have hung around the neck of a little girl. As we see in the old photographs, daughters also wore locks—especially if the family had a son as well.

45. Symbols for a scholar accompany a wish for wealth and good fortune on this lock, indicating that it was created for a male child.

46. A peony adorns this wealth and good fortune lock. Each curled tip of the neckring might represent either the horn of a cow or the end of a *ruyi*.

47. The silversmith's hallmark could appear anywhere—the front, back, bottom, or top—of a lock. A hallmark typically includes two or three Chinese characters.

CHAPTER THREE: GROOMING KITS AND FRAGRANCE CARRIERS

1. Three to five tools hang from long chains on most grooming kits from the Qing dynasty. Most common are the earpick, nailpick, and tweezers. This example, with a basket centerpiece symbolizing abundance, features rare carved silver monkey links on the chain.

2. The decorative bottle gourd centerpiece on this grooming kit symbolizes longevity, good fortune, and fertility. The stopper unscrews; but the narrow passage only opens into the upper chamber, whose pierced design makes it non-functional as a medicine holder.

3. These grooming kits, featuring an unusually large number of tools, also include foxtail chains and symbolic swords. Despite the open pattern of

the centerpieces, they are quite heavy.

4. A silver bat hovers over two women and a man with an umbrella, which tells us that this is a scene from the novel, *The White Snake Pagoda*.

5. The tools on this grooming kit dangle from a carved jade musical stone, and must have hung from the sash of a very wealthy man.

6. Two grooming tools—the earpick and the nailpick—often hang from simple minority grooming kits. The monkey is associated with high rank, fertility, and good health: the bottle gourd brings longevity and fertility.

7. To use one of these grooming kits, simply turn the double sheath upside down and two tools—earpick and nailpick—fall forward. The chains all feature a rosette pattern and might be from the same region.

8. To use the tools in these grooming kits, one pushed the knob up or down the shaft. The smallest kit includes calligraphy. The kit with the Chinese figure slide may be unique. Push the figure down and an earpick appears, push him up and a nailpick materializes.

9. This long minority grooming kit features not one, but three centerpieces of carved jade in graduated sizes in addition to jade beads on the chains. The matching fish bell dangles certainly belong to the piece, but the jade and carnelian are most likely replacements. The upper chain lends considerable weight to the piece, which jingles with every movement. People certainly heard the wealthy owner of this piece approaching.

10. Two silver lions play with a ball above a centerpiece featuring a scholar with a *ruyi* riding a deer, a hovering bat, and a young boy fanning the scholar. Since a deer symbolizes the salary of an official, and the person riding this one holds a *ruyi*, the amulet obviously represents a scholar-official.

11. A fine silversmith used the repoussé technique for the silver bat and the centerpiece, which both resemble the kit in Figure 4. On this centerpiece, however, we find a bearded official beneath a tree peering at the sun. The chain also features rosettes.

12. Piercing enhanced the dragons chasing the pearl of potentiality on this grooming kit, which also includes a butterfly. The bells below the dragons, which do not match those above, undoubtedly replaced lost tools.

13. The silver butterfly, symbolizing longevity, joy, and marital happiness, often serves as a centerpiece on Chinese grooming kits. Here the butterflies (including an unusual enameled one which surfaced without its tools), always hang upside down. The larger wings allow more space for the lugs holding the chains.

14. Since the lion on this grooming kit is playing with a ball, we know it is a male and symbolized courage, energy, wisdom, and protection for the wearer.

15. The old jade grooming kit on the left contains few of its original chains and dangles, but retains its charm. The double lions with the revolving ball rank on the second set are highly distinctive. (Grooming kit on the right compliments of Adele Anderson)

16. Unusual centerpieces also embellish small grooming kits. The three-dimensional calligraphy denotes marital bliss, while the bat hovers over coins and a longevity symbol. The woven centerpiece offers a variation on the endless knot, while the circle represents either a coin or the wheel of law.

17. Multiple symbols often appear on the same grooming kit. On the left: a Buddhist endless knot, peaches for fertility, and a fish for abundance lead down to a basket of fruit with a plum blossom for abundance, fertility, and longevity. On the right: a single fish for abundance, and the *sheng*—a mouth organ—for fertility, hang above a boy riding an ox, which symbolizes the Buddhist path to nirvana.

18. A wealthy Han official might have worn this grooming kit featuring an elaborate jade carving encased in silver. The double happiness symbol in the jade, the two bats, the two coins, and the plant with seeds tell us that it was probably a wedding present. (Compliments of Brooke Jaron)

19. Wealthy clients often requested that their grooming kits be gilded. On the left, carved jade lies encased in a gilded frame. The grooming kit was re-gilded after purchase to restore it to its former glory. (Compliments of Joan Ahrens) In the second example, the gourd depicting the flowers of the seasons is purely decorative, as are the tiny monkey links on the chain. The two fish symbolizing marital bliss suggest a dowry or wedding gift.

20. Carved jade, old amber beads, silver fish

dangles, and an intricate purse shape transformed this long minority grooming kit into a real treasure. *Articles of Personal Adornment*, by Yang, Ma, Huang, and Jin, identifies a similar piece as a Qing dynasty Bai artifact from Dali.

21. The chain on this minority grooming kit connects coin-shaped links for wealth with carved jade lotuses symbolizing purity in the midst of corruption, harmony, and marital bliss.

22. This grooming kit stands out because of its uniquely carved jade centerpieces. On the lower piece, we see a peach for longevity and the *ruyi* wish-granting scepter. Above, the stonecarver fashioned a lotus leaf and a fish for wealth.

23. Flowers often fill basket centerpieces, and plum blossoms adorn the bases. Note the different styles of chains used on these sets.

24. Compare the variations in the bases of the basket centerpieces on these grooming kits. The chains all differ, but the tools on two of the sets are similar.

25. On a grooming kit, a silver baby symbolizing fertility can often be found amidst the flowers in a basket. Many women received such kits as dowry presents.

26. A bat, symbolizing happiness and prosperity, often formed the base of a basket centerpiece or rested inside of one. On the right, a second bat insures good fortune.

27. Two carnelian dangles hang from these grooming kit ensembles, which also include other wedding symbols, such as the double fish or double flower. The dangles may be original to the kits or could have replaced matching silver pieces.

28. Silversmiths also engraved basket shapes onto flat sheets of silver and then cut out the designs. Remarkably, the smaller basket—despite its pierced surface—has a different design engraved on each side.

29. These minutely detailed grooming kits exhibit finer workmanship than usual. A large scroll portraying a magpie and plum blossoms, a lotus, and a *ruyi* cover the large centerpiece. A basket, a sword, books, and a conch shell appear above that, and at the top, we find a bat and two coins. Rooster and bat dangles complete the ensemble. The tools include a strange spoon, reputedly for incense.

30. Numerous grooming kits surface with a

mustache comb, instead of tweezers, in the center. The combs were probably replacements but tell us that the grooming kits were worn by men. The peony centerpiece represents wealth and advancement.

31.   In Qing dynasty China, a tongue scraper removed germs and freshened one's breath. It often hung from expensive grooming kits such as this one, which retains all of its original implements.

32.   The purse-shaped carrier on this grooming kit held cotton or cloth soaked in herbal fragrances. The top chain is not original, but allows the purse to open.

33.   Some of the grooming kits with fragrance carrier centerpieces have lost their lids, others have been soldered shut; and still others function as well as they originally did. Several still contain bits of cotton. The tiny eyes of the guardian lion on the lid of the largest example move in and out to "see" in all directions.

34.   Someone patched this fragrance carrier together a long time ago, but the unique style and workmanship make it worth keeping.

35.   The minority exhibit at the Shanghai Museum calls a receptacle similar to the one on this grooming kit a powder horn.

36.   This grooming kit features the outlines of a butterfly and endless knot, unique shafts on the grooming tools, a small gourd with revolving base, and a six-sided opium container.

37.   Simply engraved, the single cylinder needle case on this grooming kit gave the owner, probably a woman, a place to keep her sewing needles. A coin for wealth and the Buddhist's endless knot tell us what else she considered important.

38.   The jade lotus and grooming tools hanging from this minority double needle case are not original. According to the family of the old woman who owned this piece, they replaced similar pieces that were lost. Floral designs enhance the sheath of the triple tube needle case on the right.

39.   The amulet above the triple needle case on this grooming kit portrays a dragon for male vigor and fertility on one side and a scholar-official riding a qilin on the other. This is most unusual, since each side is pierced. Endless knots, fruit, a butterfly, and bell dangles complete this intricate assemblage.

40.   The needle case on this grooming kit is the only example that I have ever seen with an inner cylinder covered with repoussé work. The sheath of the case includes a couple on one side, the God of Longevity and the God of Rank on the other.

41.   Gilded grooming kits contain some of the most unusual amulets. The basket contains flowers and a butterfly soldered to the basic design, as was the double swastika, representing 10,000 efficacies and associated with immortality. Above this we find the endless knot with a longevity symbol, two peach dangles for fertility, and bells with the magpie and plum design. In the center of the illustration, a gilded bat frames a piece of carved jade. On the right, the gilded centerpiece lost its tools, but not its beauty. A plug of old ivory with a Peking glass bead fills the opening.

42.   The large silver basket filled with flowers might have originally been covered with kingfisher feathers inside the ridges that outline the design. A musical stone and *ruyi* adorn the top; a large reticulated fish replaces a lost tool on the bottom.

43.   This domed centerpiece appears on grooming kits and other adornments found in Inner Mongolia. Some suggest it may be a rendition of a lotus.

44.   There seems to be no limit to the possible sizes of the domes, or the number found on a single grooming kit.

45.   A Chinese man or woman in the Qing dynasty wore a silver fragrance carrier as both a deodorant and an air freshener. The large artifact lost its upper chain, but not the gilded center of the lotus.

46.   This group of fragrance carriers exhibits a variety of shapes and designs. Most examples have the same design on both lateral surfaces, but the one on the upper right features lotus blossoms on one side and magpies with plum blossoms on the other.

47.   Typical blue, green, and yellow enameling highlights this remarkable Qing dynasty purse-type fragrance carrier. A butterfly rests on a *ruyi* for the hook, tiny rat and bird charms dangle from the chain, and rows of dangles swing with every movement.

48.   Pierced designs cover many cylinder-shaped fragrance holders. Floral designs cover some, scenes swirl around others. The double tube

exhibits symbols for the scholar around the character for longevity on each side. The second from the right wished the recipient longevity, wealth, and nobility, which tells us that a man probably wore it.

49.   These three cicada fragrance carriers bear a strong resemblance to certain needle cases, but the carriers incorporate a pierced torso to allow the fragrance to escape. (Compliments of Robert K. Liu)

50.   Odd bits and pieces of beads and chains turned this beautiful enameled cicada fragrance carrier into a gaudy pendant on a contemporary necklace.

51.   On the left, we find another garish assemblage using a gorgeous old enameled cicada fragrance carrier. This one, with its telltale beads, probably surfaced after the Cultural Revolution. The simpler cicada on the right more closely resembles the way these artifacts hung.

52.   The fragrance carrier on the right contains a circle of red material on one side, faded gray on the other, and cotton in between. I believe the gray material was once blue. If so, a Buddhist might have owned this piece to combine the blue of the sky with the red of fire to create natural energy, as well as a pleasant odor.

53.   Like the expensive needle cases, costly older fragrance carriers bore a different scene on each side. Note the small vase. In Chinese mythology, the rabbit resides in the moon and pounds out the elixir of immortality. On the other side, the depiction of a young couple tells us that this was probably a dowry or wedding present.

54.   The scenes on fragrance carriers derive from art (the squirrel and the grapes), folklore (the dragonfish who made it through Longmen Gate), mythology (the three Fu Lu Shou), and Chinese custom (the young scholar going to Beijing).

55.   Many rectangular fragrance carriers surfaced in the Shanghai area. The majority include small doors on the sides, which slide up and down. Although these cases have elaborate scenes on the fronts and backs, the thin silver cases seem very fragile.

CHAPTER FOUR: QILINS

1.   Qilins without riders, symbolizing wisdom, justice, longevity, and cosmic harmony, often

surface in southwest China. Note the variations in each qilin's coat, mane, tail, and dorsal spine. Most qilins appear anatomically correct on each side.

2. Since the qilin is a mythological creature, silversmiths drew on their own imaginations and artistic ability to create them. Compare the workmanship on the old, soldered example on the left with the higher quality artifact on the right.

3. Buddhists often portray a qilin carrying the Book of Law on its back. In this example, the tail resembles a lotus pod and tufts of hair flare up from the hooves. A young Buddhist boy studying for the civil service examinations probably wore this. Boys continued to wear such amulets on special occasions into their teens.

4. A baby seated on a qilin gave the beast a different meaning. The qilin in this example symbolizes fertility and the desire for a son. As the bringer of children, the qilin might be compared to the European stork.

5. The qilin in Figure 4 has an open back, enabling us to examine the silversmith's expertise in repoussé work on the reverse.

6. Some qilins carrying babies, such as this one, possess anatomically correct fronts and backs. In this heavy example, the baby carries a wish-granting *ruyi* and holds on to the qilin's horn.

7. In this example, the silversmith might have been trying to create Guanyin, the Goddess of Mercy and bringer of children, riding a qilin. Guanyin is often portrayed holding a baby. The typical official riding a qilin carries only a lotus blossom or a *ruyi*, and possibly the *sheng*. The loose flowing robe on this figure also differs from an official's robe, which is cinched at the waist and hugs the legs. If the rider is Guanyin, a woman wore this qilin.

8. The qilins carrying barefooted children from the minority regions of southwest China stand out because of the children's huge bare feet. The minorities did not practice foot-binding. At first sight, these two pieces seem very similar, but closer examination reveals major differences in the details of both child and qilin. Qilins of this type feature the front of the child on both sides.

9. The rider on the qilin at the left carries a sword to cut through ignorance as his owner studies to pass the civil service examinations. At the upper right, a small qilin and rider hang from a thick cloth neckring. In the example on the bottom, the back of an unusual qilin's head resembles an open lotus pod filled with seeds for fertility.

10. The gilding has worn thin on this wonderful old qilin and rider, but the original chains and matching fruits remain in place. Double happiness symbols adorn the ends of the chains, suggesting a wedding gift.

11. To make a qilin unique, a silversmith often incorporated moving parts. In this illustration, qilins enjoy moveable tongues, eyes, or whiskers. At the upper right, the rider holds a scroll in hands that extend out from his body. The artisans added hats to three of the riders after forming the body, and forged horns and flowing ribbons from strips of silver.

12. Considering the fact that enameled pieces chip with time, these two flamboyant pieces surfaced in remarkable condition. The abundance of red enameling, which appears maroon or pink, is surprising.

13. In lieu of special effects, some patrons preferred an artistic depiction of a qilin and rider. Here, the happy, well-fed official gallops to his destination on a qilin who seems to bellow.

14. In this rendition, an official flies through the clouds with his ruyi scepter in hand. Note the unusual closed mouth on the qilin, and the feet that seem to be sailing through the air.

15. This artisan added curled wire nostrils that move back and forth on this extraordinary qilin. The rider, wearing a serene expression, holds a prod for the horse in one hand, and a blue enameled *ruyi* in the other. A silversmith created this heavy, beautifully detailed piece for a wealthy client.

16. Engraved dangles bearing Chinese surnames hang from the feet of some qilins. Note the gourd shapes and the three-dimensional lotus blossom in the official's hand.

17. The *sheng* that the official on the qilin carries in this example is the finest depiction of this reed instrument I have ever seen. An umbrella for nobility and protection might be the item in his other hand. Several parts, including the rider's hat and a section of one horn, have broken off, but the detail on the rest is still remarkable. The beads were added much later.

18. The drooping lotus in this official's hands is most unusual. He is also hatless, but wears a Buddha-like expression of serenity.

19. This costly qilin, with a separate tongue and miniature necklace, carries an official with a separate lotus blossom and *sheng* in his hands. The silversmith formed the figure—as well as the qilin's blanket—separately, and bolted them to the animal, which actually stands on its legs.

20. These two qilins and riders hail from the Republic era. This type can be identified by the rider wearing a man's suit instead of a gown, a bowler instead of an official's hat, or by the flags they often carry. Look for other erroneous symbols. In the top example, the official carries plum blossoms.

21. This huge qilin and rider measure over 11 cm wide and incorporate the usual *sheng* and lotus.

22. On the reverse of Figure 21, note the anatomically correct back and the hallmark of the silversmith on the official's robe.

23. The silversmiths who made these two qilins saved their clients money by adding only flat backs to the pieces (see Figure 24).

24. The back of the top figure is plain silver with two tiny coin-shaped holes and the hallmark of the silversmith. On the bottom, we find a most unusual engraved back. (Bottom qilin compliments of Joan Ahrens)

25. These qilins and riders range in size from 4.2 cm to 11.3 cm wide.

26. Friends and relatives probably presented the smallest qilins to baby boys. In the upper right examples, the face resembles a monkey's. This could be a reference to the monkey king or simply this silversmith's lack of talent.

27. Some of these qilins seem a bit overweight, but I think obesity symbolized abundant wealth in an era when the masses were starving.

28. Like the qilins, many of the riders also appear overweight. The heavy-jowled official on the left embodies prosperity, as does the bulging stomach of the rider on the right.

29. Notice the posture of these riders. One has to wonder where the silversmiths found inspiration. Did they use family members, officials they knew, or just their imagination?

30. Neither of these large artifacts includes a back plate, but the fronts are most interesting. In the top

figure, the silversmith meant to create a qilin carrying an official with a lotus blossom, but he shaped a lion's head instead. The designer of the elaborately pierced qilin on the bottom hooked a chain to the front of the qilin's forehead and to the top of his tail. Miraculously, the qilin still hangs well.

31. Backless qilins cost less, but still offered interesting detail in the coats of the qilins and the robes of the officials. On the upper left, we even find a small bat for happiness hovering over the pair.

32. These four medium-sized qilins and riders surfaced with all their dangles intact. The heavy artifact in the upper right is solid silver, whereas the other three seem to be hollow. Each official has a topknot of hair, carries a lotus, and has an opening for his eyes and mouth. Note the differences in the coats of the qilins.

33. In this illustration, one official carries the books of the scholar—or possibly the Buddhist Book of Law—in addition to a lotus blossom. A *sheng* sits on the ground beneath the feet of two qilins. Note the inner sides of the legs on several of them.

34. These large qilins, each measuring over 9 cm wide, look similar until one focuses on the tilt of a rider's head or the detail of a qilin's mane. The costlier one on the right is heavier, hallmarked, and made from a higher grade of silver.

35. Variety exists even among the smaller qilins. The obesity of the rider in the upper left, the gilding on the upper right, the grass beneath the feet on the lower left, and the strange saddle trappings on the lower right deserve our attention.

36. Compare the minute detail of these two very similar qilins, each hallmarked by their silversmiths. We only find this level of detail in the saddles, qilins, and officials on the finer, heavier pieces. Flares of fire, a symbol of compassion in a wise ruler, streak across the qilins' flanks.

37. After examining a number of qilins, the oddities tend to pop out. In the two artifacts on the left, the officials seem to have no feet and the qilin in the lower left appears polka-dotted. On the upper right, a pair of books rests between the qilin's feet and the qilin's tail ends with real flair. On the lower right, the silversmith could not decide which way to fashion the tail, so he gave his qilin two of them.

38. The officials on these examples appear similar, but the qilins differ greatly from their "beards" to their tails. In this instance, it is the one on the left that is hallmarked.

39. In this illustration, the happy official on the top is solid and heavy, the one on the lower left hollow but heavy, and the one on the right is hollow and light (and bears the only hallmark). The one on the lower left bears the same design on both sides, right down to the design on the official's knees; but the other two appear anatomically correct on the reverse.

40. Note the difference in the quality of the repoussé work on these flat artifacts. A buyer saved a great deal of money with this lightweight style, and he could still order either a baby astride a qilin, or a successful civil service candidate riding on one.

CHAPTER FIVE: COLLARS, NECKRINGS AND TORQUES

1. An infant collar, little more than an expandable silver ring, hung around a baby's neck to keep him safe from disease and harm. Some minority groups felt that such a collar fooled the evil spirits into thinking the baby was nothing but a worthless dog.

2. Some of the larger infant collars were thicker and worn into childhood. When the child finally outgrew one, it was often melted down to make an amulet.

3. The lock on this infant ensemble unfastens to open the neckring, which is held together by the lock at one end, and a flat engraved chain with a huge peach dangle at the other.

4. Chains hang from this small neckring to hold the flat, lightweight hundred-family protection lock.

5. This neckring spreads to fit around a baby's neck. Since the pendant represents Wen Shu, the Buddhist God of Wisdom riding his lion, the ensemble protected a baby boy and wished him well on his civil service examinations.

6. The chains on this neckring probably held silver dangles originally. The dragon chasing the pearl of potentiality on the lock offers longevity, prosperity, and nobility.

7. This neckring, with its double happiness symbol soldered in place, adorned a woman at her wedding. We cannot be sure about the lock, since locks were interchangeable.

8. The dragon on the centerpiece, the lock with the qilin and official, plus the inscription for longevity, prosperity, and nobility, tell us that this neckring belonged to a boy.

9. Both women and children wore the neckrings with double dragons. On the lock hanging from this one, the twin *Hehe* bring harmony, blessings, and wealth. On the other side, a carp swims through lotus blossoms for affluence year after year.

10. The shanks of the locks on this type of neckring fit through the mouths of the dragons so they had to be fully functional. On this lock, the symbols for a scholar, a couple with a child, a lotus blossom for fertility, and an inscription wish the recipient a houseful of wealth and nobility.

11. An unusual engraved lock with a baby and lotus blossoms hangs from this neckring. On the neckring, tips with Chinese calligraphy replace the usual dragonheads.

12. On this neckring, one simply pulls open the side of the engraved lock to remove it.

13. This neckring looks well used. The lock depicts an elderly figure in a chair, an official standing over a longevity symbol, and a young boy with books running toward them. Calligraphy on the back sends a wish for honor, wealth, and longevity.

14. One end of this neckring fits into the other. On this butterfly-shaped lock, a young boy carrying books meets someone in the clouds as a nobleman looks on from below.

15. A huge wedding lock hangs from this neckring. A woman plays a musical instrument beside an urn, a vase holding calligraphy brushes, and a bowl of fruit. Books, calligraphy brushes in a vase, scrolls, and a chessboard cover the man's table. It is possible that the silversmith was trying to describe the couple's attributes.

16. If you remove the central plaque on this neckring, you can lift the lock off the hooks hidden by the plaque. On the lock, the *Hehe* twins flank a table laden with fruit in front of other mythological figures. The back also contains double longevity symbols.

17. Soldered to one end, the minority lock on this heavy neckring will never get lost.

18. This engraved torque resembles a style found in the Tang dynasty. Here, two fish hide in the lotus leaves for years of abundance and marital bliss.

19. To open this tiny torque, swing out the right side. The hollow, dark interior makes the raised, pierced floral design appear three-dimensional.

20. Plum blossoms and peonies swirl across the endless knot soldered to the left end of this intricate torque, which is hinged to swing open. To close, insert one tip into the other behind the centerpiece.

21. This blue-enameled torque is also hinged. The centerpiece features a bearded old man with a staff and *ruyi*, a figure with a flywhisk, and a young boy kneeling between them.

22. This heavy twisted torque probably adorned the neck of a man of the Dong minority during the Lunar New Year festivities. It weighs 244 grams.

23. This set of six torques—weighing an incredible 2,681 grams—must have been difficult for a young Miao woman to wear at a festival, but it certainly advertised her wealth.

24. Dragons and fish wish the owner of this hollow torque fertility and abundance. Two dragons chase the pearl of potentiality in the front, culminating in two stylized dragonheads and a single fish on either side. Considering the duplicated symbols, I think we can assume this was used for a wedding.

25. Someone cut through the silver ring on this torque (upper right), and this seems strange since it pulls apart behind the centerpiece. The symbols for the Immortals surround the three Fu Lu Shou on the lock, while engraved plum blossoms and other longevity symbols curve around the torque.

26. A silversmith created this huge double happiness symbol pendant speckled with couples for a wedding. Note the Eight Buddhist Emblems and wish for good fortune. The centerpiece contains a rare depiction of the God of Longevity on his stag, with a bat for happiness. More symbols for longevity adorn the hinged torque.

27. Raised symbols for longevity cover this torque, which includes a centerpiece with a lion for protection. The lock, shaped like a butterfly, includes a woman with a baby, a bearded man with a flywhisk, and two figures with long swords. The lock opens and the back is plain.

28. On this torque, raised scenes appear to depict either an allegory or the path of life. The sides culminate in a plain ring. The dragons, soldered to the bottom, include the hallmark of the artisan. On this type of artifact, both sides of the back bear the same hallmark—as if they were made separately and then matched in the final construction.

29. The scenes on this torque are cut out and raised so that they appear three-dimensional. Once again, two dragonheads adorn the middle, followed by the magpie and scenes that lead us to a couple in a house beneath a plum blossom, lotus, and fish. The lock, which is functional, portrays a scene from a drama and has an interchangeable back.

30. A centerpiece depicting a couple and an old man were added to this torque covered with floral designs. A scene from a drama enhances the large lock, which employs a fixed shank and lacks a back, but does bear a hallmark.

31. Fruits, flowers, and magpies swirl around the top of this large torque, which terminates in an enameled centerpiece with plums and peaches, soldered to one side of the opening. Three characters from the Chinese drama entitled *"The Yellow Crane Tower"* adorn the huge lock, along with fruits, flowers, and the symbols for a scholar. I believe this is a boy's lock on a wedding torque. The original lock was probably enameled to match the centerpiece.

32. This torque is also decorated with silver fruits and flowers and includes a centerpiece soldered to one side of the opening. On the lock, a figure carrying a plum blossom branch rides on a qilin as young people wave symbols of prestige and power.

33. Numerous flowers swirl around this torque, which measures 29 cm high. The centerpiece, soldered to the torque, depicts Liu Hai with his famous toad. Beneath them hangs a carp holding a lock which portrays the three Fu Lu Shou and all of the Eight Immortals.

34. Green tourmaline stones and gilded beads covered with a lotus design fill this gilded torque. A depiction of Liu Hai adorns the gilded centerpiece. The lock depicts a scene from a military drama. The back reads: "May your house be filled with gold and jade."

CHAPTER SIX: TALISMANS AGAINST MISFORTUNES

1. A Qing dynasty Chinese woman wore a tiny, anatomically correct silver baby boy to insure the safe birth of a son. Some babies appear naked, some wear a *doudou*, others are more elaborately dressed. The visible male appendage makes sense if we remember the split pants worn by infants and toddlers.

2. On many silver babies, the back is also fully rendered. Oddly, the head often includes a round indentation. Each bears the distinctive design of the artisan.

3. Some silver babies wear an outfit that looks like a pair of pajamas, while others—possibly those from a later period—wear one that resembles a suit. Some of these artifacts feel solid and heavy; others are hollow.

4. A silver baby often appears to be walking or even running. This might refer to the wearer's desire for a child's rapid advancement, or her yearning for his swift arrival.

5. On six of the fourteen silver babies in this illustration, the backs duplicate the fronts. Several carry a lotus blossom; while one drapes it around his neck.

6. This heavily detailed young boy holding a teapot (representing fertility) hangs on a long chain strung with charms for additional fruitfulness. The entire ensemble, suspended from a silver cicada with layers of wings, undoubtedly hung from the sash of a man hoping for a son.

7. The large baby and dented turtle strung on auspicious red yarn, as well as the smaller rounded figure, all contain pellets that rattle to entertain an infant. The identical silver boys on a single chain represented either a wish for numerous sons, or the legend of the wife who bore twin sons for her 50-year-old husband to reward his piety.

8. An oval crotal bell often hung from the wrist, ankle, or clothing of a baby to frighten away evil spirits.

9. A round bell also scared away demons and helped a parent keep track of a wandering toddler.

10. This large bell, dented with time and use, entertained at least one infant as a rattle. The symbols of all Eight Immortals adorn the top.

11. The large tiger head rattle charmed an infant, while the smaller examples probably hung from his clothing.

12. Complex scenes adorned the sides of seal-shaped bells on the conveyance of high officials.

13. Bells of this design hung from the eaves of a noblewoman's sedan chair.

14. Chains, adorned with charms and terminating in a bell, held back the curtains of a sedan chair.

15. Large crotal bells were sold in pairs. Two bells hung from the sedan chair of a minor official; but as many as eight decorated the conveyance of an important personage, making sure that everyone knew he was passing.

16. Tiny lotus slippers occasionally contained a bell hidden in the wooden heel, making the wearer more enticing. (Compliments of Beverley Jackson)

17. Silversmiths produced bells in the shapes of fruits, animals, and even dragonfish. These often hung from chains on the bottoms of locks, qilins, and even needle cases.

18. Fruit-shaped bells often included seeds in the design, and represented fertility.

19. A small silver bottle gourd—representing fertility, healing, longevity, and wealth—often served as the centerpiece on a grooming kit, or dangled from a chain. The gourd on the lower left held a powdery substance, but most of these artifacts do not have removable stoppers.

20. Larger and more elaborately decorated silver bottle gourds served as either toggles or sash hangings. All of these held medicine. Enameling coated the more expensive pieces.

21. The double gourd, representing heaven and earth, included stoppers facing in opposite directions. None of these open, but the artifacts with three lugs on the bottom probably held grooming tools. The other two, solid and heavy, functioned as toggles.

22. Solid or simply outlined, heavy or light, plain or detailed, the popularity of the bottle gourd design gave silversmiths ample opportunity to use their creative powers.

23. Traditional blue and yellow enameling covers this hanging, which includes a bottle gourd, two musical stones, and odd chains.

24. The smooth, hollow silver gourds on the left closely resemble the plant, while the gourds on the right contain pellets and rattle when shaken.

25. A silver ox symbolized spring, fertility, strength, and domestic bliss. Note the differences in the way silversmiths rendered this animal.

26. This ox with a vase on its back represents a wish for domestic bliss and fertility, with the basket for continued abundance.

27. A young boy plays the flute as he rides his ox, symbolizing the realization of nirvana for Buddhists.

28. On two of these figures, we see the traditional boy with his flute. On each of the others we find a baby with a lotus blossom, representing fertility.

29. The magic white donkey of Daoist Immortal Zhang Guolao could be stored in a pouch or bottle until needed. Facing a journey, Zhang simply removed the animal and sprayed water on him to transform him to full size. The donkey carried his master 1,000 miles a day, symbolizing perseverance and making this amulet a popular gift for a student.

30. Zhang Guolao's donkey often appears engraved on flat sheets of silver, which obviously cost less than the repoussé pieces. The donkey for perseverance and the dog for protection on the same hanging might have been presented to a young man going to Beijing to take his civil service examinations.

31. A silver horse amulet represented different groups in the Qing dynasty. The large Tibetan windhorse, with his elaborate saddle and chain reins, dispelled demons and illness. The small Chinese horses symbolized endurance, while the similar Mongol pony wears the typical halter of bells around its neck. The silver rider on the galloping horse probably hung around the neck of a young boy.

32. Symbols of peace in retirement, these silver goats are depicted in remarkable detail.

33. These silver lions surfaced in Yunnan Province. The head and tail of each revolves, and the eyes and tongues move. The one on the left is hollow, but the example on the right is solid silver and extremely heavy. Dangles also hang from the one on the left, although he has lost his ears. The one on the right wears a small bell hanging from his neck. Could they have been made in the same silversmith's shop?

34. These single and double lions all frolic with a ball, which identifies them as male. Lions symbolized courage, energy, and wisdom.

35. The silversmith created a separate tongue and ears for this lion, which probably hung from the neck of a young boy on special occasions.

36. The largest silver amulet of a lion I have ever seen, this highly detailed beast incorporates moveable ears, a separate tongue, sharp teeth, and the artist's signature engraved on the back. The original dangles and chain are missing, and have been replaced by the type of beaded chain added after the Cultural Revolution.

37. Merchants favored the knot picks depicting rats with serrated backs to cut the string used on packages. Scholars received them as well, to help unravel questions and answers on civil service examinations.

38. Large solid silver tortoises, symbols of longevity and steadfastness, denote the secrets of heaven and earth. Note the plain chain on one and the handsewn stuffed cloth neckring on the other.

39. This gilded silver pig with an ingot on its back represents wealth, fertility, and virility.

40. The rooster, which frightens away evil spirits with its crowing, offers security.

41. A pair of silver mandarin ducks represents marital bliss, whereas a single duck protected Buddhists from demons. Notice the differences in the feet.

42. The Chinese wore a silver dog for protection since a dog's bark frightened away evil spirits. Members of the nobility favored Pekinese as pets, and many silver dog amulets possess fancy collars.

43. A silver fish symbolizes abundance, wealth, and fertility. Two fish represented marital harmony, and this symbol adorned many wedding gifts. These reticulated fish seem to swim with every movement.

44. Solid fish also enjoyed popularity, as did the three-legged toad, which represents longevity. Notice the enameling.

45. The Chinese believed that monkeys bestowed health, protection, and success. Sun Wukong, the Monkey King from the novel *The Journey to the West* often appears in full regalia in the center. On the left, he is shown stealing the peaches of immortality from the garden of the Queen Mother of the West. On the right, he wears an iron helmet to control his impulses since he could cover 6,000 miles in a single bound.

46. This gilded official riding a pig represents a wish for wealth, virility, and good fortune on the civil service examinations.

47. The amulets depicting officials riding dogs and the rooster symbolized protection and success for the young male recipient. The official riding a rat conveyed expectations for wealth and success.

CHAPTER SEVEN: RINGS, EARRINGS, AND BRACELETS

1. Fruit, flowers, and calligraphy appear on small silver rings for women. The ends fold over each other, making the rings expandable.

2. Enameled rings originally cost more than plain silver, but often chipped or faded with time.

3. Familiar flowers adorn larger rings from the Qing dynasty. Even more important than the beauty was the symbolic message. The lotus and plum blossom designs enjoyed great popularity.

4. Animals and birds blended with fruits and flowers on the larger rings.

5. Frogs appear on rings as symbols of longevity, due to their long life span, and fertility, since folk belief held that a frog's seed fell from heaven with the dew.

6. Rings featuring stacks of books and gods playing chess to determine the length of a man's life appealed to scholars.

7. Traveling opera companies sold rings with scenes from their performances as souvenirs. Other large rings depicted scenes from folklore and mythology.

8. Lions top these unusual rings. The bells on the long chains dangled beneath the hand and jingled with every movement. The lions protected their wearers, as did the bells, which frightened away evil spirits.

9. Thimble rings—wide bands with circular holes to push the needles from beneath the fabric—came in different widths and thicknesses. Note the areas worn smooth by use.

10. Members of military regiments used puzzle rings in drinking games. The ring in the center reveals how the circlets were connected.

11. Here we see the back of a puzzle ring with the circlets in place. Note the popular symbols on the others.

12. Tibetans and Mongols incorporated large old chunks of turquoise or coral into their rings.

Traders probably sold the coral pieces with holes in the center as beads.

13. Tibetan men wore the saddle rings around their long hair or on their headbands.

14. Tiny blue kingfisher feathers often covered dangling earrings made for wealthy women or members of the Court.

15. Minority women also loved to wear silver earrings coated with enamel or kingfisher feathers. These feature dragons, flowers, bats and the usual multitude of dangles.

16. The long (14.5 cm) earrings from the Yi minority, feature bats for happiness. Shorter earrings, such as the gilded pair on the upper right, often include dangling rings.

17. Some earrings, such as the multi-circular pair, weigh so much that they tear the ear lobes of the Miao women who wear them. Each earring in this pair weighs an astounding 62 grams.

18. Note the different types of dangles on these earrings.

19. Silver earrings, such as the pair in the top center, often include a circlet of jade. Others were gilded for the wealthy. The two remaining pairs are reputed to have been recovered from tombs, but surfaced in the United States.

20. Many earrings of this period focused on single and double dragonheads with the elusive pearl.

21. Prospective bridegrooms usually sent a pair of wedding bracelets to their betrothed through an intermediary. A Han woman wore one of these enameled bracelets on each wrist.

22. A fish swimming among lotus plants on these Miao bracelets sends a wish for the couple to live in affluence year after year.

23. Dragons chasing a pearl swirl around each bracelet in this pair. Beads inside the circlets frighten away evil spirits. Minor differences characteristic of handmade items appear on the twosome.

24. The set of Miao dragon bracelets on the top is hollow, while the solid pair in the middle is extremely heavy. The matched pair on the bottom—probably Han—features raised longevity symbols and bats for happiness.

25. Rattan bracelets with repoussé or engraved strips of silver purportedly cured arthritis.

26. This jade and silver bracelet featuring scholar

symbols promised good health, success, and protection.

27. Chainlink flexible bracelets usually terminated in two dragonheads and a pearl, which could be unscrewed to open the piece. This type surfaces in either plain or enameled silver.

28. Small bangles for baby girls often expanded for years of wear. Open-ended bracelets bent around the child's wrist.

29. Note the different interpretations that silversmiths gave the dragon and pearl motif on these bangles. Some feature thick edging; others have none. Some artisans crammed every centimeter with minuscule designs; others opted for less detail. Some included pellets to make the bracelets jingle; others did not.

30. These extra-wide minority bracelets and bangles depicting fish, flowers, bats, crabs, endless knots, and scholars' objects are not as heavy as they appear since they are hollow.

31. Stylized dragons chase a pearl over silver mesh in the extra wide minority bracelet. All twelve animals of the zodiac encircle the smaller but heavier example above it.

32. Each of these single bangles seems to be a pair. Several contain beads. Note that some display identical designs on both sides of the centerline, whereas others prefer different motifs.

33. A solid silver bracelet may be braided, twisted, engraved, enameled, or covered in repoussé. Most of these bear the hallmarks.

CHAPTER EIGHT: AMULETS FOR SECURITY AND SUCCESS

1. The military God of Wealth, shown here in ancient armor, always carries an ingot in his hands. These expensive silver amulets double as needle cases and might have held the sewing needles of the wives of wealthy merchants, officials, or scholars.

2. The God of Wealth in the center appears complete, down to the dangles on his military hat. Gilding covers the figure on the right.

3. This smaller figure carries a sack of money, but might still represent the military God of Wealth. As such, it would have hung from a man's sash.

4. Liu Hai, another God of Wealth, tries to control his three-legged toad on these amulets. In

the upper left, we find him with a foot on the toad, and in the lower right, actually riding him. The pair represents wealth and longevity.

5.	The *Hehe*, also called the Heavenly Twins, surface as either twin boys or men—one carrying a lotus blossom and the other, a covered box. Symbols of wealth and harmony, they were especially popular with those in business.

6.	On these silver pieces, we find Shouxing, the God of Longevity, with his bald pate, white beard, and peach for longevity. The amulet depicting Shouxing riding a deer with a bat behind him forms a rebus for the three Fu Lu Shou.

7.	These miniature shrines depict Guanyin, the Goddess of Mercy, on either the inside or the outside. Worshipped by men and women alike, she usually sits or stands on a lotus blossom carrying a child, vase, lotus, or pearl. Occasionally, she is portrayed with her hands folded.

8.	Maitreya, the Laughing Buddha destined to succeed Buddha himself, brings peace and prosperity. Note the telltale bare chest, wide smile, and either long hair or long ears. He is often shown carrying a fish. In comparison, the two babies riding a fish symbolize only fertility and abundance.

9.	A silver *ga'u*, or relic container, protected both Tibetan and Mongol men and women on their journeys. A man might wear a dozen at once, suspended across his chest and hanging from his neck. Women wore certain styles for adornment, as well as security. This *ga'u* held a fragment of a monk's robe and a *tsa tsa* molded from clay and possibly mixed with the ashes of a respected spiritual teacher.

10.	The hole in the center of this large *ga'u* (still attached to a leather cord), originally held either a painted thangka or a tiny metal or clay image of Buddha. Symbols of Buddhism cover the top. Both monks and laymen wore this style.

11.	Silver frame *ga'us* include hand-painted thangkas for protection. Note the garuda and the symbols of Buddhism on the lower one.

12.	Hand-stitched leather encases the old trefoil-shaped Tibetan *ga'u* on the right to protect it. The casing allows room for the lugs on this shrine shape that a man preferred. The *ga'u* on the upper left hung around a woman's neck.

13.	Twisted and filigreed silver wire dotted with coral or turquoise stones embellish the tops of these old *ga'us*, which were worn by women.

14.	Symbols of Buddhism fashioned in repoussé adorn the square *ga'u*; foliate and geometric patterns cover the round one.

15.	In Qing dynasty China, a wealthy religious man wore a miniature shrine hanging from his waist on a journey. A tiny door, with a round hole and an image of a deer, lifts to reveal a figure of Buddha. Miniature guardian lions top these enameled cases.

16.	On this plain silver shrine, the door slips over the house containing the miniature Buddha, and the engraved cover slides down over the shrine to protect it.

17.	This shrine evolved into the centerpiece for a beaded chain necklace after the Cultural Revolution. At least we can still raise the door and see the tiny figure.

18.	This simpler, engraved paktong shrine might be older than the others.

19.	On this amulet, which resembles an actual shrine, the miniature silver doors spread open to reveal the miniature god inside.

20.	The Qing dynasty Chinese wore miniature silver scissors to sever any contact with evil spirits. On one example, we find buckets for prosperity, babies for fertility, and scissors for protection.

21.	Amulets for achievement, longevity, abundance, marital bliss, good fortune, and protection dangle from this sash hanging.

22.	These silver tripods embodied protection from corruption, as well as a wish for the birth of successful sons.

23.	The large tripod wished the virtuous recipient a house full of gold and jade, along with protection. Considering the pair of mandarin ducks and set of deer, it was probably a wedding present.

24.	This tripod, with its "thirteen tai-bao" inscription, is a puzzler, but it might have been meant to offer the wearer protection from corrupt officials.

25.	A buyer could also choose from a simpler engraved flat amulet in the shape of a tripod. The large one offers the recipient a wish for good fortune and the ability to "rise like the sun," while the smaller one blends protection, wealth, and fertility.

26.	A silver ingot-and-coin-shaped amulet insured wealth and success. The silver horse carrying a coin adds rapid advancement and endurance. In the lower right, Liu Hai and a deer atop the ingot insure wealth. The bats with the coin form a rebus for "blessings before your eyes."

27.	The figure inside the sycee holding a coin is either the God of Rank or an official. Plum blossoms add a wish for longevity and endurance.

28.	A child sitting in an ingot adds fertility to wealth. This solid, heavy example still bears some of its enameling.

29.	Note the variety in the hangings with coins and ingots. The amulets with coral, which feature a coin shape engraved on the other side, came from Mongolia.

30.	The Eight Trigrams, invented by Emperor Fuxi around 3,000 B.C., continue to be used for divination and adornment on silver amulets. The yin-yang often fills the center. This impressive piece includes the Eight Symbols of the Daoist Immortals on the reverse and features an unusual scalloped edge.

31.	Calligraphy on the back of the Eight Trigrams predicts a successful career and a long and happy marriage. Symbols for fertility and longevity indicate a wedding present.

32.	This old Tibetan healing amulet features the twelve animals of the zodiac encircling the Eight Trigrams. In the center, every line in the square adds up to fifteen.

33.	Silver occupational amulets offer good fortune and harmony in one's career. They often include an abacus, a book, a pair of shears, a foot measure, a mirror, a sword, and a shape that might have represented a musical instrument.

34.	The reverse of the amulets in Figure 33 depict either a flat, woven basket similar to the one used in a child's first year celebration or the animals of the zodiac surrounding the Eight Trigrams.

35.	Occupational amulets do not have to be round. They also vary greatly in size.

36.	The reverse of the amulets in Figure 35 depicts the Eight Trigrams and the yin-yang.

37.	This enameled silver amulet represents the highest official in the Emperor's Court. A wealthy young boy must have worn it to insure his future success.

38.	High stepping officials symbolized rapid advancement in one's career.

39. The flowers of the four seasons on this silver drum offer wealth and distinction, while the pomegranate represents fertility. Carnelian beads form the ends of the drum.

40. Were these double happiness amulets wedding gifts or were they actually worn at the ceremony? We'll probably never know for sure. The larger one includes wishes for longevity and a hundred years of wedded bliss.

41. The double fish (for conjugal bliss) and the endless knot often appear together on the same hanging.

42. Symbol of perseverance, courage, and industriousness, this finely detailed silver Hakka woman carries a fishing pole and basket of fish in one hand, and ribbons she has woven in the other. Note the tiny earrings, bracelets, and details of her clothing.

43. In this illustration, the tiny silver Hakka women all carry their baskets of fish, but some have lost their poles. Compare the cool hats with their fringes.

44. The silver Hakka women often lose one or more of their accessories, but they still fascinate us with the great diversity in their craftsmanship.

45. The artisans who fashioned these pieces appear to have been highly skilled in portraying facial expressions.

46. As symbols of abundance, silver basket amulets often held bats for happiness, coins for wealth, flowers for longevity and purity, and even babies for fertility.

CHAPTER NINE: HAIR, HEAD, AND HAT ADORNMENTS

1. Many silver hairpins featured bats, butterflies, and flowers, but smiths found ways to design any subject matter from babies to ducks.

2. Carved carnelian-tipped hairpins made for Buddhists often combined the red of fire in the stone with the blue of the sky in the enameling. The tips resemble flames of fire.

3. Carved jade appears in many shapes and shades of green on hairpins. All offer good health and protection from harm to the wearer.

4. Wire held carved jade on silver hairpin frames. The enormous hairpin on the right certainly attracted attention. Kingfisher feathers compliment the jade on the diadem and small Buddha hairpin.

5. Branches of coral found new life as carved dragons and birds on the ends of silver hairpins. Strands of tiny beads often hang from the tips of such pieces.

6. A silversmith left the center of a double-ended hairpin plain, since it would be hidden behind the owner's hair.

7. Straight-pinned, double-ended, or triple-ended, these silver hairpins exhibit fine detail and workmanship. The Buddhist Symbols, the Five Poisons, longevity symbols, lotus and plum blossoms, and the symbols for a scholar are some of the designs to look for.

8. These Qing dynasty hairpins were certainly worn by a very wealthy woman— possibly a member of the Court—who tried not to let the dangles move as she walked.

9. As on other enameled Qing artifacts, the colors blue, green and yellow predominate.

10. Multi-sections and multi-layers could often be found on costly enameled hairpins.

11. Many flat Manchu hairpins—with fine repoussé or engraving—survived intact.

12. On expensive gilded hairpins, both Manchu and Han women expected and received the finest workmanship. The Eight Symbols of the Daoist Immortals, depictions of the gods, and Chinese calligraphy were all presented with clarity and beauty.

13. *Ruyi*-shaped hairpins often employed removable tops for easier storage and simpler insertion into the hairdo.

14. In the top center, the halberds for good fortune and happiness, the vase for peace and harmony, the double fish for marital happiness, and a musical stone for prosperity form a common grouping on this gilded hairpin. A jade monkey slides down the pole on the left, pink tourmaline still enhances the one on the bottom, and an endless knot appears on the right.

15. Tiny blue kingfisher feathers adorned gilded hairpins for the wealthy. All of these creations end in an earpick. In the top center, a double fish, a musical stone, a lotus, and an endless knot tell us this probably belonged to a Buddhist.

16. Pearl and either glass or stone beads often highlight more expensive kingfisher hairpins. On these, we find red glass, carnelian, and pearls.

17. The more expensive the hairpin, the more complex the design. Dangles, vibrating antennae, layers of petals, leaves, and butterfly shapes are featured here.

18. Many kingfisher hairpins lose their feathers over time. Some collectors prefer these to the perfect pieces. Note the reticulated fish, the "jumping" grasshopper, the elaborate bat, the three phoenixes, and the maiden with a carved bone face.

19. Gilded kingfisher diadems often feature bats and flowers, or even layers of flowers.

20. Wealthy women wore wedding coronets covered with kingfisher-coated symbols on their wedding day, and after that, on important feast days such as the New Year celebration. Buddhist symbols and dragons enhance this one.

21. Silver depictions of the Eight Daoist Immortals and the God of Longevity often appear sewn to the fronts of children's hats or to the sides of hats worn by certain Chinese minority women. The diversity of style is evident in these examples.

22. Complete sets of silver Immortals with the God of Longevity were sold sewn to cardboard so that each figure could be examined. Note the carved jade pieces accompanying the gilded set.

23. Silver gods, flowers, and dragons adorned the hats of children and women.

24. Calligraphy with images of gods or the Immortals, amulets with dangles, ox heads with horns, and a three-dimensional dragon survived the ravages of time, which destroyed the textiles they originally embellished.

25. A hat could include one or more silver calligraphy characters. This set includes plum blossoms and a lotus on each one.

26. The Eight Immortals had designated steeds and are occasionally depicted riding them.

27. Elaborate repoussé embellished hair barrettes which fit into a coiffure.

28. Note the numerous rows of dangles on this bamboo and silver comb. Were the sword shapes symbolic decoration or did they help to keep the comb in place?

29. The bamboo and silver comb utilized the pins to secure the comb. The example beneath it is solid silver enhanced with repoussé.

30. Silver combs with repoussé came in all shapes and sizes and fit into the hairdo. The largest examples covered the head like a crown.

31. Spheres adorned the crowns of hats for young boys and men. The three smallest silver spheres and the one covered with scholar symbols were probably sewn to a young boy's hat. The gilded sphere with the red crystal topped the hat of an official. Spheres with appropriate stones or glass became mandatory for high officials in 1727.

32. A successful examination candidate who hadn't yet received his official appointment probably wore this gilded hat finial with a gilt spike. A jewel of rank would replace the spike after his appointment.

33. Silver images of Maitreya, the Laughing Buddha, adorn the infant's eagle hat, which also features an embroidered vase filled with halberds, a musical stone, a longevity symbol, flowers, and two fish.

34. The full set of Eight Immortals and the God of Longevity adorn this windhat for an infant, which includes a back flap and a hole in the crown.

35. The rim of this eight-segment hat for a young boy also includes the silver symbols for the Eight Immortals and Shouxing.

36. A silver tiger head for protection, kingfisher-covered amulets, and pompoms adorn the front of this child's hat from southwest China. (Compliments of Brooke Jaron)

37. The back of Figure 36 shows the way amulets with dangling bells and wind flap charms were sewn to hats.

38. According to Qing dynasty belief, the three tiny silver tigers protected the little boy who wore this hat and also gave him courage.

39. This tiger hat, complete with teeth, eyes, and ears, has an imitation official's sphere sewn to its crown.

40. On the back of Figure 39, we find bells to frighten away evil spirits and a tiny pair of scissors to cut off all contact with demons.

41. Minority women in Yunnan Province wore these "bird hats" or "phoenix hats". Except for the tail and a small portion of the top, the surfaces appear covered with silver amulets backed by cardboard to protect the material. Look for Immortals, dragons, lions, phoenixes, dragonfish, calligraphy, and circlets among the amulets. (Top example: compliments of Beverley Jackson)

42. We also find headbands covered with silver amulets. Like the hats, they include a large central flower containing a cabochon of glass, stone, or amber.

CHAPTER TEN: UTILITARIAN SASH HANGINGS

1. On Qing dynasty eating kits, the silversmith used repoussé, engraving, or chasing methods to decorate the silver overlays. The tops of the knives or chopsticks often repeated the designs.

2. Soldiers, trackers, nomadic tribesmen, and Imperial employees all wore such eating kits, especially when traveling. A heavy cord strung through a metal ring on the sheath secured the kit to the sash or plaque.

3. On this ensemble, we find a silver protective *garuda* with snakes streaming out of his mouth. Notice the hand-woven cord, triple tassels, and the endless knot.

4. The design on the overlay of the sheath in this illustration is repeated on the handle of the knife. Stylized dragons gambol across the silver.

5. These two eating kit sheaths might have been created as a set for a nomadic husband and wife. The knife handles differ, but each fits and seems appropriate.

6. Double dragons (or possibly dragonfish) chase the elusive pearl on the bottom of this sheath, while another dragon peers down from the top.

7. Hand-tooled designs encrusted with coral and turquoise cabochons cover the silver in this example. A qilin, a dragon, a fan, and a conch shell embellish the silver, which probably belonged to a high-ranking military officer or civil official.

8. The silver overlay on this ivory eating kit includes malachite and coral cabochons. The silver design on the rosewood handle of the knife matches the sheath.

9. Smaller, thinner, and lighter eating kits incorporated sheaths of tortoiseshell and sharkskin.

10. Tibetan eating kits frequently hung from a leather and silver chatelaine strung through a belt. On these examples, chunks of coral embellish designs featuring variations of the guardian *kirtimukha*.

11. Silver plates decorated many leather tinder pouches, which always featured steel strikers on the bottoms. Lifting a flap, one often finds a bit of cotton, some string, or a piece of flint. To start a fire or light his pipe, a man held the piece of flint against a clump of tinder and hit it with the striker.

12. The top flaps of these similarly shaped leather tinder pouches employ either engraving, piercing, or repoussé for the designs.

13. The tinder pouch in the top example includes the striker bottom, but the lower one does not, telling us that it is a money pouch. Tinder pouches lack depth in their design, whereas money purses offer space to hold a number of items.

14. The Eight Buddhist Symbols garnish this silver-covered iron pen case, which held and protected wooden pens used for writing letters and signing documents.

15. This tobacco case takes its shape from animal bone, and is embellished with silver bands at the top and bottom. A chunk of carved wood encased in silver plugs the top.

16. All three of these opium boxes were spring-loaded for easy access. One is covered with calligraphy, another includes a poem by Li Bai next to an elaborate enameled scene, and the third offers a silver rendition of a man's shoe.

17. Spectacle cases of wood covered in sharkskin often employed a silver trim to keep the covering from chipping.

18. Some wealthy scholars commissioned spectacle cases decorated with raised silver designs glued to the front.

19. Silver toggles operated as counterweights to secure accessories to a sash. Aquatic animals embellish the disk-shaped toggle, while enameling highlights the bat.

20. This gilded-silver symbolic seal hanging includes many amulets for good fortune, marital bliss, fertility, and longevity. It obviously hung from the sash of an official.

21. The symbolic seal pendant on this necklace is all that is left of a hanging similar to the one in Figure 20. The chain and beads were added after the Cultural Revolution.

22. Tibetan officials used these seals of silver plated iron to sign documents. Lampblack provided the ink. (Compliments of Brooke Jaron)

23. Silversmiths employed repoussé to create the Eight Symbols of the Daoist Immortals and scenes from mythology on these cylindrical containers. They might have held prayers written on paper and wound around the inner shaft.

24. A bamboo mustache comb with a silver handle, central shaft, and two crossbands hung from the sash of a man in the Qing dynasty. Note the different cut out designs on the handles of these examples, and the toggles that counterbalanced the artifacts.

25. Occasionally, the central shaft of a mustache comb also bore decoration. On the upper right, a stylized swastika for 10,000 blessings covers the shaft. Note the beads on the cords of these examples, and their small embroidered pouches.

26. On the right, we find a mustache comb with an unusual twisted silver handle and central shaft engraved with plum blossoms for longevity. On the left, the owner added odd beads to the old cord as he collected them.

27. Enameling covers one shaft of a mustache comb in this example, while repoussé enhances another. The solid silver representation of a woman's comb probably hung on a grooming kit as a centerpiece. When a Hakka woman died, her comb was broken in half to sever all ties, so this unbreakable silver comb might have been the centerpiece on a wedding gift denoting a perpetual bond.

28. A solid silver mustache comb often bore its silversmith's hallmark and a handle in the shape of a dragonhead. The comb in the center, obviously created for a wealthy client, also includes a sheath with elaborate repoussé to protect it.

29. Many medical implements also hung from sashes. The medicinal spoon, which doubles as a thogchak, hails from Tibet. The gourd, one of the largest I've ever seen, held medicine. The Tibetan tiger claw and the Han animal tooth—both encased in silver—functioned as acupuncture needles to relieve pain. The medicine bottle, with ingot-shaped dangles, is shaped like a Buddhist jar containing the elixir of heaven.

CHAPTER ELEVEN: MANDARIN AND MINORITY ARTIFACTS

1. Unusual enameled Buddha-head beads, an anchor bead, a pendant, and thirty counting beads adorn this Court necklace made from carved fruit pits. A civil official above the fifth rank wore a single necklace to formal Court functions, while high-ranking women could wear as many as three at a time.

2. Qing dynasty fingernail guards, measuring from 3 cm to 15 cm long, protected a noblewoman's long fingernails. These examples feature bats, lotus blossoms, endless knots, coins, and the Eight Symbols of the Daoist Immortals. (Compliments of Joan Ahrens)

3. Buyers purchased fingernail guards in pairs. The set worn on the right hand differed from that worn on the left. Note the pair of tortoiseshell guards with enameled silver tips. (Tortoiseshell guards: compliments of Joan Ahrens)

4. On the authentic fingernail guards, one lower flap folds over onto the other for an adjustable fit. Silver guards without this feature, such as the one on the bottom, were souvenirs exported after the Qing dynasty. A reinforcing plate added ventilation and strength to the back of the shield.

5. The cranes on this rare pair of Qing dynasty gilded sleeve buckles oppose one another, and the flowers swirl in opposite directions. Sewn to the sleeves of a gown, such buckles prevented the wearer's sleeves from smearing his (or her) calligraphy or paintings.

6. Books, scrolls, and urns surround the endless knot on the top buckle. A bowl of peonies for wealth and distinction adorns the lower with its unusual gilded edge.

7. On the reverse side of the artifacts in Figure 6, we see the way sleeve buckles fastened together. Rectilinear in shape, they fit the curve of the arm.

8. Various plants, including the bamboo, lotus, peony, plum blossom, orchid, and chrysanthemum represented incorruptibility, distinction, longevity, and wealth. The crane and deer on the bottom buckle simply add to these sentiments.

9. Compare the figures and backgrounds of these two similar artifacts. Unfortunately, someone apparently mistook the top one for a belt buckle and tried to straighten it.

10. Lions, fish, bats, and butterflies abound on these sleeve buckles, which also include numerous flowers. A wealthy young boy probably wore the smaller one.

11. Poems and messages extolling the benefits of opium use cover these paktong containers. The size of the message increased incrementally with the size of the box.

12. Men felt that opium increased their sexual pleasure, and carried their own supply to brothels in containers such as these. Silvery sleeves depicting proper young ladies covered erotic scenes. The containers fit into embroidered pouches hung from a man's sash.

13. Enameling, engraving, or repoussé might decorate an opium box. Scenes, still life, symbols, and flowers enhanced rectangular, round, and hexagonal-shaped containers. Note the various ways the boxes open.

14. Hexagonal opium boxes often dangled from the grooming kits and hangings of the various minorities. Interestingly, the traditional lotus and plum blossom designs —not poppies— cover the lids. The large round container still contains aged and caked opium from a bygone era. The smaller round one, similar to opium cases, held lime because of the shaker top.

15. Women of the Bai minority of Yunnan Province favored the triangular apron holders featuring the dragonfish or the butterfly. Note the neckring and dangles on the right.

16. This gilded apron holder, sewn to an embroidered apron from the Yi minority, illustrates the way such a holder was worn. It simply hooked to a button on a blouse or dress. (Compliments of Adele Anderson)

17. All four of these Yi apron holders feature the Dragon Gate of Longmen. If the sturgeon made it through the gate, they turned into dragonfish, symbols of perseverance. Babies or flowers fill the centers; phoenix birds frame the sides.

187. Here we find three Yi apron holders depicting a scene from the novel *A Journey to the West*. The story, set in the seventh century, features a monk who travels to India with a priest, a monkey, and a pig, to bring Buddhism back to China.

19. Smaller apron holders from the Bai, Dong, and Miao minorities feature bats, butterflies, baskets, babies, fish, and even a phoenix. The enameled examples are most unusual.

20. The lengths, widths, styles, and weights of these different minority neck chains vary greatly. Hook designs include baskets, lions, butterflies, longevity symbols, and even *ruyi*.

21. This heavy, long chain probably held amulets as it displayed the wearer's wealth. Such chains adorn wealthy Tibetans.

22. On this chain, a small image of Maitreya

appears inside each basket for abundant peace and prosperity. The hooks at the top are shaped like butterflies. Weighing 320 grams, this chain is fastened to an article of clothing, a headdress, or another neck chain.

23.   A woman in the Dai minority wore these gilded phoenix collar buttons on her wedding day. The birds, with a single lug behind the torso, were sewn to the collar so that the dangles hung down. Note the antique green and red glass beads.

24.   Buttons of this type, sewn to the high collars of blouses, shirts, or vests, were common among the Dai and Yi minorities. Pairs of bats, fish, and dragons indicate that these adornments were probably wedding attire.

25.   This large beautifully enameled butterfly surfaced in Kunming. It hangs from a double strand of plain silver beads interspersed with enameled ones depicting gourds, books, and rhinoceros horns.

26.   A longevity symbol forms the torso of the bat on the central ornament, while smaller bats, balls, and symbolic swords hang beneath it on this unique old necklace.

27.   A heavy solid silver butterfly, a set of balls within balls, a fish, and a gourd make this hanging a most impressive show of wealth with good wishes for longevity, prosperity and fertility.

28.   A pair of phoenixes and two officials guard a woman with a baby inside a temple on this hanging. The woman and baby might represent either the Goddess of Mercy and the children she would bring, or else a woman wishing to have a son.

CHAPTER TWELVE: ARTIFACTS WITH BEADS

1.   A gilded silver pendant, covered with kingfisher feathers and coral clusters, often hung from a coral rope chain necklace around the neck of a woman in the Imperial Court. Such artifacts often surface with chipped feathers; but the coral chains remain in remarkably good condition, owing to the intricate pattern of the weaving.

2.   The top of this bracelet is silver repoussé. Behind it, large coral beads were strung on a stiff wire circle to form this intricate bangle. The value of the coral now exceeds that of the silver.

3.   Gilded silver kingfisher pieces mingle with coral branches, pearls, carved jade, and carnelian beads in this old wedding crown. Despite the chipped stones and lost feathers, the artifact remains awash in color.

4.   Coral beads and branches enhance these hairpins created for noblewomen in the Qing dynasty.

5.   Carvers displayed their expertise creating the coral, jade, and turquoise heads of these silver hairpins.

6.   An old chunk of coral adds its color and symbolism to a silver plate attached to the top of a Tibetan leather needle case. The *garuda* offers the owner protection from kidney failure, plague, and cancer. On the other, we find a divinatory turtle.

7.   On this Mongol hairpin, the coral represents fire and the turquoise represents the sky. Fire and sky fused to bring harmony to the universe.

8.   Here, coral and turquoise chunks accentuate a Mongol amulet box, grooming kit centerpiece, and clothing ornament.

9.   Since these amulets, highlighted with bits of coral, are soldered shut, they probably hung from a headdress. Between the two bats, the coral and turquoise form the shape of a gourd.

10.   This large Tibetan pendant includes two fish for marital bliss and a balance of the yin and yang, two horses for endurance, and the conch shell for authority. On the back, an engraved lotus promises incorruptibility. A man certainly wore this piece.

11.   Several silver baskets hang from this post-Cultural Revolution necklace employing coral and turquoise beads. Note the differences in the colors of the coral and the turquoise, and the mismatched chains.

12.   Coral and carved bone beads transformed this remnant of an old grooming kit into a necklace.

13.   We see great similarities in the bead patterns on these three necklaces utilizing antique silver amulets. Originally, the pieces hung on simple chains and symbolized protection, redemption, and marital bliss.

14.   This enameled double gourd originally offered a wish for fertility to the recipient, but now seems overpowered by the beads of coral, turquoise, and bone. Even the dangles detract. Try to imagine it hanging from a silver chain with plain silver dangles.

15.   These pieces featuring a silver baby standing in an ingot and a figure in a lotus position holding a Buddhist wish-granting stone no longer function as needle cases. The addition of the beads and chains makes it impossible to raise their tube covers.

16.   Even fragrance carriers evolved into pendants on beaded necklaces. This one still includes the original foxtail chain and the musical stone with double fish amulet. Unfortunately, the dangling carnelian beads clash with the coral and turquoise, detracting from the symbols of the Daoist Immortals on the main artifact.

17.   For Tibetans, turquoise represented the "stone that stole its color from the sky" and fought off evil spirits and disease. Here, headdress ornaments incorporate the deep blue shade of the stone that Tibetans favored over their native green variety.

18.   Considered to be the product of conifer trees, turquoise was rarely embedded in silver by the Chinese. The example on the left is a rare exception.

19.   An old carnelian cabochon set in a gilded centerpiece highlights this large Tibetan plaque, which adorned the front of a woman's dress.

20.   Trying to impress buyers from the West, the Chinese added new carnelian beads to these amulets.

21.   Huge necklaces were created after the Cultural Revolution by stringing carnelian and enameled beads onto large wire rings culminating in double dragon centerpieces that usually held silver qilins. In this example, oval orange carnelian and blue enameled beads form the ring for the silver dragons and the large silver qilin and official.

22.   To form this necklace, a lock depicting a qilin and rider was added to the enameled double dragon centerpiece, closing a ring of carnelian and enameled silver beads. The turquoise and carnelian dangles replaced silver bells.

23.   Oval orange carnelian beads alternate with

beads of white agate and blue enameled silver on this neckring. A gilded double dragon centerpiece holds the qilin with matching chains and bells.

24. At first glance, this necklace looks like an antique treasure; but the ill-assorted chains, dangles, and odd beads tell us that it is a twentieth-century creation using a Qing dynasty qilin.

25. Another stringer utilized a miniature shrine as the centerpiece for this necklace with carnelian, turquoise, and enameled silver beads. Fortunately, one can still raise the door to view the tiny statue inside.

26. Certain minority groups in southwestern China loved to add jade carvings to their grooming kits. In this example, we find three different floral shapes on the original chain but the jade and glass dangles hanging from the second piece are obvious replacements. Note the elaborate tools.

27. This grooming kit incorporates carved jade into its main construction. Both the musical stone and the ingot contribute symbolic value to the piece.

28. In the Bai minority, silver chains hold huge carved jade pendants. The carved peony on the jade represents wealth and distinction. Butterflies on the chain added longevity.

29. A circular jade *pi* (symbolizing heaven) compels our attention on this hanging, which also includes double fish, silver bells, and beads of coral.

30. Dangles of jade—a few with moveable parts—now hang from silver baskets, urns, and musical stones. The silver pieces were originally centerpieces on small grooming kits.

31. Jade, coral and turquoise dangles were haphazardly added to the bottoms of these qilins.

32. Silver beadcaps enhance the carved pieces of jade on these hangings. Considering all the turquoise and coral beads and inlays, these artifacts probably originated in either Mongolia or Tibet.

33. Elaborate knotting and rare old beads turned these Qing dynasty mustache combs into collector's items for both bead lovers and silver connoisseurs. Unfortunately, vendors often remove such beads and sell them separately.

34. Dealers used new string to add beads and tassels to these antique Mongolian headdress ornaments. While these pieces might appeal to tourists as souvenirs of the Ghost Market, buyers need to realize that they are contemporary fabrications.

35. Recent assemblages combine silver pieces with beads and odd carvings on cheap string, destroying the integrity of the amulet.

Index